21 世纪旅游管理学精品图书

INFORMATION & OPERATION FOR OUTBOUND TOURISM

出境领队知识与实务

王 君 主 编

余益辉 副主编

ZHEJIANG UNIVERSITY PRESS
浙江大学出版社

图书在版编目(CIP)数据

出境领队知识与实务:英文 / 王君主编. —杭州:
浙江大学出版社,2021.8(2025.1重印)
ISBN 978-7-308-21499-5

Ⅰ.①出… Ⅱ.①王… Ⅲ.①国际旅游—旅游服务—
高等职业教育—教材—英文 Ⅳ.①F590.63

中国版本图书馆 CIP 数据核字(2021)第123491号

出境领队知识与实务

CHUJING LINGDUI ZHISHI YU SHIWU

王 君 主编

策划编辑	李 晨	
责任编辑	李 晨	
责任校对	郑成业	
封面设计	春天书装	
出版发行	浙江大学出版社	
	(杭州市天目山路148号　邮政编码310007)	
	(网址:http://www.zjupress.com)	
排　版	杭州朝曦图文设计有限公司	
印　刷	广东虎彩云印刷有限公司绍兴分公司	
开　本	787mm×1092mm　1/16	
印　张	14.75	
字　数	340千	
版 印 次	2021年8月第1版　2025年1月第2次印刷	
书　号	ISBN 978-7-308-21499-5	
定　价	49.00元	

版权所有　翻印必究　印装差错　负责调换

浙江大学出版社市场运营中心联系方式:0571-88925591;http://zjdxcbs.tmall.com

编委会

主　编：王　君

副主编：余益辉

编　委：徐劼成　陈　玥　丁　方　傅周丹

前　言

在改革开放进一步扩大、加深,"一带一路"倡议得到越来越多国家认同、支持的大好形势下,出境旅游蓬勃发展并出现新的业态。党的二十大报告指出,我们要深化文明交流互鉴,出境旅游从业者面临新的挑战:需要了解的目的地国家数量更多了;游客对他们的外语要求提高了;随着目的地国家的增多,出现突发情况的形式、概率都在增加;随着中国的国际形象、地位的变化,出境旅游从业者在涉外工作中的思想政治意识也需跟上时势的发展。因此,如今的出境旅游从业者,必须全方位提高自己,以适应新的形势的需要。正是为了培养出合格的、能适应新形势出境旅游的从业者,我们决定编写这本教材,希望为浙江乃至全国的旅游人才,尤其是出境旅游人才的培养做出一点贡献。

本教材以大洲为模块,以国家为章,精选了五大洲10个中国游客的主要目的地国家进行介绍。每一章分为两部分:第一部分是国家概况,主要包括总览、历史和人民、文化和教育、主要景点这4个单元;第二部分是出境领队实务,包含情景对话和案例分析。情景对话部分描述了在旅游过程中发生的情景,比如在出入境海关的情景,生动有趣。案例分析部分列有旅游突发事件案例及按照相关的法律法规解决的方法,实操性强。

本教材的写作特点:一是部分采用双语编写,主要是国家概况部分使用中英双语,中英双语在内容上互为补充,可以让使用者更容易掌握相应内容;二是内容相对全面,涵盖了五大洲主要国家;三是知识与实操相结合,给使用者提供宝贵的工作技巧、经验;四是将思想政治教育适时地融入教材,以进一步提高国人的国际形象。

本教材不仅面向旅游专业的学生,也面向所有对出境旅游有着浓厚兴趣的社会人士,我们采用扫二维码观看视频的形式,图文并茂地向大家介绍旅游目的地国家知识及应急处理方案。

本教材在编写过程中广泛查阅了相关图书、期刊、网站,在此向相关作者表示诚挚的谢意! 囿于编者的认知能力、学术水平和思想智慧的限制,本教材难免存在缺憾。不当之处,敬请广大同行及读者指正。

编　者

2025 年 1 月

CONTENTS

Chapter 7   Spain/西班牙

Chapter 8   Russia/俄罗斯

Chapter 9   Australia/澳大利亚

Chapter 10   Egypt/埃及

Chapter 1

Japan/日本

Part One
Briefing on Japan/日本概况

Unit 1 Overviews/总览

I Basic Information/基本信息

National Flag/国旗	National Emblem/国徽
The national flag of Japan is a rectangular white banner bearing a crimson-red disc at its center. This flag is officially called Nisshōki, but is more commonly known in Japan as Hinomaru (the "circle of the sun"). It embodies the country's sobriquet: Land of the Rising Sun.	The imperial seal of Japan, also called the chrysanthemum seal, chrysanthemum flower seal or imperial chrysanthemum emblem, is one of the national seals and a crest (mon) used by the emperor of Japan and members of the imperial family. It is a contrast to the paulownia seal used by the Japanese government.
日本国旗是一面长方形的白旗,中间有一个鲜红色的圆盘。这面旗被官方称为"日章旗",但在日本更常见的是称为"日之丸"(字面意思是"太阳圆轮")。这也体现了日本的别名:旭日之国。	日本国徽是一枚皇家徽记,在日本,由于法律并没有确立正式的国徽,因此习惯上,日本皇室(天皇家)的家徽"十六瓣八重表菊纹",即菊花纹章被作为日本代表性的国家徽章而使用。

Other Basics/其他基本信息	
Full Name/国家全称	Japan/日本国
Other Names/其他名称	Nippon or Nihon/日本
Total Area/国土面积	378,000 km²/37.8万平方千米
Population/人口	约1,2562,000(2021年3月)
Nationality/民族	Yamato people/大和族
Capital/首都	Tokyo/东京
National Anthem/国歌	Kimigayo("His Imperial Majesty's Reign")/《君之代》
National Flower/国花	Chrysanthemum/菊花
National Bird/国鸟	Green Pheasant and Crested Ibis/绿雉与朱鹮
Divisions/行政区划	One metropolis(Tokyo), one circuit(Hokkaido), two urban prefectures (Osaka prefecture, Kyoto prefecture), forty-three subprefectures, under which cities, towns, and villages are established/1都(东京都)、1道(北海道)、2府(大阪府、京都府)、43县,其下再设立市、町、村
Language/语言	Japanese/日语
Major Political Parties/主要政党	Liberal Democratic Party, Constitutional Democratic Party, the Komeito Party, Japanese Communist Party, and Japanese Restoration Party/自由民主党、立宪民主党、公明党、日本共产党、日本维新会
Government Type/政府类型	Constitutional Monarchy/君主立宪政体
Religious Belief/主要宗教信仰	Shinto and Buddhism/神道教、佛教
Currency/货币	Yen/日元
Time Difference with Beijing/与北京时差	+1(Summer Time+1)/早一个小时

Ⅱ Physical Geography/自然地理

Japan is located on the west bank of the Pacific, with a land area of about 378,000 square kilometers including Hokkaido, Honshu, Shikoku, Kyushu and more than 6,800 other small islands, so it is also known as the "Nation of Thousand Islands". 75% of the country is mountainous and hilly, so the forest coverage is high. However it is not suitable for farming. Only 11.1% of the land area is under cultivation. As a result, Japan's population is concentrated in coastal areas, ranking 37th in the world in population density.

Japan has great temperature differences all year round. Japan has a subtropical monsoon climate. But deeply affected by the ocean, its marine feature is obvious. As its islands stretch from southwest to northeast and span about 20 degrees of latitude from north to south, the climate varies greatly.

Located at the extinct boundary between the Eurasian and Pacific plates, Japan is in an area combined with western Pacific island arc, coastal mountain and trench. Japan is also located in the Pacific Ring of volcanoes. One in ten of the world's volcanoes are located in Japan. According to the statistics, among all the world's earthquakes of magnitude 6 or above, more than 20 percent occurred in Japan.

日本位于太平洋西岸,陆地面积约37.8万平方千米,包括北海道、本州、四国、九州4个大岛和其他6,800多个小岛屿,因此也被称为"千岛之国"。国土面积的75%属山地丘陵地带,因此森林覆盖率高,但不适合农耕。耕地面积仅占日本国土的11.1%。因此,日本的人口多集中在沿海地区,日本的人口密度在世界排名第37位。

日本一年四季温差很大。日本国土以亚热带季风气候为主,但其深受海洋影响,海洋性气候明显。由于日本的岛屿自西南向东北延伸得很长,南北跨越纬度约20度,所以全国各地的气候有很大的不同。

日本位于亚欧板块和太平洋板块的消亡边界,为西太平洋岛弧—海岸山脉—海沟组合的一部分。日本位于环太平洋火山地震带,全球有十分之一的火山位于日本。据统计,全世界里氏规模6级以上的地震中,超过20%都发生在日本。

Ⅲ Government and Administration/日本政府机构

The government of Japan is a constitutional monarchy in which the power of the emperor is limited and is relegated primarily to ceremonial duties. As in many other states, the government is divided into three branches: the legislative branch, the executive branch, and the judicial branch.

日本政府是君主立宪制,天皇的权力是有限的,主要是仪式性的职责。与许多其他国家一样,政府分为三个部门:立法部门、行政部门和司法部门。

1. The National Diet/议会

Japanese Parliament is generally referred to as the National Diet, consisting of the House of Representatives and the House of Councilors. It is the supreme organ of power and the sole legislature. The House of Representatives has 465 members for four-year terms. National Diet can pass a motion of no confidence in the cabinet and the prime minister has the power to dissolve the House of Representatives early for new elections. The House of Councilors has 245 members and serves six-year terms, with half elected every three years.

In power, the House of Representative is superior to the House of Councilor. The National Diet shall be convened from January to June every year for a period of 150 days, and at other times an emergency or special session may be convened as required.

议会泛称国会,由众、参两院组成,为最高权力机关和唯一立法机关。众议院定员465名,任期4年。国会可通过内阁不信任案,首相有权提前解散众议院重新选举。参议院定员245名,任期6年,每3年改选半数,不得中途解散。在权力上,众议院高于参议院。每年1月至6月召开通常国会,会期150天,其他时间可根据需要召开临时国会和特别国会。

2. The Cabinet/内阁

The Cabinet of Japan is the executive branch of the government of Japan. It consists of the Prime Minister, who is appointed by the Emperor after being designated by the National Diet, and up to nineteen other members, called Ministers of State. The Prime Minister is designated by the National Diet, and the remaining ministers are appointed and dismissed by the Prime Minister. The Cabinet is collectively responsible to the National Diet and must resign if a motion of no confidence is adopted by the National Diet.

日本内阁是日本政府的行政部门。它由首相和多达19名被称为国务大臣的其他成员组成。首相由国会任命,其他内阁成员由首相任免。内阁对国会负有集体责任,如果国会通过内阁不信任案,内阁必须辞职。

3. Judiciary/司法

Judicial power in Japan belongs to the Supreme Court and its subordinate courts. The "three instances at four levels" system is adopted. The Supreme Court is the court of final appeal, which hears unconstitutional and other major cases. The high court is responsible for the second instance, and there are altogether 8 courts in Japan. The chief justice (President) is nominated by the Cabinet, appointed by the emperor, and 14 judges are appointed by the Cabinet, subject to the review of the national vote. Judges at other levels are nominated by the Supreme Court and appointed by the Cabinet for 10-year terms that are renewable. Judges at all levels shall not be removed from office unless formally impeached.

日本的司法权属于最高法院及下属各级法院。采用"四级三审制"。最高法院为终审法院,审理违宪和其他重大案件。高等法院负责二审,全国共设8所。最高法院长官(院长)由内阁提名,天皇任命,14名判事(法官)由内阁任命,需接受国民投票审查。其他各级法院法官由最高法院提名,内阁任命,任期10年,可连任。各级法官非经正式弹劾,不得罢免。

Unit 2 History and People/历史和人民

Ⅰ History/历史事件

It is said that Japan was founded on February 11, 660 BC. In the 4th century, Japan had its first unified regime and established the centralized system of the emperor in the reform. Culturally, it was deeply influenced by the Sui and Tang dynasties of China. For 600 years after the 12th century, Japan was effectively ruled by several samurai regimes including the shogunate, which included the politically turbulent northern and southern dynasties and the warring states period. In the 17th century, the edo shogunate issued the order of locking up the country, which ended in 1854 when the American fleet forced it to open port. After that, under the pressure from the western powers, Japan started reforms. First, the emperor took back political power from the shogunate. Then, in the Meiji restoration in the mid-19th century, Japan carried out large-scale political and economic reform and introduced European science and technology. Japan's society then realized industrialization and modernization, implemented the constitutional monarchy of the emperor's dictatorship, and officially incorporated Hokkaido as its territory. Since the end of the 19th century, Japan began to expand abroad, first annexing Ryukyu, and then taking the Taiwan Island, the Korean Peninsula, the Sakhalin Island and other places. In the 20th century, Japan became one of the imperialist powers recognized by all countries and the only big power in the eastern world at that time. Japan launched the war of aggression against China in 1931 and later became one of the Axis Powers. In 1941, it expanded the battlefield to the western Pacific as part of World War Ⅱ. In 1945, after the atomic bomb bombed Japan, it finally declared unconditional surrender. After the defeat, under the leadership of the Allies, Japan has maintained a unitary parliamentary constitutional monarchy with an Emperor and an elected legislature called the National Diet.

传说日本于公元前660年2月11日建国,在公元4世纪出现首个统一政权,并于大化改新中确立了天皇的中央集权体制。文化上深受中国隋唐两代的影响。12世纪后的600年间,日本由幕府等数个武士阶级政权实际统治,其间包括政治纷乱的南北朝与战国时代。17世纪起江户幕府颁布锁国令,至1854年被美国舰队迫以开港才结束。此后,日本在西方列强进逼的时局下,首先天皇从幕府手中收回政治实权,接着在19世纪中期的明治维新进行大规模政治与经济改革,引入欧洲的科学与技艺。日本的社会于是实现了工业化及现代化,施行天皇专权的君主立宪制,将北海道正式纳为领土。自19世纪末起,日本开始进行对外扩张,首先吞并琉球,之后占领台湾岛、朝鲜半岛、库页岛等地进行殖民式统治。进入20世纪时,日本已成为当时各国承认的帝国主义列强之一,也是当时东方世界唯一的大国。1931年,日本开始对中国发动侵略战争,后来成为第二次世界大战的轴心国之一。1941年,日本扩大战场至西太平洋,成为第二次世界大战的一部分。最终于1945年在本土遭受原子弹爆炸后宣布无条件投降。战败后,在同盟国的领导下,日本维持了单一的议会君主立宪制,由天皇和选举产生的立法机构组成,称为国民议会。

1. Taika Reforms/大化改新

The Taika Reforms was a series of social and political reforms in Japan in 645 AD. The main content was to abolish the system of the dictatorship of the powerful clan at that time, and set up a centralized state by imitating the system of the Tang Dynasty of China, which had a profound influence on the development of Japan's history.

大化改新是公元645年时日本的一连串社会政治改革。其主要内容是废除当时豪族专政的制度,并效法中国唐朝体制成立中央集权国家,对日后日本历史发展影响深远。

2. Meiji Restoration/明治维新

After the overthrow of the shogunate, the Meiji government implemented a series of reform measures to enrich the country and strengthen the army, gradually abolishing the old feudal system and establishing a new system to promote the development of capitalism, which was called "Meiji Restoration" in history.

幕府被推翻以后,明治政府为实现富国强兵,推行了一系列改革措施,逐步废除了旧的封建体制,建立起新的制度,促进了资本主义的发展,历史上称为"明治维新"。

3. World War Ⅱ/第二次世界大战

During the World War I, Japan's economy developed rapidly. The domestic political situation was dominated by the Control Faction who knocked out the Imperial Way Faction. Since then, Japan has carried out large-scale aggression against East Asian countries, including China. Due to the fact that the Control Faction changed the country's political system from the outside to the inside, Japan became the main aggressor in the Pacific and Far East of World War Ⅱ.

On August 15, 1945, Japan accepted the Potsdam Proclamation and agreed to an unconditional surrender.

第一次世界大战时期,日本经济发展迅速。统制派军人击倒皇道派军人从而掌握军政大权。此后,日本开展了对包括中国在内的东亚各国的大规模侵略。由于统制派军人由外而内改变国家政体的思想,日本成为第二次世界大战远东以太平洋战场上的主要侵略者。

1945年8月15日,日本接受《波茨坦公告》,并无条件向盟军投降。

Ⅱ People and Figures/人民及名人

Japan is a multi-ethnic country. In addition to Yamato, the indigenous minorities are the Ryukyu and Ainu (including the Orok and Nivkh, who were expelled from Russia), as well as the lower-ranking tribesmen within the Yamato. Foreigners living in Japan or naturalized as Japanese are mainly from the People's Republic of China, the Korean peninsula, Brazil, the Philippines and other countries and regions.

日本是一个多民族国家。除了大和族之外,日本本土少数民族是琉球族和阿伊努族(还有被俄罗斯驱逐的鄂罗克人与尼夫赫人),此外在大和族内部还有地位较低的部落民。居住在日本或归化为日籍的外国人主要来自中华人民共和国、朝鲜半岛、巴西、菲律宾等国家和地区。

1. Emperor Meiji/明治天皇

Emperor Meiji (November 3, 1852—July 30, 1912), was the 122nd Emperor of Japan (1867—1912) according to the traditional order of succession. He presided over the Meiji period, a time of rapid change that witnessed the Empire of Japan rapidly transform from an isolationist feudal state to an industrialized world power.

明治天皇(1852年11月3日—1912年7月30日),依传统的继承顺序为日本第122代天皇(1867—1912年在位)。明治天皇在位的时期,是一个日新月异的时期,见证了日本帝国从一个孤立主义的封建国家迅速转变为一个工业化的世界强国。

2. Oda Nobunaga/织田信长

Oda Nobunaga (June 23, 1534—June 21, 1582) was a powerful feudal lord of Japan in the late 16th century who attempted to unify Japan during the late Sengoku period, and successfully gained control over most of Honshu. He overthrew the Ashikaga shogunate, which nominally governed Japan for more than 200 years and brought an end to the chaos that had lasted more than 100 years. Oda Nobunaga is regarded as one of three unifiers of Japan along with his retainers Toyotomi Hideyoshi and Tokugawa Ieyasu.

织田信长(1534年6月23日—1582年6月21日),是活跃于16世纪的战国大名,曾在日本战国后期试图统一日本,并成功地控制了本州的大部分地区。他推翻了名义上管治日本200余年的足利幕府,使持续百年以上的乱世步向终结。织田信长与丰臣秀吉、德川家康一起被称为日本战国三杰。

3. Toyotomi Hideyoshi/丰臣秀吉

Toyotomi Hideyoshi（March 17, 1537—September 18, 1598）was a preeminent feudal lord, warrior, general, samurai, and politician of the Sengoku period who is regarded as Japan's second "great unifier". He succeeded his former liege lord, Oda Nobunaga, and brought an end to the Sengoku period. The period of his rule is often called the Momoyama period, named after Hideyoshi's castle. After his death, his young son Hideyori was displaced by Tokugawa Ieyasu.

丰臣秀吉(1537年3月17日—1598年9月18日)是日本战国时代末期至安土桃山时代的大名,武士,战国时期的政治家,是日本的第二个"伟大的统一者"。他接替了他的前领主织田信长,结束了战国时代。他统治时期常被称为桃山时代,以丰臣秀吉的城堡命名。在他死后,他小儿子的地位被德川家康替代。

4. Tokugawa Ieyasu/德川家康

Tokugawa Ieyasu（January 31, 1543—June 1, 1616）was the feudal lord of the warring states period of Japan and the general of the first generation of the Edo Bakufu, the actual head of Japan from 1598 to 1616.

德川家康(1543年1月31日—1616年6月1日)是日本战国时代的大名及江户幕府第一代征夷大将军,于1598年至1616年为日本实际元首。

Unit 3 Culture and Education/文化和教育

I Culture /文化

On the one hand, Japan constantly absorbs foreign cultures. On the other hand, it has its own characteristics. From the 4th century to the 9th century, east Asian cultures were brought to Japan by people from across the globe. After that, Japanese envoys to China in the Sui and Tang dynasties brought Chinese Buddhism culture to Japan. Flower, tea and incense were all introduced to Japan along with the Chinese Buddhism. It became an important part of the traditional Japanese art, and was called the "elegant way" of Japan. Then around the 10th century, Japan reduced its communication with the east Asian continent and began to develop a national culture with its own characteristics, and Kyoto became the cultural center. In the mid-16th century, European culture was introduced to

Japan. Later, due to trade protection and ban on Christianity, the spread of European culture in Japan halted. It was not until the 19th century that Japan, under the diplomatic pressure of the United States, signed the Treaty of Kanagawa with the United States of America and opened trade in Shimada and Hakodate. Only then did European culture revive in Japan and later became an important member of Japanese culture.

During the Meiji Restoration period, Japan implemented a number of modernization reforms. Along with the good economic situation, the domestic cultural ecology also improved, and a large number of outstanding literary writers and artists emerged. During the Taisho period, Japan introduced a lot of American popular culture, such as music and movies. After the 1920s, the Japanese fascist regime was established and strict restrictions were imposed on foreign cultures. After the World War II, the Allies democratized Japan, relaxed its restrictions on foreign cultures, and maintained its pluralism. In recent years, Japanese culture has become international, and its anime and video games have a great influence overseas. Japan currently has 17 world heritage sites, 13 of which are cultural and 4 are natural. Japan, along with Britain and the United States, is known as a "cultural power in the world."

日本一方面不断吸收外来文化,另一方面亦有自身的特色。自公元4世纪到9世纪,就有渡来人带来东亚文化。往后日本的遣隋使和遣唐使为日本带来了汉传佛教文化,花道、茶道和香道都是伴随着汉传佛教传到日本的,是日本传统艺术的重要一环,并称为日本的"雅道"。随后到10世纪左右,日本与东亚大陆的交流变少,开始发展具有独自特色的国风文化,而京都则成为日本的文化中心。16世纪中叶,欧陆文化传到日本,后来因贸易保护政策和基督教禁令,欧陆文化在日本的传播停滞。直至19世纪,日本才在美国的外交压力下签署《日美神奈川条约》,开放了下田及箱馆两港口通商,欧陆文化在日本才得以重新复兴,后来更成为日本文化的重要一员。

明治维新时期,日本实施多项现代化改革。伴随着经济好转,国内文化生态亦有所起色,出现了大批杰出的文学作家及艺术家。大正时期经济景气,这段时期日本引进了美国不少流行文化,如音乐、电影等。20世纪20年代以后,日本法西斯政体确立,对外来文化实施严格的限制。第二次世界大战后,同盟国在日本实行民主化,放宽了日本对外来文化的限制,维持了其多元性。近年来日本的文化迈向国际化,动漫和电子游戏在海外拥有很大的影响力。日本当前共有17项世界遗产,其中13项是文化遗产,4项是自然遗产。日本与英国和美国一同被誉为"世界文化大国"。

Ⅱ Education/教育

At present, Japan has compulsory education of six years in primary school and three years in secondary school, and most students go on to high school education after receiving compulsory education. In 2010, the higher education enrollment rate was 98 percent, which was the highest in the world, and the university enrollment rate was 45.5 percent. Japan also has the world's highest literacy rate at 99 percent. After the World War Ⅱ, six years of primary and three years of secondary compulsory education began to be popularized in Japan. In the 1970s, high school education was popularized, and university education began to be popularized gradually at the end of the 20th century. At the beginning of the 21st century, Japan shifted the focus to the popularization of graduate education. The goal is to increase the number of graduate students from 100,000 at the end of the 20th century to 200,000. Lifelong national education is also a new highlight of Japanese education in the 21st century. The public education and cultural network, such as citizen halls, libraries and museums, has been spread all over Japan.

目前,日本实行小学6年、中学3年的义务教育,大部分学生在接受完义务教育后还会继续进入高中。2010年高等教育入学率为98%,位列全球第一,大学入学率也高达45.5%。日本的识字率亦为全球之冠,达到99%。第二次世界大战之后,日本陆续开始普及6年小学和3年中学的9年义务教育。20世纪70年代,高中教育普及化,直到20世纪末,大学教育也开始逐步普及。21世纪开始,日本将教育大众化逐步迈向重点发展研究生教育,目标是要把研究生的人数从20世纪末的10万人增加至20万人。国民终身教育也是21世纪日本教育的新亮点。公民馆、图书馆、博物馆等公共教育文化体系已经遍布日本全国各地。

Unit 4 Major Attractions/主要景点

Ⅰ Mount Fuji/富士山

Located in Honshu at 3,776.24 m, Mount Fuji is the highest volcano in Japan and 2nd-highest in Asia. It is an active stratovolcano that which erupted in 1707—1708. Mount Fuji lies about 100 kilometers south-west of Tokyo, and can be seen from there on a clear day. Mount Fuji is a exceptionally symmetrical cone, which is snow-capped for about 5 months a year. It is commonly used as a symbol of Japan and frequently depicted in art and photographs, and visited by sightseers and climbers as well.

富士山位于本州岛,是日本最高的火山,海拔3,776.24米,属于亚洲第二高的岛屿火山。它是一座活跃的层状火山,上一次喷发是在1707—1708年。富士山位于东京西南约100千米处,天气晴朗时可以从东京看到。富士山是一个非常对称的圆锥体,每年有5个月左右时间被雪覆盖。富士山作为日本的象征,经常出现在艺术作品和照片中,吸引了络绎不绝的观光者和登山者前来参观。

II Ginza/银座

Ginza is one of the main business districts in the central district in Tokyo, Japan, and known as "the most expensive place in Asia". It is famous for its high-end stores and symbolizes the prosperity of Japan. As a shopping paradise, it has a complete collection of the brand names from all over the world. Huge shopping malls stand on both sides of the street with fashionable and personalized clothes everywhere.

银座是日本东京中央区的一个主要商业区,号称"亚洲最昂贵的地方"。银座以高级购物商店闻名,象征着日本的繁荣。这里汇聚着世界各地的名牌商品,街道两旁巨型商场林立,时尚、个性的服饰随处可见,算得上是一个购物的天堂。

III Kyoto/京都

Kyoto is a city in Kinki, Japan, roughly equals the downtown area of the Kyoto city today. Built in the 8th century, it served as the capital of Japan from 794 to 1869 before the capital was moved to Tokyo, and later developed into an important political and cultural center in medieval and modern Japan. After over a thousand years of development, Kyoto ranks with Tokyo as the most representative cultural showcase of Japan.

京都是位于日本近畿地方的都市,约等同于今日京都市的市中心区域。其历史起于8世纪建立的"平安京",于794年起被定为日本首都,至1869年迁都东京为止,此后其发展成为日本中古及近代重要的政治与文化中心。历经千年的发展,京都与东京并列为现今日本最具代表性的文化橱窗。

Part Two
Outbound Tour Guide Operation/出境领队实务

Unit 1　Situational Dialogues/情景对话

Ⅰ　Dialogue 1　Check-in/Luggage Check-in

(*A : clerk of the airline*　*B : tour leader*)

A: Good morning, sir, what can I do for you?

B: Good morning. I'd like to make group check-in for my tour group. I'm the tour leader.

A: OK. Would you please show me your passport?

B: Here you are.

A: You are going to fly to Tokyo, right?

B: Yes.

A: Your flight number is NH930 from Hangzhou Xiaoshan International Airport to Tokyo Narita Airport. Am I right?

B: Yes, that's right.

A: How many people are there in your group?

B: 11, including me.

A: OK. Does the whole group need to be seated together?

B: As far as possible. These two are a couple, would you please arrange them together? This lady needs a window seat. This one needs an aisle seat. Thank you.

A: OK. I'll try my best. How many pieces of luggage do you want to check in?

B: I have 2 suitcases, a handbag, and a shoulder bag altogether. By the way, what is the free baggage allowance[①]?

A: Every passenger may check in 2 pieces of luggage with the maximum weight allowance 23 kilos each excluding hand luggage. Please make sure there are no explosive, inflammable, poisonous, and other kinds of dangerous articles in your luggage. Besides,

important documents, currencies, valuables, and other articles that need special custody are not allowed to be packed in your checked luggage.

B：OK, got it.

A：Please make sure there are no spare lithium batteries of any kind in checked luggage. Mobile power supply (Charge Pal) is regarded as spare lithium battery and can only be carried in hand luggage.

B：OK.

A：By the way, liquid more than 100 milliliters needs to be checked in.

B：OK.

A：And you are not allowed to carry on board arms, knives under control, sharp and lethal weapons.

B：Sure.

A：Would you please put your check-in luggage on the conveyor belt one by one?

B：OK.

A：This one is overweight. It's 28 kilos. You may get something out, or you need to pay excess luggage charges. Actually we allow the passengers to take two items of hand luggage and the free allowance is 10 kilos each.

B：I have taken some out. Please check it again.

A：Put it on, please.

B：All right. It's OK.

A：Here is your passport and boarding pass[2] with luggage claim tags[3] attached. Your flight will be departing from Gate 10 at 13：40 and the boarding time is 13：10.

B：OK. Thank you very much.

A：You are welcome. Enjoy your flight.

B：Bye.

Notes：

①free baggage allowance：免费行李限额。

②boarding pass (card)：登机牌。

③luggage claim tag：行李领取牌。

Ⅱ Dialogue 2　Onsen Hotel in Japan

(A: tourist　B: tour leader)

B: Good morning ladies and gentlemen. Mentioning Japan, people naturally think of onsen (hot spring), tatami, and Japanese cuisine. An onsen hotel is the right place where tourists can experience the charming Japanese traditional customs. And that's what we are going to do today.

A: Do we have to take our shoes off to enter an onsen hotel?

B: Some traditional Japanese hotels ask the guests to take their shoes off. If shoes-off is mandatory, there will be a higher place by the entrance as an indicator. Besides, whether there are in-house shoes like slippers available also shows whether you need to take your shoes off.

A: Is the check-in of an onsen hotel different from that of a general hotel?

B: Not much different in formalities which include showing ID certificate and filling in the necessary forms. As hot spring bath and dinner in the hotels in hot spring area are the most important enjoyment, many people would choose a package of dinner-accommodation-breakfast. Therefore, many hotels require guests to check in after three o'clock p.m. and check out before ten o'clock a.m.

A: Do we have to take off our shoes to enter the room?

B: Yes. Please don't walk into the tatami room with your slippers on.

A: Is there any staff member to explain about the room?

B: In Japanese style hotels, the usual case is that a waitress in kimono will show the guests to their rooms and explain to them the do's and don'ts in the room.

A: Are there only Japanese style guestrooms in an onsen hotel?

B: Mostly yes. But some hotels also have rooms of western style or western and Japanese combined.

A: What are the differences between the guestrooms of Japanese style and western style?

B: Japanese style rooms have tatami. Instead of bed, a large and low wooden table is arranged in the room. Bedding is set on tatami in due time. You can enjoy in your room the unique Japanese experience of sitting as well as sleeping on the tatami.

A: Is there pajama in the room?

B: A simple style of kimono called "bathrobe" is available in the room. You can wear it in your room as pajama, and you can also leave your room in it.

A: I wonder how to put on a bathrobe.

B: First, put your arms through the sleeve holes. Then, put the left front piece over the right piece and tie the belt with a knot. In cold season, the hotels may offer short overcoat or large sleeve cotton robe for you to put on over the bathrobe.

A: Where are the meals set?

B: For some hotels, meals are set in the guestrooms, and for some others, they are arranged in a large room together with other guests.

A: Is the bedding set at a regular time?

B: Different hotels have different ways to do it. Generally speaking, the bedding is set in the time when the guests are having dinner elsewhere. If the guests have dinner in the room, the bedding is set after the dinner with the guests' presence.

A: Why do Japanese like hot spring?

B: Japanese is a nation who loves soaking in the tub since ancient. A bath warms up the body and alleviates fatigue. In a hot spring, one can enjoy the spacious bathing pool and stretch his/her arms and legs to relax the mind and relieve the stress. People also believe that hot spring helps cure many diseases and therefore is conducive to people's health.

A: What is the so called onsen after all?

B: Onsen refers to the natural hot spring bathing pool. The hot water comes from underground and is said to contain the minerals that beautify the skin and heal physical illnesses.

A: It's not a mixed bath of men and women, is it?

B: The usual hot springs have separate bathing pools for men and women. What needs to be noted is that, in some places, they alternate the pools for men and women in different period of time.

A: How about children?

B: There isn't a unified age limit for children of different sex in the bathing pool. Different regions have different practices. Kyoto has the lowest limit of 6 years old while Hokkaido has the highest of 11 years old. Notices about the limit of age and height are put up in many hot springs. If you have children with you, you'd better check it.

A: Are there anyone who are not supposed to take hot spring bath?

B: Avoid having it right before or after a meal or right after alcohol drinking or strenuous exercises. In addition, the Japanese hot springs usually refuse those with tattoos.

A: What should one bring with for hot spring bathing?

B: Many hotels ask the guests to bring the bath towel from their rooms. For those with long hair, a hair ring is necessary. You'd better not wear jewelry or watch. Shampoo, hair conditioner, and bath cream are usually provided.

A: May we wear swimming suits in hot spring pools?

B: A hot spring pool is not a swimming pool, so swimming suits are not allowed. A hot spring consists of shower area and bath area. Before getting into the pool, clean your body and hair in the shower area. During the shower, keep yourself seated to avoid spreading hot water to others. If you have long hair, tie it up so that it will not get into the water. As for the towel, don't let it touch the water. The proper way is to keep it on your head or on the side of the pool. Finally, on your way to the change room, dry your body with towel.

A: There are so many rules.

B: Yes. Hot spring is part of Japanese culture. So learn about the basic etiquette of it and enjoy your time to the best at the onsen hotel.

Ⅲ Dialogue 3 Japanese Buddhism and Japanese Monks

(A:Mr. Li   B: Suzuki)

A: Suzuki, when I was in Japan, I saw a monk's wedding at a temple! How come a monk can get married!?

B: That's not strange at all. The Japanese monks can not only get married but also eat meat. They can even live out of temple and have other careers such as a owner of a bar or restaurant.

A: How amazing! Why can Japanese monks be so different? Could you tell me about it?

B: In fact, for Japanese monks, it is not imperative to follow the principles of Buddhism in their cause of cultivation. Instead, the cultivation of mind is what they really value. They see "eat meat and drink wine but keep Buddha in your mind" as their motto. However, they were not like this from the beginning. They used to follow many strict and detailed rules and regulations.

A: I see. But what caused the change?

B: It all started from Shinran, the founder of Japanese Pure Land Buddhism in Kamakura period.

A: Why, is it he who started the practice of monk's getting married?

B: That's right. Born in a noble family, Shinran became a monk when he was 9 years old and spent 20 years on Mount Hiei, practicing Buddhism arduously. One day when he was 29, he had a dream in the Hexagonal Hall built by Prince Shotoku. In the dream, Goddess of Mercy preached to him, saying that if he could get married in accordance with the predestination, the goddess herself would marry him in the incarnation of a beautiful girl and he would have a wealthy life and be reincarnated in the Pure Land of Eternal Happiness. Therefore, Shinran got himself married, which was a taboo for monks at that time. However, what influenced the Japanese monks the most is "the Release of the Ban on Meat Eating and Marriage" issued after The Meiji Restoration.

A: What is "the Release of the Ban on Meat Eating and Marriage"?

B: "The Release of the Ban on Meat Eating and Marriage" was issued in 1872. Before that, only the monks of Pure Land Sect could get married. With the release of the ban, all monks in Japan can get married and eat meat and drink alcohol as well.

A: I see. Many thanks.

B: You are welcome.

A: Could you tell me about some interesting Japanese monks?

B: Do you know monk Kanho from Yakushi Temple? He is a monk lead singer who founds a band named Kissako and combines music with Buddhism. His music "The Heart Sutra" hits a record of over 15 million times of play in the social media platforms in China.

A: How incredible!

B: Monks are racking their brains to attract more young people to their temples. Gyousen Asakura is the 17th abbot of SYOONJI in Fukui County. In 2016, he started Techno Dharma Assembly, where he projected the real-time bullet screen on the Buddha Hall. The magic combination of colorful lights, e-music and Buddhist chanting, plus the 3D Holographic Laser Projection, creates a wonderful scene. The integration of Buddhist chanting and e-music is loved by all ages.

A: The assembly sounds cool. I'd like to see it someday. You mentioned that there are monk bars in Japan, where the monks are selling the drinks. Is that true?

B: Yes. From the manager to the clerk, all of them are registered monks. A monk bar is different from an ordinary bar in that it has Buddha statue enshrined in the Buddha niche and there is a daily routine chanting ceremony at eight o'clock p.m.

A: This is hard to imagine in China. Are there any monks in Japan who are still devoted to Buddhist cultivation then?

B：Of course. "The thousand-day pilgrimage" to Mount Hiei in Kyoto is an example. The pilgrimage takes about 7 years. For the first three years, the pilgrims would walk and pray for 100 days in each year. In the fourth and the fifth year, they would walk and pray for 200 days respectively. Every day, they would start walking from two o'clock in the morning for about 6 hours to cover a distance of 30 kilometers. They need to worship more than 260 temples and Buddha statues including the Domtar, the Sitha, Yokokawa, Hiyoshi Taisha, and so on. After 700 days of walking and worshiping in 5 years, they need to "enter the hall", to wit, to retreat in Acalanatha hall for nine days, during which they not only refuse to have any food, water, sleep or even lying down, but also fetch water from the Arghya well as sacrifice to Acalanatha and chant the Buddhist sutra in the hall for 100, 000 times every day. The sixth year is called "Hundred Ascetic Days in Akayama", in which the pilgrims would worship and walk 60 kilometers each day. The seventh year is "The Grand Tour in Kyoto", which is a 100-day worshiping tour with 84 kilometers' walking each day. The following cultivation is 100 days on Mount Hiei, where they would walk 30 kilometers daily.

A：What a strong will they have!

B：In 1988, John Stevens, an American monk in Japan, published his book *The Marathon Monks on Mount Hiei*. For the first time this mysterious thousand-year old oriental way of cultivation was made known to the world. The term "Marathon monks" has made Mount Hiei the Mecca for the Marathon lovers from all over the world. Xiao Li, I'm sure you have a better understanding of Japanese Buddhism and monks now.

A：Yes, of course. I've learned a great deal from your explanation. Thank you so much.

B：Don't mention it. It's my honor to be able to help you.

Unit 2　Case Study/案例分析

Ⅰ　案例一:游客意外受伤的处理

　　钱先生准备参加旅行社组织的赴日本旅游团。旅行社的业务员告诉钱先生:为了保障旅游者的权益,旅行社都将按照规定办理保险,而且旅游行程安排合理,节奏缓慢,特别适合像钱先生这样的老年旅游者。随后钱先生随旅游团队到达日本。由于是第一次出境旅游,钱先生十分不适应靠左行的交通习惯,在过马路时不幸摔倒,导致左脚扭伤,花费6,000多元。钱先生要求旅行社为其向保险公司索赔。但旅行社说林先生的受伤属于意外,旅行社没有过错,不能纳入旅行责任保险的赔偿范畴。钱先生则认为旅行社事先告知已为自己购买保险,但没有说明责任保险与意外保险的区别,更没有向他推荐意外保险,旅行社工作有疏忽,必须为此承担相应的责任。

1. 纠纷防范与应对

告知义务是法律赋予旅行社的法定义务,是旅行社在组团和服务时必须履行的义务。

(1)旅行社履行告知义务的法律规定。

①《消费者权益保护法》规定,经营者对有可能危及人身、财产安全的商品和服务,应当向消费者做出真实的说明和明确的警示。

②《旅行法》规定,旅行社对可能危及旅游者人身、财产安全的事项应当向旅游者做出真实的说明和明确的警示。

③旅游经营者、旅游辅助服务者对可能危及旅游者人身、财产安全的旅游项目未履行告知、警示义务,造成旅游者人身损害、财产损失,旅游者请求旅游经营者、旅游辅助服务者承担责任的,人民法院应予以支持。

(2)旅行社履行告知义务的范围。

①告知的期限范围。从旅游者向旅行社咨询开始到旅游合同履行完毕,这期间都是旅行社履行告知义务的阶段。告知义务的履行必须贯彻旅游服务的全过程。

②告知内容的范围。旅行社告知的内容大至旅游目的地的法律法规、民情风俗,小到气候变化、餐饮特色,等等。

(3)旅行社如何履行告知义务。

①告知义务内容必须具体明确。

②履行告知义务必须看清楚对象。

③履行告知义务必须针对不同的产品,不能千篇一律。

④履行告知义务,以书面形式为好。

(4)旅行社履行告知义务纠纷处理的基本原则。

①履行告知义务是旅行社的法定义务,在服务过程中必须认真完全履行合同,否则将要承担相应的法律责任。

②在赔偿时,应考虑旅游者个人的行为能力。

2. 领队注意事项

①领队自身需了解各类相关保险业务。

②行前需告知,行程中需提醒。

③事情发生时,脱身处理,保留证据,并做好安抚工作。

Ⅱ 案例二:游客执意参与泰拳对练受伤的处理

1. 案例简介

赵先生和单位同事参加前往泰国的旅游,按照旅游行程,赵先生等要去参观泰拳对练表演项目。到现场后,赵先生希望共同参与表演。当赵先生向领队提出要求参与表演时,领队坚决反对,赵先生同团的同事闻讯也是力劝其放弃,但赵先生坚持要参与。最后地陪只得转告表演者,有旅游者希望与他切磋,表演者也是婉言谢绝,但赵先生固执地要参与表演。在屡次劝说无效的情况下,表演者和赵先生开始了对练,结果只用了一个回合,赵先生的手臂骨折。领队立即把赵先生送往医院救治,然后写出事实经过,请赵先生的同事、地陪和泰拳表演者签名。赵先生要求旅行社承担医疗费用等共计3万余元。

2. 案例分析

请问:

(1)赵先生的医疗费用等损失应当由谁来承担?

(2)旅行社是否有赔偿赵先生损失的义务?

专家意见:

(1)赵先生的医疗费用等损失应当由他自己来承担。赵先生作为完全民事行为能力人,应当明白自己参加拳击表演可能产生的后果。领队等劝阻他不要参加表演,就是希望不要发生伤害事件。赵先生不听劝阻,自己就应当为此承担责任。

(2)旅行社没有赔偿赵先生损失的义务。领队劝阻赵先生参加拳击表演,已经履行了安全保障义务。赵先生的损害,完全是他自己不听从劝告,参加不适合自身条件的旅游活动而导致旅游过程中出现的人身损害,其损失和旅行社无关。

Chapter 2

Republic of Korea/韩国

Part One
Briefing on the Republic of Korea/韩国概况

Unit 1　Overviews/总览

I　Basic Information/基本信息

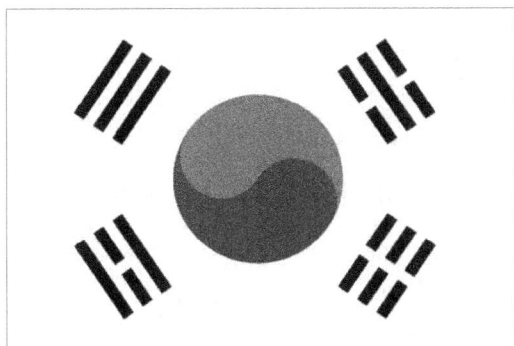

National Flag/国旗	National Emblem/国徽
The flag of the Republic of Korea, also known as the Taegukgi, has three parts: a white rectangular background, a red and blue Taegeuk in its center, and four black trigrams, one at each corner. They represent heaven, earth, water and fire. The flag base is white, symbolizing the purity of the Korean people and their love for peace. 韩国国旗称为太极旗,中央的太极象征宇宙,蓝色为阴,红色为阳。4个角落的卦在左上方的是乾,右下方为坤,右上方为坎,左下方为离,分别代表天、地、水、火。国旗底色为白色,象征韩国人民的纯洁和对和平的热爱。	The national emblem of the Republic of Korea is in round shape. A five-petal hibiscus with a Yin and Yang fish pattern in the center. The ribbon says "Republic of Korea". 韩国国徽为圆形。圆面为五瓣的木槿花,中间为阴阳图案。绶带上写着"大韩民国"。

Other Basics/其他基本信息	
Full Name/国家全称	Republic of Korea/大韩民国
Total Area/国土面积	103,290 km²/10.329万平方千米
Population/人口	52,000,000（2021年3月）
Nationality/民族	Korean/韩民族
Capital/首都	Seoul/首尔
National Anthem/国歌	"Patriotic Song"/《爱国歌》
National Flower/国花	Hibiscus/木槿花
National Bird/国鸟	Magpie/喜鹊
Divisions/行政区划	The major administrative divisions are eight provinces, one special self-governing province, six metropolitan cities（self-governing cities that are not part of any province）, one special city and one metropolitan autonomous city/主要的行政区划为8个道、1个特别自治道、6个广域市、1个特别市、1个特别自治市
Language/语言	Korean/韩语
Major Political Parties/主要政党	Democratic Party, Liberty Korea Party/共和民主党、自由韩国党
Government Type/政府类型	Presidential Republic/总统共和制
Religious Belief/主要宗教信仰	Protestantism, Buddhism, Catholicism/基督新教、佛教、天主教
Currency/货币	Won/韩元
Time Difference with Beijing/与北京时差	+1（Summer Time+1）/早1小时

Ⅱ Physical Geography/自然地理

The Republic of Korea is located in the south section of the Korean Peninsula in northeast Asia, surrounded by sea on three sides, bordering the Democratic People's Republic of Korea in the north, the People's Republic of China across the Yellow Sea in the west, and Japan in the east and southeast across the Sea of Japan, covering an area of about 103,290 square kilometers, accounting for about 45% of the peninsula's area.

The Republic of Korea's terrain is high in the north and low in the South. Most of it is mountainous. The Republic of Korea's plains are mainly distributed in the south and west along the rivers and in coastal areas, mostly with the elevation of below 200 meters above sea level. The main moutains in ROK include Taebaek Moutains, Sobaek Moutains and Ziling Moutains. The Taebaek Mountains, which runs along the east coast from Huanglong Mountain in the north, is the longest mountains in the Korean Peninsula, with a total length of about 500 kilometers and an average elevation of 1,000 meters, forming the backbone of the Southern Korean Peninsula.

The Republic of Korea tends to have a temperate continental humid and subtropical humid climate. The four seasons are distinct. Spring and autumn are short; summer is hot and humid; winter is cold and dry. Temperatures in most parts of the Republic of Korea can exceed 30 ℃ Celsius in summer. Winter is cold, with the lowest temperature in inland areas down to −20 ℃.

韩国地处东北亚的朝鲜半岛南段,三面环海,北部与朝鲜接壤,西与中国隔着黄海相望,东部和东南部与日本隔着日本海相邻,面积约 10.329 万平方千米,约占半岛面积的45%。

韩国地势北高南低,东高西低,大部分是山地。韩国的平原主要分布在南部和西部的河流及海岸地带,海拔多在 200 米以下。韩国的主要山脉包括太白山脉、小白山脉和车岭山脉。北起黄龙山纵贯东海岸的太白山脉是韩鲜半岛最长的山脉,全长约 500 千米,平均海拔 1,000 米,构成朝鲜半岛南部的脊梁。

韩国属温带大陆性湿润和副热带湿润气候。一年四季分明。春、秋两季较短;夏季炎热潮湿;冬季寒冷干燥。夏季韩国大部分地区气温都会超过 30 ℃。冬季气温寒冷,内陆地区最低气温可达−20 ℃。

Ⅲ Government and Administration/韩国政府机构

The Repubilc of Korea has a government divided into three branches: executive, judicial, and legislative. Since the 1960s, the Repubilc of Korea has fully developed a system of liberal democracy. In 1987, the Repubilc of Korea held its first fair and open presidential election.

韩国政体由行政、立法和司法三权组成。自 20 世纪 60 年代以来,韩国已经成功发展自由民主制。1987 年,韩国举行第一次公平开放的总统选举。

1. Legislative/立法机构

The National Assembly is a unicameral legislature of the Republic of Korea. According to the law, it shall be composed of at least 200 seats for each four-year term. More than 80% of the seats shall be elected by the national vote, and the remaining 5% or more shall be elected by the proportional representation system.

大韩民国国会是韩国一院制立法机关,按法律规定应由至少200个议席组成,每届任期四年,其中80%以上的席位由国民投票选举产生,5%以上的席位通过比例代表制产生。

2. Judiciary/司法机构

The Repubilc of Korea's Judiciary is independent of the Repubilc of Korea's Executive and Legislature. The Republic of Korea's courts are in three levels: the grand court, the high court, and local courts, including specialized patent courts, family courts, and administrative courts.

韩国司法机构独立于韩国行政和立法机构。韩国法院分为大法院、高等法院和包括专门性的专利法院、家庭法院和行政法院在内的地方法院三个级别。

3. Executive/行政机构

The Repubilc of Korea's executive branch implements presidential system, which is the core system of the Repubilc of Korea's separation of powers system. The president of the Republic of Korea is directly elected by the Repubilc of Korea's people for a five-year term. The constitution of the Republic of Korea states that the president cannot be re-elected in order to prevent any individual from holding power for long periods. The Repubilc of Korea's president exercises executive power through a State Council of 15–30 members.

韩国的行政部门实行总统制,是韩国三权分立制度的核心体制。大韩民国总统由韩国国民直接选举产生,任期为5年。为避免任何个人长期掌握国家权力,大韩民国宪法规定总统不能连任。韩国总统通过由15—30人组成的国务会议行使行政权。

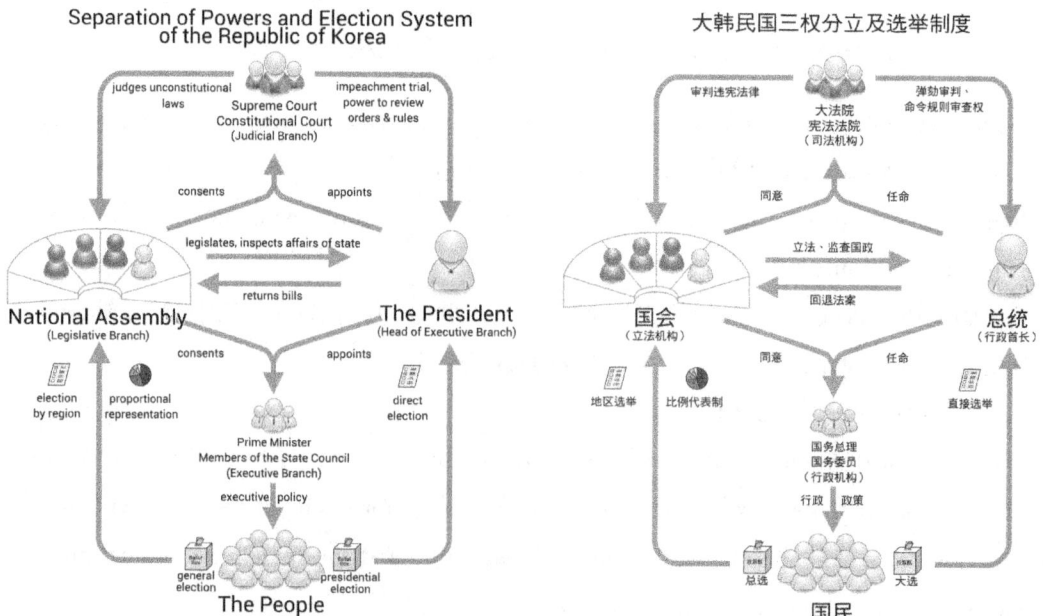

Separation of Powers and Election System of the Republic of Korea

大韩民国三权分立及选举制度

Unit 2 History and People/ 历史和人民

I History/历史

The history of the Republic of Korea began in 1948 when it was officially founded in the south of the Korean Peninsula on August 15. However, it actually began with the establishment of an interim government of the Republic of Korea in Shanghai, China in 1919.

大韩民国历史开始于1948年。1948年8月15日在朝鲜半岛南半部正式建国。韩国历史源于1919年在中国上海成立的一个大韩民国临时政府。

1. Japanese Occupation/日本占领

In the 19th century, Korea remained an "inward-looking nation", firmly opposed to western demands for diplomatic and trade relations. Since then, a number of Asian and European countries with imperialist ambitions have competed to exert influence on the Korean Peninsula. After defeating China and Russia, Japan forcibly annexed Korea in 1910 and began to colonize it.

19世纪,韩鲜依然是一个"闭关自守之国",坚决反对西方关于建立外交与贸易关系的要求。此后,一些具有帝国主义野心的亚洲和欧洲国家竞相对朝鲜半岛施加影响。日本在战胜了中国和俄国后,于1910年强行吞并韩鲜,并开始对其实行殖民统治。

2. The North-south Division/南北分裂

In February 1945, according to the arrangements of the Yalta Conference, the Korean Peninsula was jointly managed by the US, Soviet Union and China. After the end of the World War II, the Soviet Union and the United States could not agree on the condominium of the Korean Peninsula. In 1948, the peninsula was divided into two countries: the Democratic People's Republic of Korea (DPRK) and the Republic of Korea (ROK).

1945年2月,根据雅尔塔会议的安排,朝鲜半岛由美苏中三国共同托管。第二次世界大战结束后,由于苏联和美国就朝鲜半岛的共管无法达成共识,1948年,半岛被划分为南北两国:朝鲜民主主义人民共和国(简称朝鲜)以及大韩民国(简称韩国)。

3. Korean War/朝鲜战争

On June 25, 1950, a military conflict broke out between DPRK and ROK near the

38th Parallel. As a result, the Korean War broke out. At that time, the United Nations resolution led by the United States and others called for the United Nations military to support ROK. This allowed the UN to intervene in a civil war. ROK and DPRK finally signed a cease-fire agreement on July 27, 1953.

1950年6月25日,朝鲜和韩国在三八线附近发生军事冲突,由此朝鲜战争爆发。当时由美国等主导的联合国决议发动联合国军支援韩国。这使得联合国干预了一场内战。韩国同朝鲜最终在1953年7月27日签署停火协议。

II People and Figures/人民及名人

The Korean, mainly distributed in the Korean Peninsula adjacent to the northeast of China and the Russian Far East, is the main body of the Republic of Korea and the Democratic People's Republic of Korea.

朝鲜族,又称韩民族、朝鲜民族、高丽人,主要分布在朝鲜半岛及毗邻的中国东北和俄罗斯远东地区,是大韩民国及朝鲜民主主义人民共和国的主体民族。

1. Choe Chiwon/崔致远

Choe Chiwon (857—10th century) was a noted Korean Confucian official, philosopher, and poet of the late Unified Silla period (668—935). He studied for many years in the China during the Tang Dynasty, passed the Tang Dynasty imperial examination, and rose to high office there before returning to Silla, where he made ultimately futile attempts to reform the governmental apparatus of a declining Silla state. Because of his great achievements in literature, Choe Chiwon was praised by many people in both ROK and DPRK and honored as the "teacher of a hundred generations".

崔致远(公元857—10世纪)是韩国统一新罗时期(668—935)著名的儒家官员、哲学家和诗人。他在中国学习多年,通过了唐朝的科举考试,并担任要职。回到新罗之后,他试图改革衰落的新罗国家的政府机构,但最终徒劳无功。由于在文学上的极高成就,崔致远得到了朝鲜和韩国后世的众口同赞,被尊为"百世之师"。

2. Kim Koo/金九

Kim Koo (July 11, 1876—June 26, 1949) is a member of Anton's family. He stayed in China for 27 years. He is a legendary figure in the history of ROK, and known as the "father of ROK". Kim Koo was put several times in prison for various reasons after his early involvement in the Donghak Peasant Movement against Joseon dynasty. Later, due to his outstanding political leadership, Kim joined the independence movement in the Republic of Korea and became its leader. When the China Nationalist Government moved to Chongqing during the anti-Japanese period, the provisional government of the Republic of Korea led by Kim Koo also moved to Chongqing. He served as the chairman of the interim government of ROK and had good relations with the government of the Republic of China. But Japan was always on watch of him.

After the surrender of Japan, Rhee Syng-man became the first President of ROK with the support of the United States. Kim Koo fought indefatigably for the establishment of a united and independent Korea.

金九(Kim Koo,1876 年 7 月 11 日—1949 年 6 月 26 日),本贯安东金氏。他在中国待了 27 年,是韩国历史上的传奇人物,被誉为"韩国国父"。金九早年参与反对李氏朝鲜的东学党运动,之后因各种原因数度入狱。后来由于出色的政治领导力,金九加入了韩国的独立运动,且成为领导人。在中国抗日时期,国民政府迁往重庆时,金九所领导的大韩民国临时政府亦随之迁往重庆。他曾担任大韩民国临时政府主席,与中华民国政府关系良好。但当时日本则严防着金九。

日本投降后,在美国的支持下,李承晚成为韩国的首任总统。金九为建立一个统一的、独立自主的韩国进行了百折不挠的斗争。

Unit 3　Culture and Education/文化和教育

I　Culture/文化

Korean culture is derived from Korean traditional culture. Historically, while the culture of Korea has been heavily influenced by that of neighboring China, it has nevertheless managed to develop a unique cultural identity that is distinct from its larger neighbor. The modern Korean culture is the product of Korean modernization. With the development of South Korea's economy and society, the lifestyle of South Korean people, such as food, clothing, housing and transportation, has also changed, thus constructing the modern Korean culture. The popularity of Korean culture in the world is known as the Korean Wave.

韩国文化由朝鲜传统文化衍生而来。历史上,朝鲜文化深受邻国中国文化的影响,但它还是设法形成了一种独特的文化特征,与它的邻国不同。现代韩国文化是韩国现代化的产物。随着韩国经济和社会的发展,韩国人的衣食住行等生活方式也发生了变化,从而构筑了现代韩国文化。韩国文化在世界的流行被称为韩流。

II The School System/教育

The Korean school system is a 6-3-3-4 system; that is, six years of primary school, three years of junior high, three years of senior high, and four years of college. Among them, the 6 years of primary education and 3 years of junior high education are compulsory. Since the 1970s, the attainment rate of high school education in ROK has exceeded 98% as its economy took off and its national strength increased.

在韩国,基本学制是"6—3—3—4"制,即小学6年,初中3年,高中3年,大学本科4年。其中,小学6年+初中3年的9年属于义务教育阶段。从20世纪70年代开始,随着经济起飞和国力增强,韩国的高中教育普及率已超过98%。

Unit 4   Major Attractions/主要景点

I Gyeongbok Palace/景福宫

Gyeongbok Palace is the official palace of the Joseon Dynasty (1392—1910), the last unified dynasty in the history of the Korean Peninsula. Located in Seoul, the capital of the Joseon dynasty (now capital of ROK), it is the first of the five palaces in Seoul and the political center of the early Joseon Dynasty.

景福宫是朝鲜半岛历史上最后一个统一王朝——朝鲜王朝(1392—1910)的正宫(法宫)。它位于朝鲜王朝国都汉城(今韩国首尔),是首尔五大宫之首,朝鲜王朝前期的政治中心。

II Jeju Island/济州岛

Jeju Island is one of the largest islands in ROK. It is a typical volcanic island and one of the world's seven natural wonders. Formed by volcanic eruptions 1.2 million years ago, the island center boasts the highest mountain of ROK, Mt. Halla, which is 1951 meters above sea level.

济州岛是韩国最大的岛屿,是一座典型的火山岛,世界新七大自然奇观之一。它是由120万年前火山活动而形成,岛中央是通过火山爆发而形成的海拔1951米的韩国最高峰——汉拿山(Mt. Halla)。

Ⅲ Changdeokgung/昌德宫

Changdeokgung（"Prospering Virtue Palace"）is set within a large park in Jongno-gu, Seoul, ROK. It is one of the "five great palaces" built by the Kings of the Joseon Dynasty. Changdeokgung is a Chinese-style building, which still has 13 halls. It is the most complete palace of the Lee Dynasty, known as the "Forbidden City of Korea".

昌德宫位于韩国首尔市钟路区。它是朝鲜王朝国王建造的"五大宫殿"之一。昌德宫内为中国式建筑物,目前仍保存着13座殿阁,是李氏王朝宫殿中保存得最为完整的一座,被称为"韩国的故宫"。

Part Two
Outbound Tour Guide Operation/出境领队实务

Unit 1 Situational Dialogues/情景对话

Ⅰ Dialogue 1 Security Check

（*A*：*security inspector*   *B*：*tourist*）

A：Good morning. Welcome to Seoul Incheon Airport[①]. This is security check. Would you please take out your mobile, Charge Pal, umbrella, toiletries and all other metal articles from your bag and put them into this tray? And if you have a laptop in your bag, would you please take it out and put it in another tray? And take off your coat and shoes, please!

B：Sure. Shall I do this way?

A：Yes. That's right. What is the capacity of your Charge Pal?

B：It is 15,000 milliampere（mA）, which is under the limit of 20,000 mA.

A：OK. And show me your boarding pass, please! Then go into the body scanner and stand still for 3 seconds, please.

B：I wonder what this is for.

A：To make sure that no one takes any contraband such as drug, arms and ammunition.

B：I see.

A：Miss, please come over here. From the scanner, we find you have a bottle of facial cleanser over 100 ml in your bag, which is not allowed. I'll confiscate it.

B：What a pity.

A：What's this? A thermos?

B：Yes, with hot water.

A：No liquid of any kind including drinking water. Do you know the film *Lost on Journey*[②]?

B：What?

A：Because the main actor Baoqiang Wang couldn't bring himself to throw out the large bottle of milk, he had to drink the last of milk on security check.

B：Oh, milk is liquid.

A：You get it. So now you have to go through the security check process again, from the very beginning.

B：ah... how about now?

A：Well, you are in the clear now. Sorry to have bothered you. Please take your bag and other personal belongings at the other side.

B：Thank you.

Notes：

① Seoul Incheon Airport：首尔仁川机场。

② *Lost on Journey*：电影《人在囧途》。

Ⅱ　Dialogue 2　Korean Bibimbap

(*A：Minho　B：Xiao Zhang*)

A：Xiao Zhang, have you ever heard of the Korean saying "Even the beauty of Kumgang Mountain is only considered after a meal"?

B：Yes. I seem to have heard of it. Does it mean something similar to the Chinese saying "people take food as their heaven"?

A：Right. Food is extremely important, isn't it?

B：Absolutely. We are all human after all.

A：You are right. So, today we will have a try of the traditional Korean cuisine, the bibimbap, to feast both your palate and eyes.

(*at a Korean restaurant*)

A：Do you know about Korean bibimbap?

B：Just a little.

A：Korean bibimbap is not only popular on the airplane menu but also seeing a gradual rise of franchised restaurants overseas. Even Hollywood big stars in America take it as their diet food, which shows how much people love it.

B：Wow, I didn't know that the bibimbap enjoys such a high popularity.

A：Have you tried it before?

B：I have seen it many times in Korean TV series and also tried it once or twice in the

Korean style restaurants in my own country. But I don't know whether they are authentic.

A: Then you must try it here. Since you are in ROK, you have to try the authentic Korean bibimbap. What we are having now is Chonju bibimbap.

B: Awesome, really delicious. Would you please tell us more about it?

A: No problem. Besides its traditional features, people love Korean bibimbap mainly for its perfect combination of color, aroma, and taste. It is a great pleasure for the eyes, nose, and mouth. For those who try it for the first time, the perfect look of the fresh wild vegetables and the white rice greatly arouses their appetite. The finely prepared bibimbap in the brassy bowl is a masterpiece symbolizing the Korean fad. The haunting aroma from the fresh ingredients during the process stimulates people's smell and makes their mouths watering. At this moment, if you try the food, the wonderful taste of it will surely win your thumb-up and exclamation. The unique flavor of bibimbap brings people tremendous enjoyment which no other food in the world can offer.

B: Wow. Bibimbap is really great. Is it prepared in the same way in different places?

A: The ingredients differ in different places. However, the major ingredients commonly include bean sprouts, fiddlehead fern, salted beef (or fresh beef), bean jelly, and eggs. Recently, the traditional bibimbap is becoming functional, compound, convenient, and overseas-oriented. There is even the instant bibimbap customized specially for aerospace and airplane menu. And portable bibimbap is now available just like coffee and bread in Hanok village in Chonju. The portable bibimbap catered to the route and taste of different tourists is popular as well. With the increase of young people visiting Hanok village, compound types of bibimbap such as bibimbap with fried cake and mixed bibimbap have been created. Moreover, the Korean catering industry has taken measures to meet the taste of foreign tourists by reducing the pungency of it and adding mushroom and barbecue to it. If the sauce of chives is added, the flavor would be even better and more worth trying.

B: Dear me. I've never thought that the Korean bibimbap has such complexities.

A: In ROK, the most representative brands of bibimbap are Chonju bibimbap, Anton bibimbap, Tongyeong bibimbap, Jinju bibimbap and aerial bibimbap. Let me show you some pictures of them in my mobile phone.

B: Groovy. There is such a great variety of Korean bibimbap. I'm much better educated now. Next time when I come, I will try another kind of it.

Chonju Bibimbap, the Best of Bibimbap   Tongyeong Sea Squirt Bibimbap

Ⅲ Dialogue 3　Entertainment in ROK

(A: *tourist*　B: *local guide*)

A: Good morning, Miss. Thank you for telling us so much about your country yesterday. Everything you mentioned is so interesting. But I'm particularly interested in the entertainment industry in your country. Could you please tell us more about it, like the evolution of it?

B: Of course. The entertainment industry in ROK is now one of the pillar industries in the country, especially the TV dramas. But it actually doesn't have a long history.

A: Right. By entertainment industry, I actually meant to refer to the TV dramas. When did it start?

B: It was in the 1960s that the TV dramas made its first appearance. As you know, after the independence from the Japanese colonial rule in 1945 and the end of the Korean War in 1953, ROK stepped into a period of stable development. So did the film and TV industries. On January 19th, 1962, KBS broadcast the very first TV drama in ROK, *Backstreet of Seoul*. It was considered as the foregoer of Korean TV dramas.

A: That was what I did not know.

B: At that time, television was still a luxury for the majority of households and the content of the dramas was tightly controlled by the military government. Most dramas were made to educate the public and support the military government. *Backstreet of Seoul* was more like a lecture on the problems of urban life than family entertainment.

A: I see.

B: In the 1970s, TV dramas began to become a popular form of family entertainment as more households owned TV. The dramas' storylines were influenced more by the everyday lives of the people than by political agendas. For example, the dramas *Assi* and *Yeor* were about characters enduring difficult lives against the backdrop of the history on Japanese colonial rule and the Korean War.

A: How interesting!

B: In the 1980's, the variety of K-dramas increased. Being influenced by the Japanese TV dramas, the Korean TV networks began offering trendy dramas focusing on the lives and love stories of the younger generation to attract young viewers. The drama *Love and Ambition* aired in 1987 was considered a representative drama of this period.

A: Korean dramas didn't come to China until the 1990s after the establishment of diplomatic relationship between the two countries.

B: Yes. In the 1990s, trendy dramas also reached a new peak. For example, *Jealousy*, a romantic drama aired in 1994, attracted younger generation with their young characters and stylish and realistic description of the urban life, and the drama's soundtrack was also a massive hit on the record charts, motivating the TV networks to link the popularity of the dramas with merchandise sales.

A: *Jealousy*! Yes, *Jealousy* was the first Korean drama ever aired in China.

B: Is that so!

A: Yes. It eventually led to the appearance of Hallyu, or the Korean Wave in China.

B: You are absolutely right. The term Hallyu was first used by the Ministry of Culture and Tourism in ROK in 1999, when the ministry produced a music CD titled in Chinese "Hallyu—Song From Korea".

A: In China, the term was adopted by Chinese media to refer to the success of ROK popular culture.

B: Since the turn of the 21st century, ROK has emerged as a major exporter of popular culture and tourism, which have become a significant part of our burgeoning economy.

A: We did strongly feel that in China.

B: In the new century, historical dramas enjoyed a revival with the coming of fusion sageuk which incorporated a modern touch into historically inspired materials. "Fusion sageuk" means fictional stories about a real historical figure or fictional characters against a real historical backdrop. Instead of historical facts, "fusion sageuk" focuses more on the emotions and struggles of the main characters, making them more like a contemporary romantic drama.

A: I guess *Dae Jang Geum*, *Hur Jun*, *Jumong*, *Moon Embracing the Sun*, *My Love From the Star*, and *Chuno* all belong to this category, don't they?

B: Yes. I'm amazed by your familiarity with the Korean dramas.

A：It's all because of Hallyu. Thank you so much for giving me such a fascinating lesson on Korean dramas.

B：It's my great pleasure.

Unit 2　Case Study/案例分析

I　案例一：旅游途中因病意外身亡的处理

1. 案例简介

75岁的老年旅游者王先生在家人的陪同下,参加了某国际旅行社组织的韩国游。在报名时王先生家人告诉旅行社,王先生的身体状况不错,没有什么特殊的疾病。王先生在旅游期间感觉不舒服,领队和地陪马上把王先生送到医院治疗,最终不治而亡。领队复印了王先生的病历,病历上清楚地记载了王先生近期身体状况:王先生患有高血压病史,曾经因为高血压而中风,最近已停服高血压药半年多时间。旅行社帮助王先生家人料理后事,家人对此非常感谢。王先生的后事处理完毕后,其家人要求旅行社赔偿各项损失20万元,旅行社出具了王先生的病历和医院的诊断,家人才放弃了要求旅行社赔偿的请求。旅行社本着人文关怀精神,承担了家属探望王先生的住宿和交通等费用,并给予2,000元慰问金。

2. 案例分析

请问:

(1)王先生家属是否有报告其身体状况的义务?

(2)如何评价领队的服务和事后的应对?

专家意见:

(1)王先生家属有如实报告王先生身体状况的义务。在这起纠纷中,王先生家属隐瞒其身体状况,违反了有关法律规定。我国《旅游法》规定,旅游者购买、接受旅游服务时,应当向旅游经营者如实告知与旅游活动相关的个人健康信息,遵守旅游活动中的安全警示规定。

(2)领队服务和获取证据的举动值得肯定。首先是发现王先生身体不适,及时送医,履行了领队的安全保障义务。领队及时获取王先生既往病史的做法值得肯定。可以设想,如果领队不在第一时间获得王先生身体状况的证据,纠纷解决不会如此顺利。

Ⅱ 案例二:受伤未随团旅游的处理

1. 案例简介

范先生与家人一起参加了某国际旅行社的出境旅游,在报名时范先生就和旅行社说明,在旅游期间要拜访朋友。由于旅游者的集合地点是机场,按照旅行社的安排,旅游合同由领队负责与旅游者们在机场签订。但到达机场后,范先生说钱已经交了,合同签不签订都不重要,只要领队认真负责就可以。范先生在到达旅游目的地后的第二天,经领队同意后离团拜访朋友,在正常行走时被当地车辆碾过脚背,驾驶员全责,支付了全额治疗费用,并给予了适当的补偿。行程结束后,范先生要求旅行社退还全额旅游费用,理由是虽然是随团旅游,但旅游行程基本都在医院。范先生强调,如果旅行社不退团款,就到旅游管理部门投诉,要求对旅行社没有签订旅游合同行为进行处罚。最后旅行社只得妥协,全额退还旅游团款3,500元。

2. 案例分析

请问:

(1)范先生要求旅行社退还团款是否合理?

(2)旅行社退还了旅游团款,是否可以不被行政处罚?

专家意见:

(1)范先生要求旅行社退还团款不合理。因为范先生所受伤害应当由驾驶员承担赔偿责任。虽然范先生参加了旅游团,但并不意味着旅行社必须为旅游者受到的所有伤害承担责任。在这起侵权损害纠纷中,侵权责任主体非常明确,而且驾驶员已经承担了全部责任,弥补了范先生遭受的所有损失。

(2)即使旅行社退还了全额团款,仍然要受到旅游主管部门的处罚。因为按照我国《旅游法》等法律的规定,没有签订书面的包价旅游合同,由旅游行政管理部门责令改正,处2万元以上10万元以下的罚款;情节严重的,责令停业整顿1个月至3个月。

Chapter 3

United States of America/ 美国

Part One
Briefing on the United States/美国概况

Unit 1 Overviews/总览

I Basic Information/基本信息

美国

National Flag/国旗	National Emblem/国徽
The national flag of the United States is composed 13 stripes in red and white, and a bule rectangle containing 50 small white five pointed stars in the upper left corner. 50 stars represent 50 states and 13 stripes represent 13 colonies before the independence of the United States. Red symbolizes courage, white truth and blue justice. "The Star and Stripes" is a symbol of Constitution and freedom. 美国国旗的旗面由13道红白相间的宽条构成，左上角有一个包含了50颗白色小五角星的蓝色长方形。50颗小星代表了美国的50个州，而13条间纹则象征着美国最早建国时的13块殖民地。 红色象征勇气，白色象征真理，蓝色则象征正义。"星条旗"（美国国旗）是美国宪法及自由的象征。	The pattern comes from Great Seal of the United States. In fact, the United States doesn't have an official national emblem. But the pattern has become the symbol of US and it can be seen on official documents such as passport. The main image on the national emblem is the bald eagle. The bald eagle is a symbol of power, courage, freedom and immortality. It spreads its wings, holding olive branches and arrow, representing peace and force respectively. The eagle looks to the left, expecting peace. The Ribbon says E Pluribus Unum, meaning united as one. The halo above the Eagle has 13 stars, representing 13 states before the independence of the United States. 美国国徽实际上是美国官方大纹章上的图案。事实上，美国并未指定一个国徽图案。但纹章正面的图像实际上已经成为美国的象征，且经常出现在官方文件上，如护照。 国徽正面图案的主要形象是白头海雕，白头海雕是力量、勇气、自由和不朽的象征。白头海雕的双翅展开。左右鹰爪分别抓着象征和平和武力的橄榄枝和箭。鹰头目视左方，象征着期望和平。鹰嘴叼着的绶带上写着拉丁文格言"合众为一"（E Pluribus Unum）。鹰头上方的象征着拥有主权的新生国家"光环"的蓝色背景里镶着象征美国最初13个州的13颗五角星。

Other Basics/其他基本信息	
Full Name/国家全称	United States of America/美利坚合众国
Other Names/其他称呼	United States，US，USA，Uncle Sam/美国、山姆大叔
Total Area/国土面积	9,372,610 km²/9,372,610平方千米
Population/人口	330,000,000（2021年8月）
Nationality/民族	European-American，Jewish-American，Hispanic-American，Asian-American，African-American/欧裔、犹太裔、拉丁裔、亚裔、非裔
Capital/首都	Washington D.C./华盛顿哥伦比亚特区
National Anthem/国歌	"The Star-Spangled Banner"/《星光灿烂的旗帜》
National Flower/国花	Rose/玫瑰花
National Bird/国鸟	Bald Eagle/白头海鹰
Divisions/行政区划	50 states and 1 special district（Washington D.C.），3,143 counties/50个州与1个特区（华盛顿哥伦比亚特区），3,143个县
Language/语言	English/英语
Major Political Parties/主要政党	Republican Party，Democratic Party/共和党、民主党
Government Type/政府类型	Federal Republic/联邦共和制
Religious Belief/主要宗教信仰	Christian，Jewish，Muslim/基督教、犹太教、伊斯兰教
Currency/货币	US Dollar/美元
Time Difference with Beijing/与北京时差	−13（Summer time−12）/晚13个小时（夏时制晚12个小时）

Ⅱ Physical Geography/自然和地理

The United States is the second largest country in America. It comprises contiguous United States, Alaska in northwest America, and Hawaii in the Central Pacific. It covers an area of 9,372,610 km² (land area 9,158,960 km², inland water area about 200,000 km²). Most of the country is located contiguously in North America between Canada and Mexico with Pacific Ocean to the West and Atlantic Ocean to the East. The climate ranges from humid continental in the north to humid subtropical in the south.

The coastal plain of the Atlantic seaboard gives way further inland to deciduous forests and the rolling hills of the Piedmont. The Appalachian Mountains divide the eastern seaboard from the Great Lakes and the grasslands of the Midwest. The Mississippi-Missouri River, the world's fourth longest river system, runs mainly north-South through the heart of the country. The flat and fertile prairie of the Great Plains stretches to the west, interrupted by a highland region in the southeast.

The Rocky Mountains, at the western edge of the Great Plains, extend north to south across the country, reaching altitudes higher than 14,000 feet (4,300 m) in Colorado. The Sierra Nevada and Cascade mountain ranges run close to the Pacific coast. The lowest and highest points in the contiguous United States are in the state of California, and only about 84 miles (135 km) apart. At an elevation of 20,310 feet (6,190.5 m), Alaska's Denali (Mount McKinley) is the highest peak in the country and North America. Active volcanoes are common throughout Alaska's Alexander and Aleutian Islands, and Hawaii consists of volcanic islands. The supervolcano underlying Yellowstone National Park in the Rockies is the continent's largest volcanic feature. The United States has the most ecoregions out of any country in the world.

美国是美洲第二大的国家,领土包括美国本土、北美洲西北部的阿拉斯加和太平洋中部的夏威夷群岛。面积937.2610万平方千米(其中陆地面积915.8960万平方千米,内陆水域面积约20万平方千米)。美国大部分地区位于北美,在加拿大和墨西哥之间,西临太平洋,东濒大西洋。大部分地区属大陆性气候,南部属亚热带气候。

大西洋海岸平原与内陆落叶林和起伏的群山相连。阿帕拉契亚山脉将东海岸与五大湖和中西部草原分隔开来。密西西比河-密苏里河流域是世界第四大河域,南北向贯穿美国的核心区域。平坦富饶的大草原延伸至西部,东南丘陵横亘其中。

位于大草原西缘的落基山脉,南北贯穿整个美国,海拔最高处(科罗拉多州内)达4,300米。内华达山脉与卡斯克德山脉延伸至太平洋海岸。美国本土的最高点与最低点均位于加利福尼亚州,相距135千米。阿拉斯加的德纳里峰(即麦金利山)是北美最高峰,海拔6,190.5米。亚历山大群岛及阿留申群岛常见活火山,夏威夷也由火山岛组成。黄石国家公园的超级火山是北美最大的火山。美国拥有世界上最多的生态区。

Ⅲ Government and Administration/美国政府机构

The United States Government is federal republic. The President is the head of the state, government, and commander in chief of armed forces. The President is elected indirectly for a four-year term. The Cabinet consists of the President, Vice President, Secretaries, and other appointed members. The Cabinet has no right of group decision making. They worked as assistants and advisory group for the President.

美国实行联邦共和制。总统是国家元首、政府首脑兼武装部队总司令。总统通过间接选举产生,任期4年。政府内阁由总统、副总统、各部部长和总统指定的其他成员组成。内阁实际上只起总统助手和顾问团的作用,没有集体决策的权力。

1. Separation of the Three Powers/三权分立

The government is regulated by a system of checks and balances defined by the U.S. Constitution, which serves as the country's supreme legal document. The federal government comprises three branches:

Legislative: The bicameral Congress, made up of the Senate and the House of Representatives, makes federal law, declares war, approves treaties, has the power of the purse, and the power of impeachment, by which it can remove sitting members of the government. Members of Congress are elected directly by voters from states. There are 100 senators in total, 2 from each state. They work for 6 years in a term. 1/3 of them shall be reelected every 2 years. Members of House of Representatives, 435 in total, are elected according to the population proportion of each state. They work for 2 years in a term. All of them shall be reelected after the term. Both senators and members of House of Representatives can serve consecutive terms. All of them are full-time and may not concurrently hold government posts.

Executive: The President is the commander-in-chief of the military, can veto legislative bills before they become law (subject to Congressional override), and appoints the members of the Cabinet (subject to Senate approval) and other officers, who administer and enforce federal laws and policies.

Judiciary: The Supreme Court and lower federal courts, whose judges are appointed by the President with Senate approval, interpret laws and overturn those they find unconstitutional.

政府受美国宪法规定的制衡体系的监管,宪法是美国的最高法律文件。联邦政府由三个分支机构组成:

立法机关:两院制国会,由参议院与众议院构成,负责制定联邦法律、宣战、批准条约,拥有钱袋权与弹劾权,即弹劾任期内的联邦政府议员。两院议员由各州选民直接选举产生。参议员每州2名,共100名,任期6年,每两年改选1/3。众议员按各州的人口比例分配名额选出,共435名,任期两年,期满全部改选。两院议员均可连任,任期不限。参众议员均系专职,不得兼任政府职务。

行政机关:总统是武装部队总司令,可否决立法草案(受制于国会的推翻表决),任命内阁成员(受制于参议院的赞成)及其他管理与执行联邦法律与政策的官员。

司法机关:最高法院与低级别联邦法院,其法官由参议院通过后接受总统任命,其职能为解释法律与推翻违宪法律。

2. Party/政党

Republican Party was founded in 1854. Republican Abraham Lincoln was elected as the

President in 1861. Up till the year of 1933, except for 1916 years, Republican Party had been in the office of White House.

Democratic Party was founded in 1791. Slave-owner class in the Democratic Party incited people to rise in a rebellion before Civil War in 1861. The Democratic Party had been out of office for 24 years after Civil War. Cleveland was elected as the President in 1885. Since then, the Party has been out of office most of the time.

共和党成立于1854年。共和党人亚伯拉罕·林肯于1861年当选总统。此后至1933年的70多年中,除16年外,共和党一直主政白宫。

民主党于1791年成立。1861年南北战争前夕,该党的南方奴隶主煽动人民叛乱。南北战争结束后,民主党在野24年。1885年克利夫兰当选总统。此后该党又大部分时间在野。

Unit 2 History and People/历史和人民

I History/历史

1. Indigenous Peoples and Pre-Columbian History/原住民与前哥伦布时期

It has been generally accepted that the first inhabitants of North America migrated from Siberia by way of the Bering land bridge and arrived at least 12,000 years ago. The Clovis culture appeared around 11000 BC, and is considered to be the ancestor and is believed to represent the first human settlement of the Americas.

With the progress of European colonization in the territories of the contemporary United States, the native Americans were often conquered and displaced. The first interaction between Europeans and native Americans was made by the Norsemen. The Norse attempted to settle in North America about 500 years before Columbus.

人们普遍认为,距今12,000年前,第一批北美原住民从西伯利亚出发,翻过白令陆桥,到达北美。起源于公元前11000年的克洛维斯文化的先民被认为是美国人的祖先,是美洲大陆第一批居民的代表。

随着欧洲殖民在美国领土上的深入,美国土著常常被征服和流离失所。欧洲人和美洲土著之间的第一次交流是由斯堪的纳维亚人进行的。早在哥伦布前500年左右,斯堪的纳维亚人已试图定居北美。

2. European Settlements/欧洲殖民

The first Europeans to arrive in the territory of the modern United States were Spanish in 1513. The Spanish set up the first settlements in Florida and New Mexico. The French established their own as well along the Mississippi River. Successful English settlement on the eastern coast of North America began with the Virginia Colony in 1607 at Jamestown and the Pilgrims' Plymouth Colony in 1620. The Mayflower Compact, signed by the Pilgrims before disembarking established precedents for the pattern of representative self-government and constitutionalism that would develop throughout the American colonies.

With the successful establisment of British colonies in Georgia in 1732, 13 European colonies in North America were established. The 13 colonies later became the original 13 states of the United States.

第一批欧洲殖民者来自西班牙,他们于1513年来到北美,在佛罗里达以及新墨西哥建立了殖民地。法国人于密西西比河旁建立了自己的殖民地。而英国人则于1607年和1620年分别在东海岸的弗吉尼亚州詹姆斯镇和普利茅斯建立了殖民地。五月花号上的清教徒签立的《五月花号公约》则开创了代表自治与立宪制度的先例,这种制度后来在整个美洲殖民地发展起来。

随着英国于1732年成功在乔治亚州建立殖民地,13个位于北美的欧洲殖民地建立起来。这13个殖民地后来成为美国最初的13个州。

3. Independence and Expansion/独立与扩张

The American Revolutionary War was the first successful colonial war of independence against a European power. Americans had developed an ideology of "republicanism" asserting that government rested on the will of the people. They demanded their rights as Englishmen and "no taxation without representation". The British insisted on administering the empire through Parliament, and the conflict escalated into war.

The Second Continental Congress unanimously adopted the Declaration of Independence on July 4, 1776, which recognized that all men are created equal and endowed by their Creator with unalienable rights and that those rights were not being protected by Great Britain, and declared, in the words of the resolution, that the thirteen United Colonies formed an independent nation and had no further allegiance to the British crown. The fourth day of July is celebrated annually as Independence Day.

美国独立战争是第一个成功反对欧洲列强的殖民地独立战争。美国人形成了一种"共和主义"的意识形态,主张政府应当倚赖人民的意志,明确提出"无代表不纳税"的口号,反对英国向殖民地征税。而英国则坚持议会制度,于是冲突不可避免地升级成为一场战争。

第二届大陆会议于1776年7月4日一致通过了《独立宣言》,其承认人人生而平等,造物主赋予人人不可剥夺的权利,并且这些权利不受英国保护。13个英属北美殖民地组成独立国家,不再效忠英国王室。因此7月4日也被称为独立日。

4. Civil War/南北战争

Because of the great differences between the north and the south in their attitudes towards slavery, the United States of America in the north and the United States of America in the South launched the civil war, also known as the American Civil War. The South fought for the freedom to own slaves, while the Union at first simply fought to maintain the country as one united whole. Lincoln delivered his Emancipation Proclamation, and the main purpose of the war from the Union's viewpoint became the abolition of slavery. The South eventually failed in April 9th, 1865. The victory abolished the slavery, restoring the United States.

由于美国南北两方对于奴隶制的态度分歧巨大,北方的美利坚合众国和南方的美利坚联盟国展开了南北战争,也称美国内战。南方为了拥有奴隶而战,而北方联邦起初是为了维护国家统一而战。后来,林肯发表了奴隶解放宣言,战争演变为一场消灭奴隶制的革命斗争。1865年4月9日,南方宣告失败,奴隶制被废除,美国恢复统一。

5. World War I, Great Depression, and World War II/第一次世界大战、大萧条和第二次世界大战

The United States remained neutral from the outbreak of World War I in 1914 until 1917, when it joined the war as an "associated power", alongside the formal Allies of World War I, helping to turn the tide against the Central Powers.

The prosperity of the Roaring Twenties ended with the Wall Street Crash of 1929 and the onset of the Great Depression. After his election as president in 1932, Franklin D. Roosevelt responded with the New Deal, which included the establishment of the Social Security system.

During World War II while Germany conquered much of continental Europe, the United States began supplying material to the Allies in March 1941 through the Lend-Lease program. On December 7, 1941, the Empire of Japan launched a surprise attack on Pearl Harbor, prompting the United States to join the Allies against the Axis powers. The United States eventually developed the first nuclear weapons and used them on Japan in the cities of Hiroshima and Nagasaki; causing the Japanese to surrender on September 2, ending World War II.

1914年第一次世界大战爆发时,美国一直保持中立,直到1917年才与第一次世界大战

的正式盟国一道,以"协约国"的身份参加了这场战争,并帮助扭转了反对同盟国的战势。

美国兴旺的20年代随着1929年华尔街大崩盘和经济大萧条宣告终止。随后1932年富兰克林·D.罗斯福当选总统,他推行的罗斯福新政挽救了美国的严重经济危机,其中也包括社会保障制度的建立。

在第二次世界大战中,德国征服了欧洲大陆众多国家与地区。美国1941年3月签署《租借法案》,向盟国提供物资。1941年12月7日,日本偷袭珍珠港,促使美国加入同盟国对抗轴心国。美国最终开发了第一批核武器,并投掷于日本的广岛、长崎两座城市。日本最终在1945年9月2日宣布投降,至此第二次世界大战结束。

6. Cold War/冷战

After World War II, the United States and the Soviet Union jockeyed for power during what became known as the Cold War, driven by an ideological divide between capitalism and communism. After the dissolution of the Warsaw Pact in 1991, the Soviet Union disintegrated and the cold war ended. This brought about unipolarity with the U. S. unchallenged as the world's dominant superpower.

第二次世界大战结束之后,在资本主义和共产主义意识形态分歧的驱使下,美国和苏联在所谓的冷战期间争夺权力。1991年苏联解体,最终冷战结束。这使得世界变为单极,美国成为世界上占主导地位的超级大国,不受挑战。

II People and Figures/人民及名人

The United States of America has a population of 330 million (Aug. 2021). Non-Hispanic Whites accounted for 62.1%; Hispanics accounted for 17.4%, Africans accounted for 13.2%, Asians accounted for 5.4%, Mixed-blood people accounted for 2.5%, Indian and Alaska Indigenous people accounted for 1.2%, Hawaii Indigenous People and Pacific Ocean Islanders accounted for 0.2%. (A small number of people were counted repeatedly in other ethnic groups.)

美国人口约3.30亿(截至2021年8月)。非拉美裔白人约占62.1%;拉美裔约占17.4%,非洲裔约占13.2%,亚裔约占5.4%,混血约占2.5%,印第安人和阿拉斯加原住民约占1.2%,夏威夷原住民或其他太平洋岛民约占0.2%。(少部分人在其他族群内被重复统计)。

1. Abraham Lincoln/亚伯拉罕·林肯

Abraham Lincoln was born in Feb.12th, 1809. He is the 16th President of the United States of America. As a famous politician and master strategist in the history of America, President Lincoln abolished slavery system during his term. He firmly opposed the division of the country, demanded a united nation since the outbreak of Civil War and protected the unalienable right and endowed by their Creator that all men are created equal. He signed Homestead Act and delivered Emancipation Proclamation, laying a solid foundation for the victory of Civil War.

亚伯拉罕·林肯生于1809年2月12日,美国政治家、战略家、第16任总统。林肯在任期间主导废除了美国黑人奴隶制。美国南北战争爆发后,林肯坚决反对国家分裂,倡议建一个统一的国家。他维护了美利坚联邦及其领土上不分人种、人人生而平等的权利。他签署了《宅地法》,颁布了《解放黑人奴隶宣言》,为北方获得南北战争的胜利奠定了基础。

2. George Washington/乔治·华盛顿

George Washington was born in Feb. 22nd, 1732. He is the first President of the United States of America in the history, a founding father of the country. He was commander-in-chief of Continental Army in American Revolutionary War. President Washington presided over the Constitutional Convention, drawing up the Constitution. Because Washington played the most important role in the war of independence and the founding of the United States, he was honored as "the father of the United States".

乔治·华盛顿生于1732年2月22日,他是美国的开国元勋、首任总统。他在美国独立战争时任大陆军的总司令。他主持了制宪会议,制定了美国宪法。华盛顿由于扮演了美国独立战争和建国中最重要的角色,故被尊称为"美国国父"。

3. Franklin Roosevelt/富兰克林·罗斯福

Franklin Delano Roosevelt, the 32th President of America, was born in Jan. 30th, 1882. He responded the Great Depression in 1930s' well with the New Deal. In World War Ⅱ, President Roosevelt declared war on the Empire of Japan. The US helped to turn the tide against the Axis Powers.

1882年1月30日,美国第32任总统富兰克林·德拉诺·罗斯福出生。他推行新政,很好地应对了20世纪30年代的大萧条。在第二次世界大战期间,罗斯福向日本帝国宣战。美国帮助扭转了反对轴心国的局势。

Unit 3 Culture and Education/文化和教育

Ⅰ Culture/文化

The United States is home to many cultures and a wide variety of ethnic groups, traditions, and values. Mainstream American culture is a western culture largely derived from the traditions of European immigrants with influences from many other sources, such as traditions brought by slaves from Africa. More recent immigration from Asia and especially Latin America has added to a cultural mix that has been described as both a homogenizing melting pot, and a heterogeneous salad bowl in which immigrants and their descendants retain distinctive cultural characteristics.

美国是多元文化与族群的汇聚地,在这里有众多不同的传统与价值观。主流美国文化很大程度上植根于欧洲移民的文化传统,也受其他传统的影响,诸如来源于非洲黑奴的一些传统。近些年来亚洲和拉丁美洲移民文化的加入使得人们更愿意把美国描述成文化大熔炉与文化沙拉碗,移民及其后代在美国文化中保留着其自身鲜明的文化特征。

1. Food/食物

Mainstream American cuisine is similar to that in other Western countries. Wheat is the primary cereal grain and many dishes use indigenous ingredients, such as turkey, venison, potatoes, sweet potatoes, corn, squash, and maple syrup which were consumed by Native Americans and early European settlers. These homegrown foods are part of a shared national menu on one of America's most popular holidays, Thanksgiving, when some Americans make traditional foods to celebrate the occasion.

Characteristic dishes such as apple pie, fried chicken, pizza, hamburgers, and hot dogs derive from the recipes of various immigrants. French fries, Mexican dishes such as burritos and tacos, and pasta dishes freely adapted from Italian sources are widely consumed. Americans prefer coffee to tea. Americans drink three times as much coffee as tea.

The American fast food industry, the world's largest, pioneered the drive-through format in the 1940s. Fast food consumption has sparked health concerns. During the 1980s and 1990s, Americans' caloric intake rose 24%; frequent dining at fast food outlets is associated with what public health officials call the American "obesity epidemic".

主流美国食物与其他西方国家相似。小麦是美国的主要谷类作物。很多菜肴使用本土食材,例如火鸡、鹿肉、土豆、番薯、玉米、南瓜、枫糖浆等,这些都是美洲土著和早期欧洲定居者食用的。这些本土美食在传统美国节日菜单上十分常见,如一些美国人在感恩节制作传统食物来庆祝节日。

美国特色美食诸如苹果派、炸鸡、比萨、汉堡、热狗,都来源于各个不同的移民族群。比如法式炸薯条、墨西哥玉米卷饼、意大利面,这些都被广泛食用。相比于茶,美国人更爱喝咖啡。美国人喝的咖啡是茶的三倍。

美国快餐业是世界上最大的快餐业,在20世纪40年代开创了"免下车"模式。快餐行业的高速发展也给美国人带来了健康方面的隐忧。20世纪八九十年代整个美国的卡路里摄入量增长24%。不少经常光顾速食餐厅的美国人也受到了"肥胖症"的困扰。

2. Music/音乐

The rhythmic and lyrical styles of African-American music have deeply influenced American music at large, distinguishing it from European and African traditions. Elements from folk idioms such as the blues and what is now known as old-time music were adopted and transformed into popular genres with global audiences. Jazz was developed by innovators such as Louis Armstrong and Duke Ellington early in the 20th century. Country music developed in the 1920s, and rhythm and blues in the 1940s.

Elvis Presley and Chuck Berry were among the mid-1950s pioneers of rock and roll. Rock bands such as Metallica, the Eagles, and Aerosmith are among the highest grossing in worldwide sales. In the 1960s, Bob Dylan emerged from the folk revival to become one of America's most celebrated songwriters and James Brown led the development of funk.

More recent American creations include hip hop and house music. American pop stars such as Elvis Presley, Michael Jackson, and Madonna have become global celebrities.

美国黑人音乐的节奏与韵律深刻影响着美国音乐,使美国音乐区别于欧洲和非洲的传统音乐。民间音乐的元素诸如蓝调以及复古音乐得以充分的继承并逐渐流行起来。路易斯·阿姆斯特朗和杜克·艾灵顿于20世纪前期开创了爵士乐。起源于20世纪20年代的乡村音乐和40年代的节奏布鲁斯也是美国音乐的代表。

埃尔维斯·普雷斯利和查克·贝里是20世纪50年代摇滚乐的先驱。金属乐队、老鹰乐队、史密斯飞船等一批摇滚乐队席卷全球。20世纪60年代,鲍勃·迪伦在民谣复兴中崭露头角,成为美国最有名的词曲作家之一。詹姆斯·布朗则引领了疯克音乐的浪潮。

更现代的美国音乐包括嘻哈与浩室音乐。美国的流行歌手,如埃尔维斯·普莱斯利(猫王)、迈克尔·杰克逊与麦当娜成为世界流行乐坛的宠儿。

3. Sport/体育

American football is by several measures the most popular spectator sport; the National Football League (NFL) has the highest average attendance of any sports league in the world, and the Super Bowl is watched by millions globally. Baseball has been regarded as the U.S. national sport since the late 19th century, with Major League Baseball (MLB) being the top league. Basketball and ice hockey are the country's next two leading professional team sports, with the top leagues being the National Basketball Association (NBA) and the National Hockey League (NHL).

Eight Olympic Games have taken place in the United States (2028 Summer Olympics will mark the ninth time). Lacrosse and surfing arose from Native American and Native Hawaiian activities that predate Western contact. The most watched individual sports are golf and auto racing, particularly NASCAR. Rugby union is considered the fastest growing sport in the U.S.

美式橄榄球从各个方面来看都是最受欢迎的体育赛事。美国国家橄榄球联盟（NFL）拥有全世界最高的上座率。每年有数百万人在收看超级碗。从19世纪末，棒球也被视为美国的国家运动，美国职业棒球大联盟（MLB）是这项运动的最高级别联赛。篮球和曲棍球也是风靡美国的职业团体运动项目，顶级联赛是全美职业篮球联盟（NBA）和美国冰球联盟（NHL）。

美国曾举办过8届奥林匹克运动会（2028年夏季奥运会将是第9次）。长曲棍球和冲浪分别兴起于美国本土与夏威夷。最吸引人的个人运动赛事是高尔夫球和赛车，尤其是全美运动汽车竞赛协会（NASCAR）。英式橄榄球在美国被誉为发展最快的运动。

Ⅱ Education/教育

American public education is operated by state and local governments, regulated by the United States Department of Education through restrictions on federal grants. In most states, children are required to attend school from the age of six or seven (generally, kindergarten or first grade) until they turn 18 (generally bringing them through twelfth grade, the end of high school); some states allow students to leave school at 16 or 17.

About 12% of children are enrolled in parochial or nonsectarian private schools. Just over 2% of children are homeschooled. The U.S. spends more on education per student than any nation in the world, spending more than $11,000 per elementary student in 2010 and more than $12,000 per high school student. Some 80% of U.S. college students attend public universities.

Of Americans 25 and older, 84.6% graduated from high school, 52.6% attended some college, 27.2% earned a bachelor's degree, and 9.6% earned graduate degrees. The basic literacy rate is approximately 99%. The United Nations assigns the United States an Education Index of 0.97, tying it for 12th in the world.

The United States has many competitive private and public institutions of higher education. The majority of the world's top universities listed by different ranking organizations are in the U.S. There are also local community colleges with generally more open admission policies, shorter academic programs, and lower tuition.

美国公共教育由州和地方政府管理，由美国教育部通过限制联邦拨款进行规范。在大部分州,儿童从6或7岁(幼儿园或1年级)至18岁(一般是从12年级到高中毕业)接受义务教育。部分州学生可提前一至两年完成义务教育。

　　大约有12%的美国孩子上教区学校或非教派私立学校。只有约2%的孩子在家学习。美国是世界上人均教育投入最高的国家。2010年美国小学生人均教育投入超过11,000美元,高中生人均投入超12,000美元。约80%的美国学生选择就读公立大学。

　　全美25岁及以上年龄段调查显示,84.6%的人拥有高中学历,52.6%的人拥有大学学历,27.2%的人拥有学士学位,还有9.6%的人拥有硕士学位。基本识字率约为99%。联合国评定美国教育指数为0.97,居世界第12位。

　　美国拥有众多极具竞争力的公立和私立高等学府。各排名机构公布的世界名校排名中,美国高校占据半壁江山。另外,美国还有不少社区大学,这些大学入学门槛相对较低,学制较短,学费较低。

Unit 4　Major Attractions/主要景点

Ⅰ　Yellowstone National Park/黄石国家公园

Yellowstone National Park is located in the state of Wyoming. It consists of 5 main areas. The area of Mammoth Hot Springs in the northwest is famous for its limestone steps and hot spring in the world. The area of Roosevelt has landscape in western America. Grand Canyon and Yellowstone Waterfall can be found in the center. Lake Region lies in southeast and Fountains southwest. Yellowstone National Park was made a UNESCO World Cultural Heritage Site in 1978.

　　黄石国家公园位于美国怀俄明州。它主要分五个区:西北的猛犸象温泉区以石灰石台阶和温泉闻名于世;罗斯福区是美国西部景观;中间为峡谷区,可观赏黄石大峡谷和瀑布;东南为黄石湖区;西南为喷泉区。黄石国家公园于1978年被联合国教科文组织列为世界文化遗产。

Ⅱ　Statue of Liberty/自由女神像

Statue of Liberty is America's National Monument sent by France in 1876 to celebrate the 100th anniversary of the independence of America. It has the official name of Liberty Enlightening the World. It is located along the Hudson River, New York. Statue of Liberty has a height of 45 meters and weight of 225 tons. Designed by Bartholdi, the French sculptor, the Statue dresses in ancient Greek style with a 7-pointed crown symbolizing 7 continents in the world. She holds a plate with "July IV MDCCLXXVI" on it and a torch representing freedom on her hands. Shattered shackles and chains signifies people's successful fight against tyranny. It is a symbol of the United States and testimony to the friendship between the two peoples. Statue of Liberty was made a UNESCO World Cultural Heritage Site in 1984.

自由女神像是1876年法国为庆祝美国独立100周年而设立的美国国家纪念碑。它的正式名称是"自由照耀世界",位于美国纽约海港内自由岛的哈德逊河口附近。自由女神像高45米,重225吨。这座雕像由法国雕塑家巴托尔迪设计,采用古希腊风格,头戴光芒四射冠冕,七道尖芒象征七大洲。她右手高举象征自由的火炬,左手捧着一块铭牌,上面刻着"July IV MDCCLXXVI";脚下是打碎的手铐、脚镣和锁链,象征着挣脱暴政的约束和自由。自由女神像是美国的象征,也是美法人民友谊象征。1984年,自由女神像被联合国教科文组织列入世界遗产名录。

Ⅲ Golden Gate Bridge/金门大桥

Golden Gate Bridge is located in San Francisco, USA. The bridge spans over 1,900 meters. It was built with over 100,000 tons of steel and designed by Joseph Struss. During the gold rush, it was named after a gateway to the gold. Golden Gate Bridge connects Northern California and San Francisco Peninsula. It is often seen in many American movies such as *Rise of the Planet of the Apes* and *X-Men*. The color of the Golden Gate Bridge is international orange, which is particularly eye-catching even in a heavy fog. It is widely considered a great example of architecture beauty and even a wonder in the modern world.

金门大桥位于美国旧金山,桥身全长1,900多米。它是用10万多吨钢材建成,由桥梁工程师约瑟夫·斯特劳斯设计。淘金热时期,因其如同通往金矿的一扇大门而得名。金门大桥的北端连接北加利福尼亚,南端连接旧金山半岛。《猩球崛起》《X战警》等众多美国大片中也常常出现大桥的身影。金门大桥桥身的颜色为国际橘,即使在大雾中也显得格外醒目。它被广泛认为是建筑美的典范,更被认为是现代的世界奇迹之一。

Part Two
Outbound Tour Guide Operation/出境领队实务

Unit 1 Situational Dialogues/情景对话

Ⅰ Dialogue 1 Boarding Gate

(*A*：*airport staff*   *B*：*tour leader*)

B：Hi, every one. Please be gathered together to see if the family members have all arrived. Please follow me. I will check the boarding gate first. Excuse me, madam. We are going to fly to Los Angeles. Would you please tell me which gate is for the flight?

A：What is your flight number?

B：My flight number is CA183.

A：Wait a moment. Let me check.

B：OK.

A：You are going to take CA183 to Los Angeles at Gate 22.

B：How can I get to Gate 22?

A：You need to go upstairs and then turn right. Follow the sign and you will get there.

B：Thank you. By the way, is it far from here? How long will it take to go to Gate 22?

A：Not very far actually. It will take you about 15 minutes. Now it's 15：20. Your boarding time is 16：45. You need to be at the gate 30 minutes before boarding. You have plenty of time.

B：Is the duty free shops far away from the gate? I want to stroll around and buy some gifts for friends and relatives.

A：They are just on your way to the gate. The duty free shops sell numerous kinds of things from lady's skincare, make-ups to luxuries over the world. The most popular brands for lady's skincare are Lar Mer[①] and Estée Lauder[②] from America, Guerlain[③] and Dior[④] from France. There is nothing you will fail to buy, and there is something you will fail to expect.

B：Thank you very much. Can I rush over now？ Can't wait.

A：OK. My reminder, pay attention to the airport announcements in case the boarding gate for your flight will be changed for some reason. Otherwise you'll miss it.

B：Thank you.

A：Have a good trip. Bye-bye.

Notes：

① Lar Mer：海蓝之谜（美国护肤品）。

② Estée Lauder：雅诗兰黛（美国护肤、化妆品）。

③ Guerlain：娇兰（法国化妆品）。

④ Dior：迪奥（法国品牌）。

Ⅱ Dialogue 2　American Values

（*A：tourist　B：tour guide*）

A：Good morning, Mr. Guide.

B：Good morning, Sir.

A：I would like to ask you some questions if I may.

B：Sure. Go ahead, please.

A：We often hear the conception of "American Values". Can you tell me what they are?

B：It's a big topic. As far as I understand it, "American Values" differ in different context. Generally speaking, they include individualism, equality, materialism, science and technology, work and leisure, competition, action and achievement oriented and so on.

A：Very good. But can you go to some details, please?

B：Of course. Individualism, the first one, is the belief that each person is unique, special, and a"basic unit of nature". Americans tend to emphasize individual initiative and stress the need for independence. They put premium on individual expression and value privacy. This is probably the most basic of all the American values. Scholars and outside observers often call this value individualism, but many Americans use the word freedom. It is one of the most respected and popular words in the United States today.

A: Personally, I like the word freedom better than individualism too. But I wonder whether there is any difference between the freedom in Americans' eye and that in other part of the world?

B: By freedom, Americans mean the desire and the right of all individuals to control their own destiny without outside interference from the government, a ruling noble class, the church, or any other organized authority. The desire to be free of controls was a basic value of the new nation in 1776, and it has continued to attract immigrants to this country.

A: Perfect. Thank you very much. Now, what about the second one, equality?

B: It is important to understand what most Americans mean when they say they believe in equality of opportunity. They do not mean that everyone is—or should be—equal. However, they do mean that each individual should have an equal chance for success. Americans see much of life as a race for success. For them, equality means that everyone should have an equal chance to enter the race and win. In other words, equality of opportunity may be thought of as an ethical rule. It helps ensure that the race for success is a fair one and that a person does not win just because he or she was born into a wealthy family, or lose because of race or religion. This American concept of "fair play" is an important aspect of the belief in equality of opportunity.

A: Well said. As we will leave for sightseeing soon, just tell me about one more and save the rest for the next time.

B: No problem. The next one is materialism. Because of its incredibly abundant natural resources, the United States appeared to be a land of plenty where millions could come to seek their fortunes. The phrase "going from rags to riches" became a slogan for the "American Dream". Because of the vast riches of the North American continent, the dream came true for many of the immigrants. They achieved material success and many became very attached to material things. Material wealth became a value to the American people.

A: It may sound strange to you, but we Chinese have a very different understanding of "materialism". It refers to a form of philosophical monism which holds that matter is the fundamental substance in nature, and that all phenomena including mental phenomena and consciousness, are results of material interactions.

B: That's very interesting. I might as well tell you, here in America, placing a high value on material possessions is called materialism, but this is a word that most Americans find offensive. To say that a person is materialistic is an insult. To an American, this means that this person values material possessions above all else. Americans do not like to be called materialistic because they feel that this unfairly accuses them of loving only material things and of having no religious values. Nevertheless, acquiring and maintaining a large number of material possessions is still of great importance to most Americans.

A: Thank you so much for telling me in such details about the American values. The pity is we have no more time today. We'll have to keep the rest for another time. But make sure, I'll come to you again soon. Thank you again

B: You are very welcome. It's a great pleasure talking with you.

Ⅲ Dialogue 3 Thanksgiving Day in America

(*A*: *Chinese tourist*   *B*: *American tour guide*)

A: What's the day of the week today, Mr. Guide?

B: It's Thursday today, Sir.

A: Right. If I remember it correctly, today is your Thanksgiving Day, isn't it?

B: No, not yet. Today is the third Thursday of November. Thanksgiving Day is on the fourth Thursday of November. That is the next Thursday.

A: I'm sorry. I really find it hard to remember the time of some of your holidays. Our holidays are usually set on fixed calendar days while yours are scheduled in different ways.

B: You are right. But when you get used to it, it's not a problem.

A: That's true. By the way, is Thanksgiving Day a big holiday in America?

B: You bet. Thanksgiving Day is a public holiday. It is a day off for the general population, and schools and most businesses are closed. It is a federal holiday in the United States.

A: What festivities are held to celebrate the holiday?

B: Thanksgiving Day is a day for people in the US to give thanks for what they have. Families and friends get together for a meal, which traditionally includes a roast turkey, stuffing, potatoes, vegetables, cranberry sauce, gravy, and pumpkin pie. In some cities and towns, there are parades during the Thanksgiving weekend. In most areas, these festivities also mark the opening of the Christmas shopping season.

A: Mentioning turkey, I have been wondering why it is included in the celebration of Thanksgiving Day.

B: Legend has it that Plymouth's Thanksgiving began with a few colonists going out "fowling," possibly for turkeys but more probably for the easier prey of geese and ducks, since they "in one day killed as much as to serve the company almost a week." Next, 90 or so Wampanoag[①], the native Americans, made a surprise appearance at the settlement's gate, and over the next few days the two groups socialized without incident. The Wampanoag contributed venison to the feast, which included the fowl and probably fish, eels, shellfish, stews, vegetables, and beer.

A: How interesting! So the tradition has a history of almost 400 years.

B: Legend is just legend. In fact, the food selection wasn't because of the three-day feast held back in 1621 between the Pilgrims and the Wampanoag like some believe. Historians have found they ate some turkey then, but venison was the main meat eaten. Potatoes also weren't eaten at that meal, because they weren't grown in the area at the time. Pies were not on the menu because they weren't yet growing wheat either.

A: How did they get into the menu then?

B: Abraham Lincoln proclaimed a national Thanksgiving Day in 1863, but it wasn't until the 1900s that the holiday became popular across the country. In the early 20th century, things like turkey and cornbread and stuffing were something that was taught to the new, who were then immigrants, as a way of Americanizing them. As a result, many of these Thanksgiving staples became more popular.

A: You just said that Abraham Lincoln proclaimed a national Thanksgiving Day in 1863. So it was not a national holiday until then. What was the situation of Thanksgiving Day before that time?

B: Americans generally believe that their Thanksgiving is modeled on a 1621 harvest feast shared by the English colonists (Pilgrims) of Plymouth and the Wampanoag people. The New England colonists were accustomed to regularly celebrating Thanksgiving days of prayer thanking God for blessings such as military victory or the end of a drought. The U.

S. Continental Congress proclaimed a national Thanksgiving upon the enactment of the Constitution. Yet, after 1798, the new U.S. Congress left Thanksgiving declarations to the states. Thanksgiving Day did not become an official holiday until Northerners dominated the federal government. While sectional tensions prevailed in the mid-19th century, Sarah Josepha Hale, the editor of the popular magazine *Godey's Lady's Book*, campaigned for a national Thanksgiving Day to promote unity. She finally won the support of President Abraham Lincoln. On October 3, 1863, during the Civil War, Lincoln proclaimed a national day of thanksgiving to be celebrated on Thursday, November 26.

A: So, from then on the holiday is celebrated on the fourth Thursday in November, isn't it?

B: Not that soon. It was after a joint resolution of Congress in 1941 that Roosevelt issued a proclamation in 1942, designating the fourth Thursday in November as Thanksgiving Day.

Notes:

① Wampanoag: a meber of an Algonquian people who lived in Rhode Isand and Massachusetts.

Unit 2　Case Study/案例分析

Ⅰ　案例一:对旅游事故投诉的处理

1. 案例简介

上海某组团社2019年6月30日的美国东西海岸黄石国家公园团,游客分别来自北京、温州、安徽、南京、上海和香港,一团30+1人,从上海浦东机场出境。出发前,在上海浦东机场,香港人蔡先生因为没有得到旅行社的通知,需要携带港澳地区往来居民通行证在上海出境,被告知无法出境,被迫取消行程,无法参团。团队在2019年7月11日抵达盐湖城入住酒店,入住后导游并未履行安全提醒告知义务,客人朱某某和王某某使用谷歌导航搜索发现酒店附近有超市,相约在晚上8点左右自行从酒店步行前往周边的超市购物,购物结束走出超市时,不慎遇到歹徒抢劫。王某某的随身背包被歹徒抢走,背包中的钱包、信用卡和护照丢失;朱某某受伤。发生抢劫后,他们随即电话了导游和领队,导游和领队第一时间赶到案发现场,报警911。警察到达后随即做案件笔录并留有一份出警单给到当事人;随后,导游立即送受伤的朱某某前往医院检查、治疗并入院观察。朱某某因伤势原因,在盐湖城留院观察了3天,后旅行社协助其改签机票提前回国。王某某在参加完旅游行程后,通过旅行社的协助如期回国。

就此,蔡先生投诉上海组团社,因为旅行社的过失,导致自己旅行计划被取消,要求索赔。王某某和朱某某投诉旅行社导游未尽到安全告知义务,导致自己护照丢失、受伤住院和滞留境外,要求索赔。请问该如何处理?

2. 案例分析

(1)关于行程被取消的分析。

蔡先生系香港人,蔡先生如果在香港直接出境赴美是不需要携带港澳地区往来居民通行证的,但是他在上海出境则必须携带港澳地区往来居民通行证方能出境。旅行社在出行前未告知蔡先生相关事项,导致蔡先生被迫取消行程,旅行社应承担相应的责任和赔偿。

根据《旅游法》第五章旅游服务合同

第六十二条　订立包价旅游合同时,旅行社应当向旅游者告知下列事项:(一)旅游者不适合参加旅游活动的情形;(二)旅游活动中的安全注意事项;(三)旅行社依法可以减免责任的信息;(四)旅游者应当注意的旅游目的地相关法律、法规和风俗习惯、宗教禁忌,依照中国法律不宜参加的活动等;(五)法律、法规规定的其他应当告知的事项。　在包价旅游合同履行中,遇有前款规定事项的,旅行社也应当告知旅游者。

第七十条　旅行社不履行包价旅游合同义务或者履行合同义务不符合约定的,应当依法承担继续履行、采取补救措施或者赔偿损失等违约责任;造成旅游者人身损害、财产损失的,应当依法承担赔偿责任。旅行社具备履行条件,经旅游者要求仍拒绝履行合同,造成旅游者人身损害、滞留等严重后果的,旅游者还可以要求旅行社支付旅游费用一倍以上三倍以下的赔偿金。由于旅游者自身原因导致包价旅游合同不能履行或者不能按照约定履行,或者造成旅游者人身损害、财产损失的,旅行社不承担责任。　在旅游者自行安排活动期间,旅行社未尽到安全提示、救助义务的,应当对旅游者的人身损害、财产损失承担相应责任。

第七十四条　旅行社接受旅游者的委托,为其代订交通、住宿、餐饮、游览、娱乐等旅游服务,收取代办费用的,应当亲自处理委托事务。因旅行社的过错给旅游者造成损失的,旅行社应当承担赔偿责任。旅行社接受旅游者的委托,为其提供旅游行程设计、旅游信息咨询等服务的,应当保证设计合理、可行,信息及时、准确。

(2)关于人身财产安全的分析。

王某某和朱某某投诉旅行社导游未尽到安全告知义务,导致自己护照丢失、受伤住院和滞留境外,要求索赔。

首先,导游和领队在入住酒店后,应该尽到相应的安全告知义务。由于下榻酒店后,导游未尽到安全告知义务,使得朱某某和王某某忽略了海外夜间出行的安全问题,而遇到抢劫事件,旅行社需要承担相应的过失责任。因为旅行社非直接加害人,只宜对顾客做出适当的补偿。

其次,旅游者遇到抢劫后,旅行社的报警处理、送医检查并协助客人办理改签回国事宜,履行了其应尽的义务,在协助过程中所产生的一切费用,应由旅游者个人自行承担。

根据《旅行社条例》第三十九条

旅行社对可能危及旅游者人身、财产安全的事项,应当向旅游者做出真实的说明和明确的警示,并采取防止危害发生的必要措施。发生危及旅游者人身安全情形的,旅行社及其委派的导游人员、领队人员应当采取必要的处置措施并及时报告旅游行政管理部门;在境外发生的,还应当及时报告中华人民共和国驻该国使领馆、相关驻外机构、当地警方。

根据《旅游法》第六章　旅游安全

第八十条 旅游经营者应当就旅游活动中的下列事项,以明示的方式事先向旅游者做出说明或者警示:(一)正确使用相关设施、设备的方法;(二)必要的安全防范和应急措施;(三)未向旅游者开放的经营、服务场所和设施、设备;(四)不适宜参加相关活动的群体;(五)可能危及旅游者人身、财产安全的其他情形。

第八十一条　突发事件或者旅游安全事故发生后,旅游经营者应当立即采取必要的救助和处置措施,依法履行报告义务,并对旅游者做出妥善安排。

第八十二条　旅游者在人身、财产安全遇有危险时,有权请求旅游经营者、当地政府和相关机构进行及时救助。中国出境旅游者在境外陷于困境时,有权请求我国驻当地机构在其职责范围内给予协助和保护。旅游者接受相关组织或者机构的救助后,应当支付应由个人承担的费用。

(3)关于护照遗失问题的分析。

王某某的随身背包被歹徒抢走,背包中的钱包、信用卡和护照随同丢失,王某某在参加完旅游行程后,通过旅行社的协助如期回国。

首先,游客在出行前建议携带护照和签证页复印件若干份。

其次,当发生护照被盗,需要立即在当地报警,拿到报警证明。警方出具的护照丢失证明是办理旅行证或者补办护照的必备材料之一。

再次,丢失护照的旅游者需要凭借警方出具的护照丢失证明、护照和签证页复印件或其他相关的有效身份证明,在周一到周五的工作时间,前往当地大使馆补办旅行证或护照。倘若案发地没有大使馆,可以凭借警方出具的护照丢失证明和有效身份证明(复印件或照片均可)搭乘美国境内的国内航班前往有大使馆的城市补办证件。根据不同航空公司的个别规定,也可凭借警方出具的护照丢失证明和有效身份证明直接搭乘国际航班回国后补办护照。

根据《中华人民共和国护照法》第二十三条

短期出国的公民在国外发生护照遗失、被盗或者损毁不能使用等情形,应当向中华人民共和国驻外使馆、领馆或者外交部委托的其他驻外机构申请中华人民共和国旅行证。

Ⅱ 案例二:航班时间变更的投诉处理

胡先生夫妇赴美国"自由行",委托旅行社代订机票和酒店。原定返程航班起飞时间为2018年4月5日下午18:30,现提前至中午12:50,且出发前未被告知。胡先生夫妇要求赔偿"在美国少玩6小时的损失和回上海后多出来的实际住宿费"。

1. 调查事实和处理结果

(1)胡先生夫妇于2018年3月25日与旅行社签订了《委托旅行社代办合同》,仅委托为其办理代订2018年4月1日上海/洛杉矶UA199航班及4月15日纽约/上海UA198航班往返机票和在美国期间住宿的房间。旅行社已按约定完成了上述委托事务。

(2)2018年3月31日下午旅行社操作人员取得美联航的电子行程单后,发现返程航班时间提前,即用手机短信的形式及时告知了胡先生,已尽到了"委托事务处理过程中的报告义务"。

旅行社向市旅游质监所提供了双方签订的《委托旅行社代办合同》复印件、通知航班时间变更的手机短信截屏,以及美国联合航空公司的《航班变更通知》等证据,书面阐明旅行社的观点是:

①当事人双方签订的是委托代办合同,不是包价旅游合同。旅行社方已按约履行旅游者委托代订机票和酒店的义务,并无违约行为,且在知晓航班变更信息后第一时间,即用短信形式及时予以告知,尽到了报告义务。

②美联航UA198航班系公共交通工具,根据《旅游法》第七十一条的规定:"……由于公共交通经营者的原因造成的旅游者人身伤害、财产损失的,由公共交通经营者依法承担赔偿责任……"

③若胡先生向美联航提出索赔主张,旅行社可以提供帮助。

上述观点得到了市旅游质监所的认可,认定旅行社无责。

2. 经验与教训

(1)随着多元化休闲旅游市场的拓展,"自由行"旅游者不断增加。旅行社必须与其签订要求旅行社代订机票和酒店的《委托旅行社代办合同》(即原《单项委托合同》),切不可使用包价旅游合同的文本,否则将承担包价旅游合同应负的法律责任。

(2)需特别注意的是在签订委托代办合同时,也必须履行安全警示告知义务,这是一项附随义务,对有可能危及旅游者人身、财产安全的注意事项,应当事先向旅游者做出说明和警示。在签订委托代办合同时附上"旅游安全须知",让其签名确认留存。

Chapter 4

Canada/加拿大

Part One
Briefing on Canada/加拿大概况

Unit 1 Overviews/总览

I Basic Information/基本信息

National Flag/国旗	National Emblem/国徽

The national flag of Canada is red and white. Red represents the Atlantic and Pacific Ocean, and White represents the land of Canada. The red maple leaf with 11 angles represents 10 provinces and 3 territories in Canada. The maple leaf is the symbol of the country. 加拿大国旗旗面由红白两色组成,两边的红色代表大西洋和太平洋,白色正方形象征加拿大广阔的国土。中央绘有一片11个角的红色枫树叶,11个角代表着加拿大的10个省和3个自治州。枫叶是加拿大的象征。	The national emblem of Canada is a coat of arms with the Union Jack and fleur-de-lis on both sides. Four patterns on the coat of arms are 3 golden lions, a red lion, a harp and 3 lilies, representing Canada's relations with England, Scotland, Ireland and France. The lion holding a maple leaf on the top laments over the dead during the First World War. The crown represents that Queen Elizabeth II is the monarch. "A MARI USQUE AD MARE" on the ribbon suggests that Canada is located from Pacific Ocean to the Atlantic Ocean. 加拿大国徽为盾徽,两边是国旗和花。上部的四组图案分别为:3头金狮、1头红狮、1把竖琴和3朵百合花,分别象征加拿大在历史上与英格兰、苏格兰、爱尔兰和法国之间的联系。盾徽之上有一头狮子举着一片红枫叶,是表示对第一次世界大战期间加拿大的牺牲者的悼念。狮子之上为一顶金色的王冠,象征伊丽莎白二世是君主。盾形底端的绶带上用拉丁文写着"从海到海",表示加拿大的地理位置——西濒太平洋,东临大西洋。

Other Basics/其他基本信息	
Full Name/国家全称	Canada/加拿大
Other Names/其他称呼	Land of Maple/枫叶之国
Total Area/国土面积	9,980,000 km²/998万平方千米
Population/人口	38,130,000（2021年6月）
Nationality/民族	Anglo Canadian，French Canadian/英裔加拿大人、法裔加拿大人
Capital/首都	Ottawa/渥太华
National Anthem/国歌	"O Canada"/《啊，加拿大》
National Flower/国花	Maple Leaf/枫叶
National Bird/国鸟	Eurasian Beaver/欧亚河狸
Divisions/行政区划	10 provinces and 3 territories/10个州与3个地区
Language/语言	English，French/英语、法语
Major Political Parties/主要政党	Liberal Party，Conservative Party/自由党、保守党
Government Type/政府类型	Federal Parliamentary Constitutional Monarchy/联邦议会君主立宪制
Religious Belief/主要宗教信仰	Protestant Christian，Catholic/基督教、天主教
Currency/货币	Canadian Dollar/加拿大元
Time Difference with Beijing/与北京时差	-13（Summer time-12)/比北京晚13个小时（夏时制晚12个小时）

Ⅱ Physical Geography/自然和地理

Canada occupies much of the continent of North America, sharing land borders with the contiguous United States to the south, and the U.S. state of Alaska to the northwest. Canada stretches from the Atlantic Ocean in the east to the Pacific Ocean in the west. By total area（including its waters）, Canada is the second-largest country in the world, after Russia. Of Canada's thirteen provinces and territories, only two are landlocked（Alberta and Saskatchewan）while the other eleven all directly border one of three oceans. Much of the Canadian Arctic is covered by ice and permafrost. Canada has the longest coastline in the world, with a total length of 243,042 kilometers; additionally, its border with the United States is the world's longest land border, stretching 8,891 kilometers. Canada is geologically active, having many earthquakes and potentially active volcanoes, notably Mount Meager massif, Mount Garibaldi, Mount Cayley massif, and the Mount Edziza volcanic complex.

加拿大占据了北美大陆的大部分地区,南部与美国本土接壤,西北部与美国阿拉斯加连接。加拿大西濒太平洋,东临大西洋。就总面积(包括水域面积)而论,加拿大是世界第二大国家,仅次于俄罗斯。在加拿大的13个省和地区中,只有2个(艾伯塔省与萨斯喀彻温省)地处内陆,剩余11个均与海洋接壤。加拿大北部大面积被冰雪及多年冻土覆盖。加拿大的海岸线长达243,042千米,居世界之首。除此之外,加拿大与美国共享世界第一长的陆地边界,达8,891千米。加拿大地质活动频繁,发生过数次地震,境内有活火山,最著名的有米格尔山、加里波第山、凯利山和埃德齐扎火山群等。

Ⅲ Government and Administration/政府机构

Canada is a parliamentary democracy and a constitutional monarchy in the Westminster tradition, with Elizabeth II as its queen and a prime minister who serves as the chair of the Cabinet and head of government. The country is a realm within the Commonwealth of Nations, a member of the Francophonie and officially bilingual at the federal level.

加拿大是议会民主制国家,是威斯敏斯特传统的君主立宪国家,女王是伊丽莎白二世。首相是内阁主席和政府首脑。加拿大为英联邦成员、法语区联邦国,英语和法语均为政府官方工作语言。

1. Parliament/议会

The Parliament is composed of the Senate and the House of Commons. The 105 members of the Senate, whose seats are apportioned on a regional basis, serve until age 75. Each of the 338 members of parliament in the House of Commons is elected by simple plurality in an electoral district or riding. They serve for 4 years as a term.

议会由参议院和众议院组成,参众两院通过的法案由总督签署后成为法律。总督有权召集和解散议会。参议院共105席,名额按各省人口比例和历史惯例分配,任期至75岁。参议员由总理提名,总督任命。众议院共338席,众议员由按各省人口比例划分的联邦选区直接选举产生,任期4年。

2. Party/政党

(1)Liberal Party:The party in power. It was founded in 1873. Liberal Party positions themselves at the center of the Canadian political spectrum. It represents the interest of industrial monopoly-capitalist groups and middle and small-sized enterprises.

自由党:执政党,1873年成立,代表工业垄断资本集团利益并兼顾中、小企业利益。

(2)Conservative Party:The party is the official opposition. Conservative Party positions themselves on the right, representing the interest of banks, insurance, railway, energy monopoly-capitalist groups and farmers.

保守党：正式反对党，右翼政党。由联盟党和进步保守党于2003年12月合并而成，代表银行保险业、铁路运输业、能源工业垄断资本和大农场主利益。

（3）New Democratic Party：The party is an opposition. New Democratic Party is occupying the left. It represents the interest of middle and lower working class, proposing more public goods from the government.

新民主党：反对党。1961年由平民合作联盟与加拿大劳工大会联合而成。属于中左翼社会民主党性质，代表中下劳动阶层利益，主张政府提供更多公共产品以弥补市场缺陷。

（4）Bloc Quebecois：The party is an opposition. It represents the interest of Quebecois, proposing independent Quebec.

魁北克集团：反对党。1990年成立。代表魁北克人的利益，主张魁北克独立。

Unit 2　History and People/历史和人民

I　History/历史

Various indigenous peoples have inhabited what is now Canada for thousands of years before European colonization. Beginning in the 16th century, British and French expeditions explored and later settled along the Atlantic coast. As a consequence of various armed conflicts, France ceded nearly all of its colonies in North America in 1763. In 1867, with the union of three British North American colonies through Confederation, Canada was formed as a federal dominion of four provinces. This began an accretion of provinces and territories and a process of increasing autonomy from the United Kingdom. This widening autonomy was highlighted by the Statute of Westminster in 1931 and culminated in the Constitution Act of Canada in 1982, which severed the vestiges of legal dependence on the British parliament.

在欧洲殖民统治之前，各部落土著人民已经在加拿大居住了数千年。从16世纪开始，英国和法国的探险队先后在大西洋沿岸定居。由于武装冲突，法国于1763年割让了几乎所有的北美殖民地。1867年，3个英国北美殖民地组成联盟，加拿大成为拥有4个省的英国自治领。随着省和地区数量的增加，加拿大也加速了从英国自治的进程。1931年的《威斯敏斯特法案》以及1982年的《加拿大宪法法案》，使加拿大获得了立法和修宪的全部权力，加拿大事实从英国独立。

1. Indigenous Peoples/原住民

Indigenous peoples in present-day Canada include the First Nations, Inuit, and Métis. The characteristics of Canadian indigenous societies included permanent settlements, agriculture, complex societal hierarchies, and trading networks. Some of these cultures had collapsed by the time European explorers arrived in the late 15th and early 16th centuries.

今天加拿大的原住民包括加拿大第一民族、因纽特人和梅蒂斯人。 加拿大土著社会的特征包括永久性定居、发达的农业、复杂的社会等级和贸易网。欧洲探险家在15世纪末16世纪初抵达时,其中一些原住民文化已经崩溃。

2. European Colonization/欧洲殖民

In 1534, French explorer Jacques Cartier explored the Gulf of Saint Lawrence and took possession of the territory New France in the name of King Francis I. In 1583, Sir Humphrey Gilbert, by the royal prerogative of Queen Elizabeth I, founded St. John's, Newfoundland, as the first North American English colony. Canada and most of New France came under British rule in 1763 after the Seven Years' War.

1534年,法国探险家雅克·卡蒂埃来到了圣劳伦斯湾,并以当时法国国王弗朗西斯一世的名义占领了新法兰西地区。1583年,接受了英国女王伊丽莎白一世的王室特权,汉弗莱·吉尔伯特爵士建立纽芬兰,成为第一个北美英国殖民地。1756—1763年,英、法在加拿大爆发"七年战争",法国战败。1763年的《巴黎和约》使加拿大正式成为英属殖民地。

3. Confederation and Independence/联邦与独立

Following several constitutional conferences, the Constitution Act officially proclaimed Canadian Confederation on July 1, 1867, initially with four provinces: Ontario, Quebec, Nova Scotia, and New Brunswick.

Finally, another series of constitutional conferences resulted in the Canada Act, the patriation of Canada's constitution from the United Kingdom, concurrent with the creation of the Canadian Charter of Rights and Freedoms. Canada had established complete sovereignty as an independent country.

在几轮宪法会议过后,《宪法法案》于1867年7月1日正式宣布成立加拿大联邦,最初的4个省是安大略省、魁北克省、新斯科舍省和新不伦瑞克省。

最后,另一系列制宪会议产生了《加拿大法》,即加拿大宪法继承了联合王国宪法,同时制定了《加拿大权利和自由宪章》。加拿大作为一个独立的国家建立了完全的主权。

II People and Figures/人民及名人

Canada has a population of 38,130,000(2021). It is mainly composed of European descendants such as Britain and France. The indigenous people account for about 3%, and the rest are Asian, Latin American and African American. English and French are both official languages. Among the residents, 45% are Catholics and 36% are Christians.

加拿大人口为38,130,000(2021年)。主要由英国和法国等欧洲后裔组成。原住民约占3%,其余为亚裔、拉美裔和非裔美国人。英语和法语均为官方语言。加拿大居民中,45%是天主教徒,36%是基督徒。

1. Julie Payette/朱莉·帕耶特

Governor. Female, born in October 1963 in Montreal, Canada. Bachelor of International Studies, United Kingdom Atlantic United College, Bachelor of Electrical Engineering, McGill University, Canada, Master of Computer Engineering, University of Toronto. In 1992, she became an astronaut of the Canadian Space Agency and served as the chief astronaut from 2000 to 2007. She was the first Canadian to enter the International Space Station and the second female astronaut in Canadian history. In October 2017, she became the 29th Governor of Canada and became the fourth female governor in Canadian history. On January 21, 2021, she resigned as governor of Canada.

总督。女,1963年10月生于加拿大蒙特利尔市。英国大西洋联合学院国际研究学士,加拿大麦吉尔大学电子工程学士,多伦多大学计算机工程硕士。1992年成为加拿大航天局航天员,2000年至2007年担任加拿大航天局首席航天员,是首位进入国际空间站的加拿大人,也是加拿大历史上第二位女性航天员。2017年10月就任加拿大第29任总督,成为加拿大历史上第四位女性总督。2021年1月21日,宣布辞任加拿大总督。

2. Justin Trudeau/贾斯廷·特鲁多

Prime Minister. Born in December 1971 in Ottawa, Canada. He holds a Bachelor of Arts and Master of Environmental Geology from McGill University and a Bachelor of Education from the University of British Columbia. He was elected as a member of the House of Commons for the first time in 2008 and was re-elected in 2011. In April 2013, he was elected as the leader of the Liberal Party. In October 2015, the Liberal Party won the general election and in November he became the 23rd Prime Minister. In October 2019, Trudeau won the re-election.

总理。1971年12月生于加拿大渥太华市,麦吉尔大学文学学士和环境地质学硕士,不列颠哥伦比亚大学教育学学士。2008年首次当选加拿大联邦众议员,2011年连选连任。

2013年4月当选自由党领袖。2015年10月率自由党赢得大选并于11月就任加第23任总理。2019年10月特鲁多连任加拿大总理。

Unit 3 Culture and Education/文化和教育

Ⅰ Culture/文化

Canada's culture draws influences from its broad range of constituent nationalities, and policies that promote a "just society" are constitutionally protected. Canada has placed emphasis on equality and inclusiveness for all its people. Multiculturalism is often cited as one of Canada's significant accomplishments, and a key distinguishing element of Canadian identity. In Quebec, cultural identity is strong, and many commentators speak of a French Canadian culture that is distinct from English Canadian culture. However, as a whole, Canada is, in theory, a cultural mosaic—a collection of regional ethnic subcultures. On July 20, 2005, Canada became the fourth country in the world to recognize same-sex marriage. In October 2018, Canada legalized the sale and leisure use of marijuana for the first time.

加拿大文化受其各民族文化的综合影响。在加拿大,所有促进"公正社会"的政策都受宪法保护。加拿大重视平等和包容。多元文化是加拿大的重要成就之一,也是加拿大身份认同的关键因素。在魁北克尤其能体现这一点,许多评论家都谈到加拿大法国文化与加拿大英国文化的不同。从整体上看,加拿大是一种文化万花筒———一种区域民族亚文化的集合。在2005年7月20日,加拿大成为世界上第四个承认同性婚姻的国家。2018年10月,加拿大首次将销售和休闲使用大麻合法化。

1. Symbols/文化象征

The use of the maple leaf as a Canadian symbol dates to the early 18th century. The maple leaf is depicted on Canada's current and previous flags, and on the Arms of Canada. Other prominent symbols include the sports of hockey and lacrosse, the beaver, Canadian Goose, common loon, Canadian horse, the Royal Canadian Mounted Police, the Canadian Rockies, and more recently the totem pole and Inuksuk. Material items such as Canadian beer, maple syrup, tuques, canoes, Nanaimo bars, butter tarts and the Quebec dish of poutine are defined as uniquely Canadian.

枫叶作为加拿大的象征可以追溯到18世纪初。它出现在加拿大的国旗和国徽上。其他象征包括曲棍球和长曲棍球运动、海狸、加拿大鹅、普通潜鸟、加拿大马、加拿大皇家骑警、落基山脉以及最近的图腾柱和因努伊特石堆。加拿大啤酒、枫糖浆、御寒绒线帽、独木舟、Nanaimo巧克力条、黄油馅饼和魁北克奶酪薯条等都是加拿大特有的风味。

2. Sport/体育

Canada's official national sports are ice hockey and lacrosse. Golf, soccer, baseball, tennis, skiing, badminton, volleyball, cycling, swimming, bowling, rugby, canoeing, equestrian, squash and the study of martial arts are widely enjoyed at the youth and amateur levels. Canada shares several major professional sports leagues with the United States. Canadian teams in these leagues include seven franchises in the National Hockey League, three Major League Soccer teams, one team in each of Major League Baseball and the National Basketball Association.

加拿大的官方国家体育项目是冰球和曲棍球。高尔夫、足球、棒球、网球、滑雪、羽毛球、排球、自行车、游泳、保龄球、橄榄球、皮划艇、马术、壁球和武术在青年和业余爱好者中受到广泛喜爱。加拿大与美国共享几个主要的职业体育联盟。其中包括全美冰球联盟(NFL)的7支球队、全美职业足球大联盟(MLS)的3支球队、全美职业棒球大联盟(MLB)的1支球队和全美职业篮球协会(NBA)的1支球队。

Ⅱ Education/教育

According to a 2012 report by the Organization for Economic Co-operation and Development (OECD), Canada is one of the most educated countries in the world; the country ranks first worldwide in the number of adults having tertiary education, with 51 percent of Canadian adults having attained at least an undergraduate college or university degree. Canada spends about 5.3% of its GDP on education. The country invests heavily in tertiary education (more than US$20,000 per student). As of 2014, 89 percent of adults aged 25 to 64 have earned the equivalent of a high-school degree, compared to an OECD average of 75 percent.

Since the adoption of section 23 of the Constitution Act of Canada in 1982, education in both English and French has been available in most places across Canada. The mandatory school age ranges between 5–7 to 16–18 years, contributing to an adult literacy rate of 99 percent. In 2002, 43 percent of Canadians aged 25 to 64 possessed a post-secondary education; for those aged 25 to 34, the rate of post-secondary education reached 51 percent. The Program for International Student Assessment indicates Canadian students perform well above the OECD average, particularly in mathematics, science, and reading.

根据经济合作与发展组织(OECD)2012年的一份报告,加拿大是世界上受教育程度最高的国家之一;其接受过高等教育的成年人数量是世界第一,51%的加拿大成年人至少拥有本科学历或大学学位。加拿大将其国内生产总值的5.3%投入教育,在高等教育方面投入巨资(每位学生超过20,000美元)。截至2014年,89%的25—64岁的成年人获得高中或同等学力,而经合组织(OECD)国家的平均值为75%。

自1982年通过《加拿大宪法法案》第23条以来,加拿大大部分地区都提供英语和法语教育。义务教育始于5—7岁,至16—18岁完成,这也使得加拿大的成人识字率高达99%。2002年,43%的25—64岁的加拿大人接受过高等教育;对于25—34岁的人,这个比率达到51%。国际学生评估计划(PISA)显示,加拿大学生的表现远高于经合组织(OECD)国家的平均水平,特别是在数学、科学和阅读方面。

Unit 4　Major Attractions/主要景点

I Niagara Falls/尼亚加拉瀑布

Located at the junction of Ontario, Canada and New York, USA, Niagara Falls is a large waterfall on the Niagara River in North America and one great wonder of the American Continent. The average flow rate is 5,720 m³/s. Together with Iguazu Falls and Victoria Falls, they are known as the three major international waterfalls. Niagara Falls has never failed to attract people to spend their honeymoons, take a cable or do rafting.

尼亚加拉瀑布位于加拿大安大略省和美国纽约州的交界处,是北美东北部尼亚加拉河上的大瀑布,也是美洲大陆最著名的奇景之一。尼亚加拉瀑布平均流量5,720立方米/秒,与伊瓜苏瀑布、维多利亚瀑布并称为世界三大跨国瀑布。尼亚加拉瀑布一直吸引人们到此度蜜月、走钢索横越瀑布或者坐木桶漂游瀑布。

II Rocky Mountains/加拿大落基山脉

The Rocky Mountains, commonly known as the Rockies, are a major mountain range in North America. The Rockies are 4,800 kilometres long and stretch from the most northern part of British Columbia all the way to New Mexico in the southwestern United States. The mountain range is more than 70 million years old. There are 5 National Parks in the Canadian Rockies: Banff, Jasper, Kootenay, Yoho, and Waterton. There are many exciting landmarks in the Canadian Rockies including waterfalls, glaciers, the Columbia Icefield, and beautiful turquoise lakes. Millions of visitors come to the Canadian Rockies to enjoy summer activities such as hiking, mountain climbing and river rafting; and winter activities such as skiing, snowboarding and dog sledding.

落基山脉是北美的主要山脉,全长4,800千米,从不列颠哥伦比亚省的最北部一直延伸到美国西南部的新墨西哥州。山脉已有7,000万年的历史。加拿大落基山脉有5个国家公园:班夫国家公园、贾斯珀国家公园、库特尼国家公园、幽鹤国家公园以及沃特顿国家公园。这里有瀑布、冰川、哥伦比亚冰原和美丽的绿松石湖。数以百万计的游客来到加拿大落基山脉享受夏季活动,如徒步旅行、登山和漂流;还有滑雪、单板滑雪和狗拉雪橇等冬季活动。

Ⅲ University of Toronto/多伦多大学

Founded in 1827, the University of Toronto has evolved into Canada's leading institution of learning, discovery and knowledge creation. It is one of the world's top research-intensive universities, driven to invent and innovate. University of Toronto has many outstanding alumni, including 4 Canadian Prime Ministers, 15 Supreme Court Grand Justices and 10 Nobel Prize winners. University of Toronto ranks 28th in QS World University Rankings 2018.

多伦多大学成立于1827年,坐落在加拿大第一大城市多伦多。它是世界上顶尖的研究型大学之一,致力于发明和创新,被公认为加拿大综合实力第一的顶尖学府。多伦多大学有许多杰出校友,其中包括4位加拿大总理,15位最高法院大法官和10位诺贝尔奖获得者。多伦多大学在2018年QS世界大学排名中排名第28位。

Part Two
Outbound Tour Guide Operation/出境领队实务

Unit 1　Situational Dialogues/情景对话

Ⅰ Dialogue 1　Transfer

(*A*：*airport staff　B*：*tour leader　C*：*staff at the transfer counter*)

(*at the Shanghai Pudong International Airport*)

B：Excuse me, we're going to Vancouver, but transfer at Toronto Pearson Airport. Can we check in now?

A：Sure. Show me your passport, please!

B：OK.

A：Here are two boarding passes for you. One is CA048 from Shanghai Pudong International Airport to Toronto Pearson Airport for the first flight. The other is AC026 from Toronto Pearson Airport to Vancouver International Airport for the second flight. Keep safe the two boarding passes, please. And your luggage goes directly to your destination, so you don't need to claim your luggage at Toronto Pearson Airport when transferring.

B：Nice.

(*at the Toronto Pearson Airport*)

B：Excuse me, Madam. We are to transfer to Vancouver. Would you please tell me which gate we shall take?

A：What is your flight number?

B：My flight number is AC026.

A：You are flying with Air Canada[①]. You says you are transferring to Vancouver?

B：Yes. We come from Shanghai Pudong International Airport and we are going to Vancouver.

A：I see. First, you need to go to the transfer counter[②] to check your flight number. Second, you need to make sure from which terminal your flight leaves.

B：How can I get to the transfer counter?

A：Go straight ahead and you will find the transfer counter.

B：OK. Thank you.

(*ten minutes later*)

B：Excuse me, Sir. We are going to take AC026 to Vancouver. Where is the boarding gate?

C：Can I have your boarding pass, please?

B：Here you are.

C：Sorry for waiting, Madam. You are from Shanghai Pudong International Airport and you are going to transfer to Vancouver by AC026. Now you are at Terminal 4; your flight will be leaving at Gate 18, Terminal 2. You need to go downstairs and take Airport Express[3] to Terminal 2.

B：I see. How long does it take to Terminal 2 by Airport Express?

C：5 minutes. It's very fast.

B：OK. Thank you very much.

C：You're welcome. Have a good trip.

Notes：

①Air Canada：加拿大航空。

②transfer counter：转机柜台。

③Airport Express：机场快线。

Ⅱ Dialogue 2 The National Flag of Canada

(*A：Chinese tourist   B：Canadian tour guide*)

A：Good morning, Sir. Thank you for telling us so much about Canada yesterday, especially those interesting stories. I was fascinated by your broad knowledge.

B：Good morning, Miss. Thank you for saying so. It is my great honor to be your guide.

A：Maple must be your national tree. But I wonder what it has to do with your national flag. Or what stories can you tell us about your national flag?

B：First, maple tree is the national tree of Canada. In 1996, the Maple tree was officially recognized as the national Emblem. The maple leaf has been the centerpiece of the

national flag of Canada and the maple leaves have become the most prominent Canadian symbol, nationally and internationally.

A: Has the maple leaf flag been always the national flag of Canada?

B: No. It took quite a long time for the Canadians to have such a national flag. The current design of the national flag of Canada was only adopted on February 15, 1965. So in Canada, February 15 is celebrated as National Flag of Canada Day[1].

A: But as far as I know, Canada Day[2] is celebrated on July 1st to commemorate the founding of the Canadian federal government in 1867.

B: That is our National Day. They are two different Days. As for the national flag, Canada's first flag was the flag of England, since it was first claimed by British explorers. Later on, the French installed the French coat of arms as the Canadian flag. The French flag or some variant of it was used as the Canadian flag in the years to come. After the formation of the Canadian Confederation in 1867, various versions of the Canadian Red Ensign were used as the national flag of Canada. The Union Jack was also used before 1965, especially after Canada declared independence from the United Kingdom in 1931.

A: What happened to have made the change?

B: There are two major reasons for the change. First, the need for a Canadian flag completely distinct from that of the UK was felt during the Suez Crisis of 1956. The UK was one of the belligerents against the Egyptian Army, whereas the Canadian section of the peacekeeping force carried the Red Ensign, which contained the Union Jack. Canadian Prime Minister Lester Pearson, who won a Nobel Peace Prize for his role in brokering peace in the crisis, was the prime proponent of the change. Another reason for bringing about the change was that the inhabitants of Quebec, a French-speaking province of Canada, were unhappy with the Union Jack being part of the national flag.

A: Is there any reason why maple leaf was chosen to be the dominant design of your national flag?

B: It is actually a tradition. Maple trees, particularly the sap, served as an important food source to Canadian aboriginal people. After Canada was settled by Europeans, maple syrup production provided a convenient source of sugar. For several decades, "The Maple Leaf Forever"

was Canada's national song. The maple leaf was also adopted by the Canadian military as its symbol. As early as the 1700s, European settlers living in Canada already used the maple leaf as a symbol.

A: Thank you so much, Sir. It's been a great conversation. I learned a great deal about Canada from you.

B: It's my pleasure.

Notes:

①National Flag of Canada Day: 加拿大国旗日。

②Canada Day: 加拿大国庆日。

Ⅲ Dialogue 3 Marriage in Canada

(*A: Chinese tourist   B: Canadian tour guide*)

A: Good morning, Mr. Handsome.

B: Good morning, Madame.

A: I have a personal question for you if I may.

B: No problem. Go ahead, please.

A: Are you married?

B: Yes, I am. I have been married for almost three years and we have a little baby of 8 months old.

A: Congratulations! Now I think I can ask you more of those family questions.

B: Thank you. I'll try my best to answer them.

A: How do Canadian people find the partners for their marriage? Is it easy for young people to get married in Canada?

B: Except for some ethnic sectors, marriages are freely chosen by the two partners. The Canada Gender Ratio is 98 men to 100 women, which is lower than the global average of 101 men to 100 women. So in Canada, it is not so difficult for a man to find a girlfriend. Of course, the situation other way round is different.

A: You are lucky. Is divorce a problem in Canada?

B: According to the latest Statistics Canada data, approximately 38 percent of all marriages end in divorce with the divorce rate peaking around 41% in the 1980s. While the total divorce rate has been steady, there has been a steady increase in the divorce rate for three-year marriages. The divorce rate tends to decrease as the length of the marriage increases. However, in Canada, marriage is restricted to the union of a man and a woman by statute. Official marriages, officiated by either religious authorities or by municipal clerks or judges, must be dissolved by the legal procedure of divorce.

A: What about the de facto or common-law union?

B: We mention it as a second form of marriage because it gives the couple almost all the same privileges and obligations as an official marriage. Common-law union is a matter of informal declaration by the partners. Common-law conjugal recognition has recently been extended to include same-sex partners. The dissolution of common-law unions or same-sex partnerships requires no special legal proceedings, although resolution of shared property rights and support responsibilities arising from the union often require legal intervention and enforcement. In both cases, the marriage union involves mutuality of financial support, some degree of joint ownership of property, and joint responsibility for the care and support of children. Under Canadian law, all marriages must be monogamous. The de facto or common-law union is considered to be annulled should either partner take on a new conjugal partnership.

A: You just touched upon same-sex partnership. What is the situation of that?

B: Canada was the fourth country to permit same-sex marriages in the world, after the Netherlands, Belgium, and Spain. In 2005, the federal Civil Marriage Act came into force, making same-sex marriage legal across Canada. By the time of the 2016 census, there were 72,880 declared same-sex couples—0.9 percent of the total number of couples—and 33.4 percent of those same-sex couples were married.

A: In that case, your marriage law has to be adjusted, I guess.

B: You said it right. This change required that definitions for husband and wife be amended to spouse. The Income Tax Act also replaced the term natural parent with legal parent to ensure that upon divorce, support payments would include the children of both opposite-sex and same-sex couples.

A: Interesting. I wonder whether the religious people accept the idea of same-sex marriage.

B: Although some religious denominations endorse same-sex marriage, others do not. The Supreme Court has ruled that under the Charter of Rights and Freedoms, a religious official cannot be legally compelled to perform same-sex marriages if it is contrary to their religious beliefs. At the same time, government does have a duty to provide access to civil marriage, as opposed to a religious marriage ceremony, for those same-sex couples who want to marry.

A: Thank you really. I know Canada much better now.

B: My pleasure.

Unit 2　Case Study/案例分析

Ⅰ 案例一:购物引起的纠纷分析

1. 案例简介

2019年9月下旬,某组团社与客人签订的赴新马泰出境游合同中规定,全程购物次数不超过10次,每次购物时间控制在90分钟内。在马来西亚,导游发现团员在商店购物很少,于是在回酒店路上就不太讲话,在离酒店100米的地方停车,让客人步行100米走回酒店。领队边走边自言自语道:"不买东西,恐怕连饭也不给吃了。"第二天购物时,导游与团员较劲,不购物就延长购物时间;回程路上,导游帮助司机推销纪念品,客人觉得贵不买,导游动员每人交10元作为小费给司机,全车人无一不交。

在泰国,客人老张看到其他团队晚餐有红酒和月饼,即强烈要求享有同等待遇。领队以"团员出团前并没有提前说明,现在不能安排"为由,拒绝了老张的要求。晚上参加完自费项目的大部分团员与领队在车上大声说笑,没有参加自费活动的老张要求他们说话小声些,结果被一名客人奚落、谩骂,大家继续说笑。

该团回国后领队被客人投诉。

2. 案例分析

请分析领队的言行有几项问题?

答案:7项。

(1)领队人员发现地陪在100米处停车,没有及时制止。

依据:领队应维护游客的合法权益,要及时制止使游客权益受损的事。

(2)领队与地陪的关系处理得不得当。遇到不讲理的导游,我们一定不要表现出软弱的一面,让对方牵着鼻子走,陷于被动之中。

依据:在遇到导游因为生活压力而表现出有不符合旅游合同及行业标准的倾向时,我们一定要进行得体、有理、有利、有节的阻止,必要时报告组团社。

(3)领队回来的路上,一直抱怨地陪做得不好。这样有问题。

依据:忌向游客充分暴露感情。

(4)领队见到地陪向游客索要小费,应予以制止。

依据:领队是游客在旅游过程中的心理依赖。

(5)拒绝老张强烈希望有红酒和月饼的要求是不恰当的。

依据:领队应努力满足游客的合理而可能的要求,并说明费用自理。实在有原因不能满足的要说明原因并道歉。

(6)当老张要求他们参加自费旅游活动的游客轻声时,游客对他进行了奚落、谩骂,领队没有制止和采取相应的措施。

依据:领队应该认真解答,悉心照料游客;尊重游客的人权、尊严。

(7)冷落了游客老张,这样有问题。

依据:应该顾及每一个游客,特别是没有参加自费项目的游客也要兼顾,不要不顾他们的感受。

Ⅱ 案例二:航班延误的责任

1. 案例简介

2019年春节长假期间,刚拿到领队证的小李就被旅行社委派带一旅游团前往加拿大。最后一天的行程为早餐后前往土特产商店购买特产,然后从市区赶赴机场搭乘12:40的飞机回国。旅游团的客人在土特产商店买了很多特产准备回家送给亲朋好友,装箱打包完毕集合上车已是10点钟了,领队小李看了下时间,让导游催促司机加快速度赶到机场。在途中,旅游大巴又不幸发生故障,半途抛锚,等到司机修好车辆赶到机场已经是12:30。

2. 案例分析

请分析说明在这个案例中,谁应该承担责任?

答案:领队、导游和旅游大巴公司都有责任。

(1)虽然小李是刚拿到领队证的新领队,没有经验,但是在领队培训时,业务课本上讲得非常清楚,乘坐国际航班必须提早3小时到达机场办理乘机手续,这里小李为了自己的小小利益,违背了带团时必须遵守的时间及履行监督地接社行程的原则。

(2)作为当地旅行社的导游也有很大的责任,没有计划安排好行程。当旅行车抛锚时,领队和导游没有及时安排游客乘坐出租车或其他交通工具及时到达机场

(3)当地的旅游大巴公司也有相关的责任,出团前司机没有检查车况,造成途中抛锚。

Chapter 5

United Kingdom/英国

Part One
Briefing on the United Kingdom/英国概况

Unit 1　Overviews/总览

I　Basic Information/基本信息

National Flag/国旗	National Emblem/国徽

The British flag, officially called the Union Flag, is also called the Union Jack usually. Jack is a naval term for a flag hanging at the bow of a ship. The cross on the British flag combines the flag symbols of the former England (red cross with white ground), Scotland (white oblique cross with blue ground) and Northern Ireland (red oblique cross with white ground). The Red Cross edged white on the flag now represents St. George, the patron saint of England, a Christian missionary who introduced Christianity to England; The white oblique cross represents St. Andre, the Scottish patron saint; The Red oblique Cross represents St. Patrick, the Irish patron saint who spread Christianity to Ireland in the fifth century.	The British national emblem is the British Royal emblem. The central design is a shield pattern, with three Golden Lions on the upper left and lower right of the shield representing England, the red lion half standing on the yellow bottom representing Scotland, and the golden harp on the blue bottom representing Northern Ireland. The shield emblem is guarded by a crowned lion representing England and a unicorn representing Scotland. 　　Around the shield emblem, there is a French motto "Honi soit qui maly pense", which means "The evil is rewarded with evil." At the bottom of the shield hangs a Garter medal, with the French motto "Dieu et mon droit", meaning "Right of god and me." (French was used because the French-speaking Normans ruled the Britain in the English history, known as the Norman Conquest.)

National Flag/国旗	National Emblem/国徽
英国国旗，正式称呼是"联合旗"（the Union Flag），也常常称为"船首旗"（the Union Jack）。Jack 是海军用语，指悬挂在舰首的旗帜。英国国旗上的十字综合了原英格兰（白地红色正十字旗）、苏格兰（蓝地白色交叉十字旗）和北爱尔兰（白地红色交叉十字旗）的旗帜标志。现国旗的白边红色正十字代表英格兰主保圣人（将基督教传到英格兰的基督教传教士）圣乔治，白色交叉十字代表苏格兰主保圣人圣安德烈，红色交叉十字代表五世纪将基督教传播到爱尔兰的爱尔兰主保圣人圣帕特里克。	英国国徽，即英王徽。中心图案为一枚盾徽，盾面上左上角和右下角为红底上三只金狮，象征英格兰；右上角为黄底上半站立的红狮，象征苏格兰；左下角为蓝底上金黄色竖琴，象征北爱尔兰。盾徽两侧各由一只头戴王冠、分别代表英格兰的狮子和苏格兰的独角兽守护。 盾徽周围用法文写着一句格言"Honi soit qui mal y pense"，意为"心怀邪念者可耻"；下端悬挂着嘉德勋章，饰带上用法文写着"Dieu et mon droit"，意为"天有上帝，我有权利"。（使用法文是因为英国历史上曾被讲法语的诺曼人统治，也就是有名的"诺曼征服"。）

Other Basics/其他基本信息	
Full Name/国家全称	The United Kingdom of Great Britain and Northern Ireland/大不列颠及北爱尔兰联合王国
Other Names/其他称呼	the UK（United Kingdom），Great Britain，Britain，England/英国、大不列颠、英格兰
Total Area/国土面积	244,100 km²/24.41万平方千米
Population/人口	67,081,000（2020）
Nationality/民族	England，Scotland，Wales/英格兰人、苏格兰人、威尔士人
Capital/首都	London/伦敦
National Anthem/国歌	"God Save the Queen/King"/《天佑女王（吾王）》
National Flower/国花	Rose/玫瑰
National Bird/国鸟	Erithacus Rubecula Melophilus/红胸鸲，又名红襟鸟、知更鸟
Divisions/行政区划	England，Scotland，Wales and Northern Ireland/英格兰、苏格兰、威尔士及北爱尔兰
Language/语言	English/英语
Major Political Parties/主要政党	The Conservative Party，The Labor Party，The Liberal Democrats/保守党、工党、自由民主党
Government Type/政府类型	Parliamentary Democracy with a Constitutional Monarchy/议会制君主立宪制
Religious Belief/主要宗教信仰	Protestant/新教
Currency/货币	Pound/英镑
Time Difference with Beijing/与北京时差	-8（Summer Time-7）/比北京晚8小时（夏时制晚7小时）

Ⅱ Physical Geography/自然和地理

Great Britain is an island in the North Atlantic Ocean off the northwest coast of continental Europe. With an area of about 209,331 square kilometers, it is the largest of the British Isles, the largest European island, and the ninth-largest island in the world. In 2017, Great Britain had a population of about 66.05 million people, making it the world's third-most populous island after Java in Indonesia and Honshu in Japan. The island of Ireland is situated to the west of Great Britain, and together, these islands, along with over 1,000 smaller surrounding islands, form the British Isles archipelago.

The island is dominated by a maritime climate with quite narrow temperature differences between seasons. Politically, Great Britain is part of the United Kingdom of Great Britain and Northern Ireland, and constitutes most of its territory. Most of England, Scotland, and Wales are on the island. The term "Great Britain" is often used to include the whole of England, Scotland, Wales and their component adjoining islands.

England covers an area of about 130,000 square kilometers, accounting for the majority of the island of Great Britain. From west to east, the area is divided into four parts: Midland Plain centered on the Severn River Basin, Highlands about 200 meters above sea level, London Basin, and the Wilder Hills.

Wales covers an area of more than 20,000 square kilometers. It is mountainous and rugged. One fourth of Wales' land is classified as national parks and nature reserves.

Scotland and its surrounding islands cover an area of 78,000 square kilometers. The whole territory belongs to the mountain area with only the middle part relatively low and flat.

Northern Ireland covers an area of about 14,000 square kilometers and is far away from the British Isle across the Irish Sea. There are more lakes in Northern Ireland, with Lough Neagh, the largest lake in Britain, lying in the middle. The plain is along the lake.

大不列颠是北大西洋的一个岛屿,位于欧洲大陆西北海岸。面积约为209,331平方千米,是不列颠群岛中最大的岛屿、欧洲最大的岛屿和世界第九大岛。2017年,大不列颠拥有约6,605万人口,成为仅次于印度尼西亚爪哇岛和日本本州的世界第三多人口的岛屿。爱尔兰岛位于大不列颠岛以西,这些岛屿连同1000多个较小的岛屿组成了不列颠群岛。

该岛以海洋性气候为主,季节温差很小。从政治上讲,大不列颠是大不列颠及北爱尔兰联合王国的一部分,构成大不列颠及北爱尔兰的大部分领土。英格兰、苏格兰和威尔士的大部分都在这个岛上。"大不列颠"一词通常用于包括整个英格兰、苏格兰、威尔士及其邻岛屿。

英格兰全境面积约为13万平方千米,占大不列颠岛的大部分。这一地区自西向东分为4部分:以塞文河流域为中心的米德兰平原、海拔200米左右的高地、伦敦盆地和威尔德丘陵。

威尔士面积有2万余平方千米,境内多山,地势崎岖。威尔士境内有1/4的土地被列为国家公园及天然保护区。

苏格兰及其周边岛屿面积共为7.8万平方千米。全境均属山岳地带,只有中部较为低平。

北爱尔兰面积约为1.4万平方千米,隔爱尔兰海与大不列颠岛遥遥相望。北爱尔兰地区湖泊较多,英国的第一大湖——讷湖卧波其间。沿湖为平原。

Ⅲ Government and Administration/英国政府机构

The governmental model that operates in British today is usually described as a Parliamentary Democracy with a Constitutional Monarchy.

A Parliamentary Democracy with a Constitutional Monarchy is called Parliamentary Monarchy for short. Its main characteristics are that parliament is the supreme legislature of the country, the monarch is the symbolic head of state, and its duties are mostly ceremonial.

英国今天的政权模式通常被称为议会制君主立宪制。

议会制君主立宪制,简称议会君主制。其主要特点是:议会是国家的最高立法机关,君主是象征性的国家元首,其职责多是礼仪性的。

1. The Monarchy/君主制

Elizabeth Ⅱ. Her title in the United Kingdom is "Elizabeth the Second by the Grace of God of the United Kingdom of Great Britain and Northern Ireland and Her Other Realms and Territories, Queen, Head of the Commonwealth, Defender of the Faith."

The Queen is the symbol of the whole nation. In law, she is head of the executive, an integral part of the legislature, head of the judiciary, the commander-in-chief of all the armed forces and the "supreme governor" of the Church of England. She gives Royal Assent to Bills passed by parliament.

伊丽莎白二世,她的全称是"托上帝洪恩,大不列颠及北爱尔兰联合王国以及其他领土和属地的女王、英联邦元首、基督教的保护者伊丽莎白二世"。

女王是国家的象征。从法律上讲,她是行政首脑、立法机构的组成部分、司法首脑、全国武装部队总司令、英国国教"至高无上"的领袖。她任命首相和重要的政府官员,对议会通过的法案给予御准。

2. Parliament/议会制

The United Kingdom is a unitary, not a federal state. Parliament consists of the Sovereign, the House of Lords and the House of Commons.

The main functions of Parliament are: (1) to pass laws; (2) to provide, by voting for taxation, the means of carrying on the work of government; (3) to examine government policy and administrations, including proposal for expenditure; and (4) to debate the major issues of the day.

The House of Lords is made up of the Lords Spiritual and the Lords Temporal. The Lords Spiritual are the Archbishops of Canterbury and York and 24 senior bishops of the church of England. The Lords Temporal consist of: (1) all hereditary peers and peeresses of England, Scotland, Great Britain and the United Kingdom (but not peers of Ireland); (2) life peers to assist the House in its judicial duties; (3) all other life peers. The main function of the House of Lords is to bring the wide experience of its members into the process of law-making.

The House of Commons is elected by universal adult suffrage and consists of 650 members of Parliament (MPs). It is in the House of Commons that the ultimate authority for law-making resides.

英国是中央集权国家,而不是联邦制国家。议会由君主、上院(贵族院)和下院(平民院)组成。

议会的主要作用是:(1)通过立法;(2)投票批准税收方案,为政府工作提供支持;(3)检查政府政策和行政管理,包括拨款提议;(4)讨论当前重大问题。

上院由神职人员和世俗议员组成。神职包括坎特伯雷和约克大主教及24名高级主教。世俗议员包括:(1)所有英格兰、苏格兰、大不列颠及联合王国的世袭贵族/女贵族(但不包括爱尔兰);(2)协助议院司法工作的终身贵族;(3)其他终生贵族。上院的主要作用就是集中议员集体经验智慧制定法律。

下院议员由成人普选产生,共有650名议员。最高立法权掌握在下院手中。

Unit 2 History and People/历史和人民

Ⅰ History/历史

1. Four Times of Being Invaded/四次遭遇入侵

（1）The Invasion of the Roman Legion/罗马军团的入侵。

In 55 BC and 54 BC., Britain had been twice invaded by G.J. Caesar's the Roman Legion. In 43 AD, Britain was again invaded by the Roman Empire, so England and Wales were a part of the Roman Empire for nearly 400 years. The Romans built a well-developed network of roads mainly for the military purpose, which facilitated the transportation of trade（All roads lead to Rome）. They established London as the capital. They also brought the new religion, Christianity, to Britain.

公元前55和公元前54年,G.J.恺撒两度率罗马军团入侵不列颠。公元43年,罗马帝国再次入侵英国,英格兰和威尔士成为罗马帝国的一部分达近400年。为了军事目的,罗马人建立了发达的道路交通网,这同时也促进了贸易运输的发展(条条大路通罗马)。他们以伦敦为首都,把新的宗教——基督教带到了英国。

（2）Germanic Invasion/日耳曼人入侵。

After the Romans were driven away, Anglo-Saxons and other Germanic tribes invaded Britain since the early fifth century.

5世纪初,罗马人被赶跑后,盎格鲁撒克逊人和其他日耳曼部落陆续侵入不列颠。

（3）Danish Invasion（Viking Invasion）/丹麦人入侵（维京海盗入侵）。

Since the end of the eighth century, Viking pirates invaded Britain repeatedly. By the end of the ninth century, Viking pirates had established large settlements on the island of Great Britain.

从8世纪末开始,维京海盗屡屡入侵英国。到9世纪末,维京海盗已在大不列颠岛上建立大片居留地。

（4）Normandy Invasion /诺曼底入侵。

William, the Duke of Normandy in France （descendants of the Danish Vikings）, led an invasion in 1066. He entered London in October of the same year and was crowned King William I. He was historically known as William the Conqueror, by whom the Norman

Dynasty was founded. From then on, from a small country in a corner of Europe, Britain grew strong and gradually became the center of Europe, avoiding further invasion by other European nations.

法国诺曼底公爵威廉(丹麦维京人后裔)于1066年率军入侵,同年10月进入伦敦,加冕为英王威廉一世,史称"征服者威廉",诺曼王朝由此建立。从此英国变得强大,逐渐从偏居一隅的欧洲小国成为欧洲的中心,避免了被欧洲其他民族的继续入侵。

1. Historical Events/历史事件

(1) The Hundred Years War/英法百年战争。

From 1337 to 1453, the war between Britain and France for territorial expansion and throne struggle was the longest war in the world. It lasted for 116 years intermittently. At that time, it was also an era of Black Death. Under the double blow of war and epidemic, the economy of Britain and France was greatly traumatized, making life a misery for the people. Britain lost almost all of its French territory, but it also gave rise to nationalism. At the end of the war, Britain had embarked on the road of centralization. After that, it pursued a policy of "continental balance of power" towards the European continent and turned overseas to become the largest empire in the world.

1337—1453年,英国和法国为了领土扩张和王位争夺战争不断,断断续续进行了长达116年,是世界最长的战争;当时又是黑死病流行的时代。在战争和疫病的双重打击下,英法两国的经济大受创伤,民不聊生。英格兰几乎丧失所有的法国领地,但也使英格兰的民族主义兴起。战争结束时,英国已走上中央集权的道路,之后英格兰对欧洲大陆推行"大陆均势"政策,转往海外发展,成为全球最大的帝国。

(2) Enclosure Movement/圈地运动。

In the process of the disintegration of serfdom in the 14th and 15th centuries, the new bourgeoisie and the new aristocracy in Britain forced the peasants out of the land, occupied the peasants' land and public land, deprived the peasants of their ownership of and the right to use their land, restricted or abolished the original common farmland rights and animal husbandry rights, and enclosed the occupied land into private ranches and farms. This is the "Enclosure Movement" in British history.

The Enclosure Movement sacrificed the interests of farmers, accumulated original capital, provided cheap labor force and domestic market for capitalism, and laid the foundation for Britain to develop into a powerful capitalist country.

在14、15世纪农奴制解体过程中,英国新兴的资产阶级和新贵族通过暴力把农民从土地上赶走,强占农民土地及公有地,剥夺农民的土地使用权和所有权,限制或废除原有的共同耕地权和畜牧权,把强占的土地圈占起来,变成私有的大牧场、大农场。这就是英国历史上的"圈地运动"。

圈地运动牺牲了农民的利益,积累了原始资本,为资本主义提供了廉价的雇佣劳动力和国内市场,为英国发展成为资本主义强国奠定了基础。

(3) The British Industrial Revolution/英国工业革命。

The British Industrial Revolution began in the 1860s, with the technological innovation of cotton textile industry as its starting point, the improvement and extensive use of Watt steam engine as its pivot, and the realization of mechanization of machinery manufacturing in the 1930s and 1940s as its basic symbol. In the mid-18th century, Britain became the largest capitalist colonial country in the world. The expansion of domestic and foreign markets required technological reform in the workshop and handicraft industry. Therefore, the industrial revolution aimed at technological innovation first took place in Britain.

英国工业革命始于19世纪60年代,以棉纺织业的技术革新为出发点,以瓦特蒸汽机的改良和广泛使用为枢纽,以19世纪三四十年代机器制造业机械化的实现为基本完成的标志。18世纪中期,英国成为世界上最大的资本主义殖民国家,国内外市场的扩大对工场手工业提出了技术改革的要求,因此以技术革新为目标的工业革命首先发生在英国。

(4) Colonial Expansion/殖民扩张。

British colonies expanded violently in the 19th century. Ireland was merged in 1801 and the official name of Britain became the United Kingdom of Great Britain and Ireland. The British Empire refers to a great empire composed of the British mainland and its autonomous domains, colonies, territories, trusteeships and protectorates. It is the largest country with the largest territory area and the largest global colonial empire in history. At the beginning of the 19th century, the Empire reached its peak, with a population of between 400 and 500 million, accounting for one fourth of the world's population at that time; its territory was about 33.67 million square kilometers, accounting for one fourth of the world's total land area. The Empire, after the Spanish Kingdom in the 16th century, was called the "Sun-never-set Empire".

英国的殖民地在19世纪急剧扩张。1801年合并爱尔兰,英国正式名称成为大不列颠及爱尔兰联合王国。大英帝国指由英国本土及其治下的自治领地、殖民地、领地、托管地和保护国共同构成的大帝国,是有史以来领土面积最大的国家和最大的全球殖民帝国。帝国在19世纪初达到鼎盛,人口在4亿到5亿,占当时世界人口的1/4;领土约3367万平方千米,占到了世界陆地总面积的1/4。帝国继16世纪的西班牙王国之后,被称为"日不落帝国"。

（5）World Wars/世界大战。

In July 1914, World War I broke out. In 1917, Britain finally defeated Germany and maintained its sea power. The total number of soldiers killed in the war in the British Empire reached more than 500,000. The defeat of the Allies led by Germany indicated the end of the war.

In September 1939, Germany invaded Poland, World War II broke out, and Britain declared war on Germany. In the British Air War launched by Germany from July to September in 1940, the British Air Force effectively attacked the enemy. British and American troops landed in Normandy, France, in June 1944, and Germany surrendered on May 8th, 1945.

1914年7月，第一次世界大战爆发。1917年，英国最终击败德国，维护了它的制海权。战争中英帝国参战人员阵亡总数达50万以上。大战以德国为首的同盟国的失败告终。

1939年9月，德国进攻波兰，第二次世界大战爆发，英国对德国宣战。1940年7—9月在德国发动的不列颠空战中，英国空军有效地打击了敌人。1944年6月英美军队在法国诺曼底登陆，1945年5月8日德国投降。

Ⅱ People and Figures/人民及名人

The British are mostly Caucasian, commonly known as the White People. According to the latest statistics, Britain has a population of 67.08 million, one third of which live in southeastern England. English accounts for 83.9%, Scots 8.4%, Welsh 4.8% and Northern Ireland 2.9%. Most Englishmen are Anglo-Saxons. The word "England" is the homonym of "Anglo". The ancestors of Scots and Northern Ireland were Celtics.

英国人大多是高加索人种，俗称白种人。根据最新数据统计，英国人口达6,708万，其中1/3居住在英格兰东南部。英格兰人占83.9%，苏格兰人占8.4%，威尔士人占4.8%，北爱尔兰人占2.9%。大部分英格兰人就是盎格鲁·撒克逊人，"英格兰"一词即"盎格兰"的谐音。苏格兰人和北爱尔兰人的祖先是凯尔特人。

1. Queen Victoria/维多利亚女王

Queen Alexandrina Victoria (1819—1901) was the last monarch of the Hanover Dynasty in England. She was crowned at Westminster Abbey on June 28, 1838. Victoria was the second longest-serving monarch in British history, after Queen Elizabeth Ⅱ. She was in office for 64 years. Her reign (1837—1901) was the strongest "Sun-never-set Empire" period in Britain, called "Victorian Age" in British history.

维多利亚女王(1819—1901)是英国汉诺威王朝的最后一位君主，她于1837年6月20日继位，1838年6月28日在威斯敏斯特教堂加冕。维多利亚是英国历史上在位时间第二长的君主,仅次于伊丽莎白二世女王。维多利亚的在位时间长达64年。她在位时(1837—1901)是英国最强的"日不落帝国"时期,英国历史上称为"维多利亚时代"。此时,英国加大殖民扩张,在一定范围内建立和占领了很多殖民地。她在位的几十年正值英国自由资本主义由方兴未艾到顶尖,进而过渡到垄断资本主义的转变时期,经济、文化空前繁荣,君主立宪制得到充分发展。维多利亚女王成了英国和平与繁荣的象征。

2. Winston Churchill/温斯顿·丘吉尔

Winston Churchill (1874—1965) was a British politician, historian, painter, speaker, writer and journalist.

Winston Churchill was born in England in 1874. He had served as British Prime Minister twice from 1940 to 1945 and from 1951 to 1955. He was regarded as one of the most important political leaders in the 20th century, leading the British people to win the Second World War. He won the Nobel Prize for Literature in 1953 for his book *Unwanted War*.

温斯顿·丘吉尔(1874—1965),英国政治家、历史学家、画家、演说家、作家、记者。

温斯顿·丘吉尔1874年生于英格兰。他于1940年至1945年和1951年至1955年两度出任英国首相,被认为是20世纪最重要的政治领袖之一。他领导英国人民赢得了第二次世界大战。他写的《不需要的战争》获1953年诺贝尔文学奖。

3. Queen Elizabeth Ⅱ/伊丽莎白二世

Her Majesty Queen Elizabeth Ⅱ is the Queen of United Kingdom, the head of the Commonwealth and the highest head of Parliament. She was born on April 21, 1926. On June 2, 1953, she was crowned and is so far the longest-serving monarch in Britain.

伊丽莎白二世,现任英国女王,英联邦元首、国会最高首领。伊丽莎白二世于1926年4月21日出生,1953年6月2日加冕,是迄今为止英国在位时间最长的君主。

Unit 3 Culture and Education/文化和教育

Ⅰ Culture/文化

1. Shakespeare: the Symbol and Pride of English Culture/莎士比亚:英国文化的象征与骄傲

In Britain, the strong atmosphere of Shakespeare is felt everywhere. Shakespeare has been integrated into the blood of British culture like nourishment. It has become not only the pride of the British people, but also the symbol of British culture.

William Shakespeare (1564—1616), a great dramatist in the Renaissance, is a great star in British literary circles. He has a high position and great influence in the history of world culture. He is recognized as one of the three greatest poets in Europe (Shakespeare, Goethe and Dante). His plays vividly depict the social life, ideology and national customs of Europe in the 17th century and are loved by people of all ages in the world with the most publications and performances. At the same time, Shakespeare is also the most studied dramatist by experts and scholars of various countries, which makes "Studying Shakespeare" a widely influential "practical learning" in the world.

在英国,时时处处都可以感受到英国文化界弥漫着的浓郁的莎士比亚氛围,莎士比亚已经像养料一样融入了英国文化的血脉,不仅成为英国人的骄傲,也成为英国文化的象征。

文艺复兴时期伟大的戏剧家威廉·莎士比亚(1564—1616)是英国文坛的巨星,在世界文化史上地位崇高,影响巨大,是公认的欧洲三大诗人(莎士比亚、歌德和但丁)之一。他的戏剧生动地描绘了欧洲17世纪的社会生活、思想政治和民族风情,受到世界各国各时代人民的普遍喜爱,是全世界出版最多、流行最广、演出也最多的戏剧。同时,莎士比亚也是被各国专家学者研究最多的戏剧家,这使得"莎学"成为世界上一门广有影响的"显学"。

2. British Aristocratic Culture/英国贵族文化

The British aristocracy has been in existence since the Anglo-Saxon era in the fifth century. In many critical moments, they have led the country out of its predicament and become the longest-lasting stratum in the world and the greatest impetus to its own history, which is unique in world history. Therefore, some scholars say that if you do not understand the British aristocracy, you can not understand British history.

The aristocracy is a privileged class, usually hereditary. In British class-system society, the hereditary aristocracy is one of its distinctive features. Children from the aristocratic families can inherit titles from their forefathers. The aristocracy titles include Duke, Marquis, Count (earl), Viscount and Baron. Children from the aristocratic families can also inherit the fortune. And the senior tier of the aristocracy also inherits the right to be lords in the House of Lords.

Life peers are lords for their lifetime, but their children can't inherit the titles. They are made life peers out of recognition for their contributions to the UK society. For example, Margaret Thatcher, the first woman prime minister in British history and a grocer's daughter, was made a life peer when she retired as an MP.

英国贵族自公元五世纪盎格鲁·萨克逊时代开始形成,一直延续至今。在众多危急时刻,他们引领国家走出困境,成为世界上延续时间最长、对本国历史推动作用最大的阶层,在世界史中绝无仅有。故有学者称,若读不懂英国贵族,则无法理解英国历史。

贵族是一个特权阶级,通常是世袭的。在英国阶级制度社会中,世袭贵族是其显著特征之一。这些贵族家庭的孩子可以继承头衔(祖先的爵位)。贵族头衔分为:公爵、侯爵、伯爵、子爵、男爵。这些贵族家庭的孩子也可以继承财产。上层的贵族也可以继承上议院中的贵族权利。

终生贵族就是终生享有贵族的头衔,但他们的孩子不能继承头衔。他们之所以成为终生贵族,是因为他们对英国社会做出的杰出成就。例如玛格丽特·撒切尔,英国历史上第一位女首相。她是杂货商的女儿,当她以议员的身份退休时,她荣获了终生贵族的头衔。

3. English Afternoon Tea/英国下午茶

English afternoon tea is the British tradition of drinking tea and eating snacks in the afternoon. The British have a history of drinking black tea for 300 years. This is a country favoring black tea. Black tea with sugar and milk is often a necessary beverage after meals. Therefore, Britain is the world's largest black tea consumer. There is little doubt that no other nation in the world is more professional than Britain in black tea tasting.

Tea Trilogy:

Part one: Enjoying the delicious snacks;

Part two: Appreciating the exquisite tea sets;

Part three: Tasting the tea.

英国下午茶是英国人下午喝茶吃点心的传统。英国人有300年饮红茶历史,是红茶的爱好国家。加糖、牛奶的红茶往往成为餐后的必备饮料,因此英国是红茶消费量最多的国家。可以说没有一个国家对红茶的品尝水准有英国的专业。

品茶三部曲：

第一部：享用美味点心；

第二部：品赏精致的茶器；

第三部：品茶。

Ⅱ Education/教育

Britain has compulsory education for children aged 5—16. Education in Britain is generally divided into five stages. The first stage is kindergarten education from 3 to 5 years old. The second stage is primary education from 5 to 11 years old. And the third stage is secondary education from 11 to 16 years old. The compulsory education from 5 to 16 years old is stipulated by law. School-age children must attend school, and the state is responsible for the necessary tuition fees, books and supplies. There is a transitional period from high school to university. It is the senior class of middle school (or preparatory class of university) for 16—18 years old students. The fourth stage is the stage of higher education. The fifth stage is the continuing education after 16 years old. Vocational education for young people and adults (excluding regular universities) takes the forms of full-time, half-day and spare time. The length of the school system varies in different places, departments or specialties.

There are more than 100 universities and colleges in the UK, including the Russell Group, the world's leading union of universities. Oxford University and Cambridge University are the two most famous universities in the world.

英国实行5—16岁义务教育制度。英国教育一般分为5个阶段。第一阶段是3—5岁的幼儿园教育；第二阶段是5—11岁的小学教育；第三阶段是11—16岁的中学教育。5—16岁为法律规定的强制教育阶段，适龄儿童必须入学，由国家负责必需的学费、书籍和必要的供应。16—18岁是中学高级班（或大学预备班），为中学至大学的过渡期。第四阶段为高等教育阶段。第五阶段为16岁以后的继续教育，包括青年和成人的职业教育（正规大学不算在内），方式有全日、半日和业余时间。学制的长短在各地、各部门、各专业均不相同。

英国共有100多所大学和高等教育学院，包括世界著名的英国最顶尖大学联盟"罗素大学集团"，其中最闻名于世的两所大学是牛津大学和剑桥大学。

Unit 4　Major Attractions/主要景点

I　Stonehenge/巨石阵

Stonehenge is made up of huge stones, each weighing about 50 tons. Its main axis, the ancient road leading to the pillars is in alignment with the sunrise in the early morning of the summer solstice. In addition, there are two stones whose connecting line points to the direction of the sunset on winter solstice. Stonehenge means hanging stone. In the eyes of the British, this is a sacred place. It is precise to say that Stonehenge was constructed in about 4,300 years ago in around 2300 BC.

巨石阵由巨大的石头组成,每块重约50吨。它的主轴线,即通往石柱的古道和夏至日早晨初升的太阳,在同一条线上;另外,其中还有两块石头的连线指向冬至日落的方向。巨石阵的英文名字叫作"Stonehenge"。"Stone"意为"石头",henge意为"围栏"。在英国人的心目中,这是一个神圣的地方。巨石阵的准确建造年代距今已经有4,300年,即建于公元前2300年左右。

II　The Collegiate Church of St Peter at Westminster(Westminster Abbey)/威斯敏斯特教堂

The Collegiate Church of St Peter at Westminster, commonly known as Westminster Abbey, is located on the North Bank of the Thames in London. It was founded in 960.

Westminster Abbey is the place where kings or queens of all dynasties are crowned and celebrate their weddings. It is also the site of the royal mausoleum in England. Westminster Abbey is a stone book of the history of British Royal family. Voltaire, who witnessed

Newton's funeral, was deeply touched. He once wrote, "When people enter Westminster Abbey, they look not at the mausoleums of kings or queens, but at the national monuments to the greatest people who have made Britain glorious. This is the British people's respect for talent."

威斯敏斯特教堂,通称威斯敏斯特修道院,坐落在伦敦泰晤士河北岸,始建于公元960年。

威斯敏斯特教堂是历代国王加冕登基和举行婚礼庆典的地方,也是英国的王室陵墓所在地,可以说威斯敏斯特教堂是一部英国王室的石书。目睹了牛顿葬礼的伏尔泰为之深深震动。他曾感慨道:"走进威斯敏斯特教堂,人们所瞻仰的不是君王们的陵寝,而是国家为感谢那些为国增光的最伟大人物的纪念碑。这便是英国人民对于才能的尊敬。"

Ⅲ University of Cambridge/剑桥大学

Founded in 1209, Cambridge University is a world-renowned public research university located in Cambridge, England.

Cambridge University is the second oldest university in the English-speaking world. By October 2018, there have been 118 Nobel Prize winners from it (ranks No. 2 in the world). In 2018, Cambridge University was ranked No. 2 in the global universities by *Thames Higher Education* and No. 4 in the employment competitiveness of the global university graduates.

剑桥大学成立于公元1209年,坐落于英国剑桥,是一所世界著名的公立研究型大学。

剑桥大学是英语世界中第二古老的大学,截至2018年10月,共有118位诺贝尔奖获得者(世界第二)。2018年,在泰晤士高等教育的全球大学排名中居第二位,全球大学毕业生就业竞争力排名中居第四位。

Ⅳ Buckingham Palace/白金汉宫

Buckingham Palace is the London residence and administrative headquarters of the monarch of the United Kingdom. Located in Westminster, the palace is often at the center of state occasions and royal hospitality, and an important tourist attraction as well. Buckingham Palace is now open to visitors. Every morning, there is a famous handover ceremony of the imperial guards, which has become a great view of British Royal culture.

白金汉宫是英国君主位于伦敦的主要寝宫及办公处。宫殿坐落在威斯敏斯特,是国家庆典和王室欢迎礼举行场地之一,也是一处重要的旅游景点。现在的白金汉宫对外开放参观,每天清晨都会进行著名的禁卫军交接典礼,这也成为英国王室文化的一大景观。

Unit 1　Situational Dialogues/情景对话

Ⅰ Dialogue 1　Immigration Formalities

（A：*immigration officer*　B：*tour leader*）

B：Hi, everyone. We're now at London Heathrow International Airport①. OK, is everyone here?　Let's go. We shall go nonresident channel②. Please follow me. Only those who have immigration visa or PR Card③ go citizen channel.

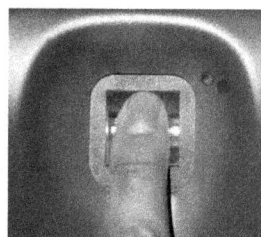

A：Welcome to UK. Good afternoon, Miss. May I see your passport, please?

B：Sure. We are a group of 20 people and here is my passport.

A：OK. What's the purpose of your visit?　On business or for pleasure?

B：We are a tour group.

A：How long will you stay in this country?

B：7 days.

A：What's your schedule for the trip?

B：We only visit Britain because of the time limit. During the stay, we'll visit London, Liverpool, Bristol, Birmingham, Manchester and Newcastle.

A：OK. Do you have return tickets to China?

B：Yes, we have. We'll go back to China from London.

A：Have you ever been to UK before?

B：Many times. I'm the tour leader.

A：Which city do you like most?

B：Magic London.

A：Magic! Good word. Do you know London much?

B：A little. London is the capital of the United Kingdom of Great Britain and Northern Ireland. It is situated in the southeast of England, sitting along the Thames River. The Inner London, the Outer London, and the London City consist of the Greater London, which is the London we usually talk about.

A：What give you the deepest impression?

B：Many. The British Museum, Tower Bridge, London Eye, Hyde Park, Buckingham Palace, and Big Ben. Especially The British Museum, which was founded in 1753, whose remarkable collection spans over two million years of human history. And we can enjoy a unique comparison of the treasures of world cultures under one roof, centred around the magnificent Great Court.

A：You are erudite and well-informed.

B：Thank you.

A：Do you have relatives or friends in UK?

B：No, I don't.

A：Where do you intend to stay while in UK?

B：Hotels. We've booked in advance.

A：How much currency does everyone have?

B：We haven't exceeded the limit of 8,000 pounds each.

A：Everything is alright. Now please let your passengers take care of their passports and go through one by one according to the order of the name list.

B：Yes. Shall I be the last one to pass?

A：As you like.

Notes：

① London Heathrow International Airport（LHR）：伦敦希思罗国际机场。

② nonresidents channel：非移民通道。

③ PR Card：Permanent Resident Card，绿卡。

II Dialogue 2 British Afternoon Tea

(*T*: *Todd*, *local guide*   *A*: *Aaron*, *tourist*)

A: So, what is our schedule for tomorrow?

T: Tomorrow is free. You can enjoy yourselves by wandering in the city, eating the specialties, doing shopping, visiting museums or just drinking tea while looking at the passers-by.

A: OK. I want to try the afternoon tea tomorrow. Anything I should pay attention to? Are there any rules I should follow when enjoying British afternoon tea?

T: Yes. The British have many traditions, but there is nothing more quintessential than taking afternoon tea. The Brits have a love affair with drinking tea. They drink more than 160 million cups of tea every day. But it was the invention of afternoon tea that turned sipping tea into a popular pastime.

A: Wow... Can you tell us more about it?

T: Sure. This social feast involves drinking good quality tea whilst nibbling on dainty sandwiches, scones with jam and cream, and a selection of small cakes. And of course, it only happens in the afternoon! It is a ritual dating back to the 1840s, designed as a light snack to bridge the gap between lunch and dinner. It went on to become a fashionable social occasion for the upper classes.

A: What is the difference between drinking tea at home and out? Is there any special place you can recommend us to have British afternoon tea?

T: Now there is a resurgence in its popularity in the UK and it's available to anyone who can afford it. Although it can be enjoyed at home, the best way to experience it is at a smart hotel or cafe. Some of the most famous places to indulge are Claridges, The Savoy or The Ritz in London. But if you're thinking of visiting such a place to tuck into a plate of sweet and savory treats washed down with a steaming hot brew, remember the rules you must adhere to: avoid being asked to leave.

A: OK. What are those rules?

T: (1) Make sure you order the correct thing. It is afternoon tea, not high tea or a cream tea. They are something different.

(2) Dress smartly. It's an important occasion. Certain places require a man wear a jacket and tie, and ladies wear a hat.

(3) When you sit down, place a napkin on your lap. It will keep your clothes clean

and can be used to wipe small crumbs from your mouth.

(4) Stir your tea correctly. Do not clink your spoon against the cup and do not leave it in the cup! Stir back and forth, not around in circles.

(5) Hold the tea cup by its handle with your thumb and forefinger together, and then use your middle finger to support and balance the cup underneath. Do not allow your little finger to stick out.

A: Anything more?

T: (6) Start by eating the sandwiches first before moving onto the sweet things.

(7) The sandwiches are called "finger sandwiches" and therefore eaten by hand not with a knife and fork. They should have their crusts cut off.

(8) Don't saw your scone in half. Ideally it should be pulled apart, creating two equal halves.

(9) When eating, take small delicate bites. This will allow you to join in conversation without always having a full mouth.

(10) Although you can ask for more sandwiches and cakes, don't stuff them in your pockets to eat later!

A: Todd, excuse me for a moment.

T: What?

A: I want to do shopping now for the formal dress for tomorrow's afternoon tea.

T: OK. Writer Henry James once noted that "There are few hours in life more agreeable than the hours dedicated to the ceremony known as afternoon tea." I'm sure once you've tried it, you will agree.

Ⅲ Dialogue 3　Travel in UK

(*T: Todd, a foreign friend　M: Mark, British*)

T: OK, Mark, we've been talking about the places you've traveled to and the things you have done there. What about your country, England? Can you recommend some good places for us to visit in England?

M: Right. Well, obviously, most people should visit London. Personally, I don't like London. It's too busy and too expensive.

T: Wait a minute. You're saying that people should visit it, but you don't like it. Why?

M: They should visit it because they have to go once to see all the famous places such the Big Ben, Trafalgar Square, Buckingham Palace, just to show they've been there. But if you arrive in London, I'd say, stay maybe just one or two days there and then move on. You can move on to other cheaper places. My favorite place in England is in the North of it. It's called the Lake District.

T: The Lake District?

M: Yeah, it is very, very beautiful.

T: So, I take it there are many lakes?

M: That's right. There got to be about twenty or thirty lakes up there and the scenery's beautiful. Famous for Peter Rabbit. Do you know Peter Rabbit?

T: Yeah, a fairy tale.

M: That's right. A children's character. The writer, Beatrice Potter, was born in the Lake District. That's where she got her inspiration.

T: So if you go to the Lake District, are you talking about camping or do you stay in like a B&B or what?

M: Yeah, you can stay in a B&B. You can camp. You can stay in pubs or inns, or there are many hotels. Things are very organized for tourists in the Lake District. Yeah, and it's not such a big area. So you can travel around there by bus, or by car, pretty easy.

T: OK, so that's two. Anymore?

M: Actually, I've never been there, but I'd probably recommend Scotland. Edinburgh Castle is very famous. Also York. The city of York in Yorkshire is very beautiful as well. It was famous for the Vikings in the old days, so it has a beautiful big cathedral and all the old Viking walls. If you like history, then England is a beautiful place to visit. There are many attractions like Stratford-upon-Avon, the birthplace of Shakespeare and Oxford, a famous university city. So if you like history, then England is great.

T: OK, well, sounds good. Thanks Mark.

Unit 2　Case Study/案例分析

Ⅰ　案例一：现金丢失的处理

朱先生参加了某旅行社组织的英国旅游团。朱先生事先准备了不少现金，计划到境外购买一些名贵商品。由于携带现金出境有限额，于是他将大部分现金放在行李箱中托运。到了目的地机场后发现行李箱已经破损，现金早已不翼而飞。朱先生认为旅行社并未事先提醒，使他遭受到了巨大损失，旅行社应当赔偿。领队认为不应当由旅行社来赔偿，原因是在行前说明会上特别强调不宜带太多现金，在当地使用银行卡即可。朱先生接到行前说明会的通知，但是并没有参加。在机场，领队再次提醒大家，不要把现金放在行李箱托运，朱先生说没有听到。领队的话却得到了许多同团客人的证实。

1. 有关财产损失的法律规定

相关法律中明确旅游经营者或者旅游辅助服务者为旅游者代管的行李物品损毁、灭失，旅游者请求赔偿损失的，人民法院应予以支持，但以下情形除外：

（1）损失由于旅游者未听从旅游经营者或旅游辅助服务者的事先声明。

（2）损失是因为不可抗力、意外事件造成的。

（3）损失是由旅游者的过错造成的。

（4）损失是由自然属性造成的。

2. 旅游者财产损失分类

（1）旅游者随身携带的行李物品的遗失或者被盗，除了交付交通部门托运的行李物品外。行李物品遗失基本属于民事行为，而被盗则属于在社会治安事件。

（2）旅游者托运行李物品的遗失或者被盗，主要是由于交通部门在运输行李物品过程中的过失和过错造成的。

（3）旅游者交付保管的行李物品的遗失或者被盗。

3. 旅游者财产损失纠纷处理存在的问题

（1）财产损失责任较难认定（责任认定有时不能轻而易举地实现）。

（2）财产损失数量较难认定（旅游者必须提供损失物品的购买凭证）。

（3）旅游活动的特点给处理纠纷带来了难度（损失较大的纠纷，很难在短时间内解决，最后只能通过司法途径解决）。

4. 旅游者财产损失纠纷处理的基本原则

(1)旅游者随身携带的行李物品遗失或者被盗。按照《中华人民共和国民法典》等法律规定,作为完全民事行为能力人,旅游者有责任看护好自己的随身携带物品,这类行李物品丢失和旅行社没有关系,只要尽到告知和提醒义务。

(2)旅游者托运行李物品的遗失或者被盗。按照《最高法审理旅游纠纷若干规定》的规定,托运的行李物品的灭失或毁灭,旅行社有义务积极协助旅游者向交通运输部门索赔。另外,贵重物品不应放在行李箱内托运。

(3)旅行社交付保管的行李物品的遗失或者被盗。作为保管人的旅行社或者饭店,应当承担全部责任。

(4)对于上述旅游者财产损失,即使旅行社和导游人员(领队)不承担赔偿责任,但旅行社应当承担协助义务。

Ⅱ 案例二:无旅行团航班信息的责任

1. 案例简介

2019年春节期间,某旅行社领队王某从香港、澳门带团回来已是临近除夕,在匆匆与旅行社OP交接完毕后,马上准备带领下一团赴印尼巴厘岛旅游。在畅游巴厘岛并结束短短的4晚6天的行程后,领队王某带领旅游团踏上了返程的归途。到了机场,安置好客人之后,领队王某拿着整团护照跑到航空公司柜台办理回程航班手续,这时却被航空公司工作人员告知该航班没有他们这个旅游团的信息。

2. 案例分析

请分析说明在这起案例中,(　　　)有责任。

A. OP有责任　　　　　　　　　　B. 领队有责任

C. OP和领队都有责任　　　　　　D. 航空公司责任

答案:C

分析:

(1)首先OP出了问题,没有把回程机票确认清楚。

(2)其次领队和OP交接匆忙,交接完后没有做出团前四核对:(1)护照与机票核对;(2)机票与行程核对;(3)机票与名单表核对;(4)护照与内容核对。

(3)领队到达巴厘岛后没有与当地的导游确认行程和返程机票。

Chapter 6

France/法国

Part One
Briefing on France/法国概况

Unit 1　Overviews/总览

I　Basic Information/基本信息

National Flag/国旗	National Emblem/国徽

The flag of France features three vertical bands colored blue, white, and red. It is also known as the French Tricolor or simply the Tricolor. Blue and red are the traditional colors of Paris. Blue is identified with Saint Martin, red with Saint Denis. At the storming of the Bastille in 1789, the Paris civil military force wore blue and red cockades on their hats. White had long featured prominently on French flags and is described as the "ancient French color". The three colors are also occasionally taken to represent the three elements of the revolutionary motto, liberté（freedom: blue）, égalité（equality: white）, fraternité（brotherhood: red）.	France has no official national emblem, but the traditional one was used in diplomatic occasions in 1912 and submitted to the United Nations in 1953. This emblem consists of: （1）A wide shield with, on the one end, a lion-head and on the other an eagle-head, bearing a monogram "RF" standing for République Française（French Republic）. （2）An olive branch symbolizes peace. （3）An oak branch symbolizes persistence or wisdom. （4）The fasces symbolizes authority and justice. The emblem has been a symbol of France since 1912, although it does not have any legal status as an official coat of arms. It appears on the cover of French passports and was adopted originally by the French Foreign Ministry as a symbol for use by diplomatic and consular missions.

National Flag/国旗	National Emblem/国徽
法国国旗以三色旗著称,分别为蓝色、白色和红色。 蓝色和红色是代表巴黎的传统颜色。蓝色是圣马丁长袍的颜色,红色则是圣但尼军旗的颜色。在1789年巴士底狱的袭击中,巴黎国民自卫军的帽子上佩戴着蓝色和红色的帽徽。白色则早已在法国国旗上占有重要地位,被称为"代表法国的古老颜色"。 这3种颜色也被用来代表革命宗旨的3个要素:自由、平等、博爱。	法国没有正式国徽,但传统上采用的徽号在1912年被采用于外交场合,并在1953年被用于呈交联合国。图案包括:(1)一个宽盾,一端是狮头,另一头是鹰头,带有字母"RF",代表法兰西共和国。(2)橄榄枝象征着和平。(3)橡树枝象征着坚忍或智慧。(4)束棒象征着权威与正义。 自1912年以来它一直是法国的象征,尽管不具有官方徽章的法律地位,但它最初由法国外交部采用,印在法国护照的封面上,作为外交和领事使团使用的标志。

Other Basics/其他基本信息	
Full Name/国家全称	French Republic/法兰西共和国
Total Area/国土面积	550,000 km²/550,000平方千米(不含海外领地)
Population/人口	65,240,000(2021年7月,不含海外领地)
Nationality/民族	93% French;7% foreign-born/93%法国人;7%外国移民
Capital/首都	Paris/巴黎
National Anthem/国歌	"La Marseillaise"/《马赛曲》
National Flower/国花	Iris/香根鸢尾
National Bird/国鸟	Gallic Rooster/高卢雄鸡
Divisions/行政区划	Metroplitan France is divided into 13 regions and 96 provinces, as well as 5 overseas single-province regions, 5 overseas administrative regions and 1 overseas dependency with special status./本土划为13个大区、96个省,还有5个海外单省大区、5个海外行政区和1个地位特殊的海外属地
Language/语言	French/法语
Major Political Parties/主要政党	The Republic in March, Socialist Party, The Republicans, etc./共和国前进党、社会党、共和国人党等
Government Type/政府类型	Unitary Semi-presidential Republic/半总统共和制
Religious Belief/主要宗教信仰	51% Christian, 40% Non-religious, 6% Islam, 1% Jewish, 2% other faiths/51%基督教,40%无宗教信仰,6%伊斯兰教,1%犹太教,2%其他信仰
Currency/货币	Euro/欧元
Time Difference with Beijing/与北京时差	-7(Summer Time -6)/比北京晚7个小时(夏时制晚6个小时)

Ⅱ Physical Geography/自然和地理

The vast majority of France's territory and population is situated in Western Europe and is called Metropolitan France, to distinguish it from the country's various overseas polities. Due to its shape, France is often referred to as l'Hexagone ("The Hexagon"). Metropolitan France covers 550,000 square kilometers, the largest among European Union members. It is bordered by the North Sea in the north, the English Channel in the northwest, the Atlantic Ocean in the west and the Mediterranean Sea in the southeast. Its land borders consist of Belgium and Luxembourg in the northeast, Germany and Switzerland in the east, Italy and Monaco in the southeast, and Andorra and Spain in the south and southwest. With the exception of the northeast, most of France's land borders are roughly delineated by natural boundaries and geographic features: to the south and southeast, the Pyrenees and the Alps and the Jura, respectively, and to the east, the Rhine river. In the Mediterranean Sea, there are Corsica island and many coastal islands.

France also has several overseas regions across the world, which are organized as follows:

(1)In South America: French Guiana.

(2)In the Atlantic Ocean: Saint Pierre and Miquelon and, in the Antilles: Guadeloupe, Martinique, Saint Martin and Saint Barthélemy.

(3)In the Pacific Ocean: French Polynesia, the special collectivity of New Caledonia, Wallis and Futuna and Clipperton Island.

(4)In the Indian Ocean: Réunion Island, Mayotte, Kerguelen Islands, Crozet Islands, St. Paul and Amsterdam islands, and the Scattered Islands in the Indian Ocean.

法国绝大多数的领土和人口都位于西欧,称为法国本土,以区别于该国的各种海外区块。法国领土形状呈六边形,面积55万平方千米,是欧盟成员国中最大的。法国本土北达北海,西北与英吉利海峡接壤,西抵大西洋,南至地中海;与东北部的比利时和卢森堡、东部的德国与瑞士、东南的意大利和摩纳哥,以及南部和西南部的安道尔和西班牙接壤。除了东北部以外,法国的大部分陆地边界大致由自然边界和地理特征划定。法国南部和东部的山脉有比利牛斯山脉、阿尔卑斯山脉和汝拉山脉,河流有莱茵河。在地中海上,辖有科西嘉岛和众多海岸群岛。

法国在世界范围内拥有众多海外省和海外领地,这些领土之间的行政区划等级和管辖形式有所不同,它们分别位于:

(1)南美洲:法属圭亚那。

（2）大西洋：圣皮埃尔和密克隆，以及安的列斯群岛的瓜特罗普、马提尼克岛、圣马丁和圣巴泰勒米。

（3）太平洋：法属波利尼西亚、新喀里多尼亚、瓦利斯和富图纳群岛，以及克利珀顿岛。

（4）印度洋：留尼汪岛、马约特岛、克罗泽群岛、凯尔盖朗群岛、圣保罗岛、阿姆斯特丹岛，以及印度洋中的分散岛屿。

Ⅲ Government and Administration/法国政府机构

The French Republic is a unitary semi-presidential representative democratic republic with strong democratic traditions. The Constitution of the Fifth Republic was approved by referendum on 28 September 1958. It greatly strengthened the authority of the executive in relation to parliament. The executive branch itself has two leaders: the President of the Republic, currently Emmanuel Macron, who is head of state and is elected directly by universal adult suffrage for a 5-year term (formerly 7 years), and the Government, led by the president-appointed Prime Minister.

The French Parliament is a bicameral legislature comprising a National Assembly and a Senate. The National Assembly deputies represent local constituencies and are directly elected for 5-year terms. The Assembly has the power to dismiss the government, and thus the majority in the Assembly determines the choice of government. Senators are chosen by an electoral college for 6-year terms (originally 9-year terms), and one half of the seats are submitted to election every 3 years. The Senate's legislative powers are limited; in the event of disagreement between the two chambers, the National Assembly has the final say. The Government has a strong influence in shaping the agenda of Parliament.

法兰西共和国是实行半总统制的单一制共和国，具有悠久的民主传统。《法兰西第五共和国宪法》于1958年9月28日由法国民众全体公民投票通过，决定了第五共和国的国家政体运作方式。它大幅度地增强了行政机关与议会的关系。所有行政机关共有两位领导人，一是共和国总统，目前的总统为埃马纽埃尔·马克龙，由普选直接选举产生，任期5年（原为7年）；二是政府总理，由总统任命。

法国议会是两院制机构，由国民议会和参议院组成。国民议会代表代表了所在选区，由民众直接选举产生，任期5年。议会有权解散政府，因此议会的多数派能够左右政府的决策。参议院成员由一个选举机构（取决于各地方议会的提名）选举产生，任期为6年（原为9年），每3年重新选举1/2的参议员。参议院的立法职能有限；当两院意见不同时，国民议会拥有最后裁决权。政府对于议会议程的安排具有很大影响。

Unit 2 History and People/历史和人民

I History/历史

1. Roman Times/罗马时代

The first written records for the history of France appeared in the Iron Age. What is now France made up the bulk of the region known to the Romans as Gaul. Over the course of the 1st millennium BC, the Greeks, Romans and Carthaginians established colonies on the Mediterranean coast and the offshore islands. The Roman Republic annexed southern Gaul as the province of Gallia Narbonensis in the late 2nd century BC, and Roman forces under Julius Caesar conquered the rest of Gaul in the Gallic Wars of 58 BC – 51 BC. Afterwards a Gallo-Roman culture emerged and Gaul was increasingly integrated into the Roman Empire.

In the later stages of the Roman Empire, Gaul was subject to barbarian raids and migration, most importantly by the Germanic Franks. The Frankish King Clovis I united most of Gaul under his rule in the late 5th century, setting the stage for Frankish dominance in the region for hundreds of years. Frankish power reached its fullest extent under Charlemagne. The medieval Kingdom of France emerged from the western part of Charlemagne's Carolingian Empire, known as West Francia, and achieved increasing prominence under the rule of the House of Capet, founded by Hugh Capet in 987.

法国历史最初的文字记载出现在铁器时代。现在的法国在罗马时代被称为高卢。在公元前1000年的过程中,希腊人、罗马人和迦太基人在地中海沿岸和近海岛屿建立了殖民地。公元前2世纪后期,罗马共和国将高卢南部吞并为纳尔波高卢省,而朱利叶斯·恺撒(恺撒大帝)领导下的罗马军队在公元前58年—公元前51年的高卢战争中征服了高卢的其余部分。随后出现了高卢罗马文化,高卢越来越融入罗马帝国。

在罗马帝国的后期阶段,高卢受到野蛮人的袭击和移民,最主要为日耳曼人。法兰克国王克洛维斯一世在5世纪后期统治了高卢的大部分地区,为法兰克人在该地区统治数百年奠定了基础。在查理曼大帝的统治下,法兰克日趋强盛。中世纪的法兰西王国出现在查理曼大帝的加洛林帝国西部,被称为西弗朗西亚,并在987年由于格·卡佩特创立的卡佩王朝的统治下日益显赫。

2. Hundred Years' War/百年战争

The death of the last direct Capetian monarch in 1328 led to the series of conflicts known as the Hundred Years' War between the House of Valois and the House of Plantagenet. The war formally began in 1337 following Philip Ⅵ's attempt to seize the Duchy of Aquitaine from its hereditary holder, Edward Ⅲ of England, the Plantagenet claimant to the French throne. Despite early Plantagenet victories, including the capture and ransom of John Ⅱ of France, fortunes turned in favor of the Valois later in the war. Among the notable figures of the war was Joan of Arc, a French peasant girl who led French forces against the English, establishing herself as a national heroine. The war ended with a Valois victory in 1453.

Victory in the Hundred Years' War had the effect of strengthening French nationalism and vastly increasing the power and reach of the French monarchy. During the period known as the Ancien Régime, France transformed into a centralized absolute monarchy. During the next centuries, France experienced the Renaissance and the Protestant Reformation. At the height of the French Wars of Religion, France became embroiled in another succession crisis, as the last Valois King, Henry Ⅲ, fought against rival factions the House of Bourbon and the House of Guise. Henry, King of Navarre, heir of the Bourbon family, would be victorious in the conflict and establish the French Bourbon dynasty. A burgeoning worldwide colonial empire was established in the 16th century. French political power reached its peak under the rule of Louis ⅪⅤ, "The Sun King", builder of Versailles Palace.

1328年,最后一位卡佩王朝君主去世,导致了瓦卢瓦家族和金雀花家族之间的一系列冲突,称为百年战争。这场战争正式开始于1337年,当时腓力六世试图从阿基坦公爵领地的世袭继承人英国爱德华三世手中夺取阿基坦公爵领地。尽管金雀花在早期取得了胜利,包括俘虏和勒索了法国的约翰二世,但在战争后期,命运转向了瓦卢瓦人。在这场战争中,著名的人物之一是法国农民女孩圣女贞德,她领导法国军队对抗英国,确立了自己的民族英雄地位。战争在1453年以瓦卢瓦人的胜利而结束。

百年战争的胜利加强了法国的民族主义意识,极大地提高了法国君主政体的权力和影响力。在被称为古代政体的时期,法国转变成为一个中央集权的君主专制政体。在接下来的几个世纪里,法国经历了文艺复兴和新教改革。在法国宗教战争的鼎盛时期,法国陷入了另一场继承危机,因为最后一位瓦卢瓦国王亨利三世与敌对派系波旁家族和吉斯家族进行了斗争。纳瓦拉国王亨利是波旁家族的继承人,在冲突中获胜,建立法国波旁王朝。16世纪,一个新兴的世界殖民帝国建立了。法国的政治权力在凡尔赛宫的建造者"太阳王"路易十四的统治下达到顶峰。

3. French Revolution/法国大革命

In the late 18th century the monarchy and associated institutions were overthrown in the French Revolution. The country was governed for a period as a Republic, until the French Empire was declared by Napoleon Bonaparte. Following Napoleon's defeat in the Battle of Waterloo, France went through several further regime changes, being ruled as a monarchy, then briefly as a Second Republic, and then as a Second Empire, until a more lasting French Third Republic was established in 1870.

18世纪末,法国大革命推翻了君主制及相关机制。这个国家作为共和国存在了一段时间,直到拿破仑·波拿巴宣布法兰西帝国成立。而当拿破仑在滑铁卢战役中失败后,法国又经历了几次政权更迭,先是君主制统治,后是短暂的第二共和国,然后是第二帝国,直到1870年建立了更持久的法国第三共和国。

4. World Wars/世界大战

France was one of the Triple Entente powers in World War I, fighting alongside the United Kingdom, Russia, Italy, Japan, the United States and smaller allies against Germany and the Central Powers.

France was one of the Allied Powers in World War II, but was conquered by Nazi Germany in 1940. The Third Republic was dismantled, and most of the country was controlled directly by Germany while the south was controlled until 1942 by the collaborationist Vichy government. Living conditions were harsh as Germany drained away food and manpower, and many Jews were killed. Charles de Gaulle led the Free France movement that one-by-one took over the colonial empire and coordinated the wartime Resistance. Following liberation in summer 1944, a Fourth Republic was established. France slowly recovered economically and enjoyed a baby boom that reversed its very low fertility rate. Long wars drained French resources and ended in political defeat. In the wake of the Algerian Crisis of 1958, Charles de Gaulle set up the French Fifth Republic. Into the 1960s decolonization saw most of the French colonial empire become independent, while smaller parts were incorporated into the French state as overseas departments and collectivities. Since World War II France has been a permanent member in the UN Security Council and NATO. It played a central role in the unification process after 1945 that led to the European Union. Despite slow economic growth in recent years, it remains a strong economic, cultural, military and political factor in the 21st century.

法国是第一次世界大战中的三重协约国之一,与英国、俄罗斯、意大利、日本、美国以及反对德国和中央政权的小型盟国并肩作战。

法国是第二次世界大战中的同盟国之一，但在1940年被纳粹德国征服，第三共和国解体，该国大部分地区由德国直接控制，而南部由维希政府控制到1942年。由于德国消耗了大量的食物和人力，导致许多犹太人被杀，生活条件恶劣。戴高乐领导的自由法国运动逐一接管了殖民帝国并协调了战时抵抗运动。1944年夏天解放后，建立了法兰西第四共和国。法国经济慢慢恢复，婴儿潮扭转了其极低的生育率。长期战争耗尽了法国的资源，并以政治失败告终。在1958年的阿尔及利亚危机之后，戴高乐成立了法兰西第五共和国。进入20世纪60年代的非殖民化使法国殖民帝国的大部分地区独立，而较小的部分则作为海外区块被纳入法国。自第二次世界大战以来，法国一直是联合国安理会和北约的常任理事国，并在1945年之后的统一进程中发挥了核心作用，在欧盟中扮演重要角色。尽管近年来经济增长缓慢，但它仍然是21世纪强大的经济、文化、军事和政治国家。

Ⅱ People and Figures/人民及名人

With an estimated 2020 population of 65.24 million people, France is the 20th most populous country in the world, the third-most populous in Europe (after Russia and Germany), and the second most populous in the European Union (after Germany). Most French people are of Celtic (Gauls) origin, with an admixture of Italic (Romans) and Germanic (Franks) groups.

据统计，2020年法国人口为6,524万，是世界第二十大人口大国，欧洲第三大人口大国（仅次于俄罗斯和德国），欧盟第二大人口大国（仅次于德国）。大多数法国人是凯尔特人（高卢人）的血统，混合了意大利（罗马人）和日耳曼（法兰克人）群体。

1. Louis ⅩⅣ of France/法王路易十四

Louis ⅩⅣ (September 5, 1638—September 1, 1715), known as Louis the Great or the Sun King, was King of France from 14 May 1643 until his death in 1715. His reign of 72 years and 110 days is the longest recorded of any monarch of a sovereign country in European history. Louis sought to create a centralized state governed from the capital and consolidated a system of absolute monarchical rule in France that endured until the French Revolution.

During Louis' long reign, France was the leading European power, and it fought three major wars: the Franco-Dutch War, the War of the League of Augsburg, and the War of the Spanish Succession. There were also two lesser conflicts: the War of Devolution and the War of the Reunions. Warfare defined the foreign policy of Louis ⅩⅣ, and his personality shaped his approach. Impelled "by a mix of commerce, revenge, and pique", Louis sensed that warfare was the ideal way to enhance his glory. In peacetime he concentrated on preparing for the next war. He taught his diplomats that their job was to create tactical and strategic advantages for the French military.

路易十四（1638年9月5日—1715年9月1日），被称为路易大帝或太阳王。从1643年5月14日起任法国国王，直到1715年去世。他在位72年110天，是欧洲历史上任何一个主权国家的君主中在位时间最长的。路易试图建立一个由首都统治的中央集权国家，并巩固了法国的君主专制制度，这种制度一直延续到法国大革命。

在路易的长期统治期间，法国是欧洲的主要强国，它打过3次大战：法荷战争、奥格斯堡同盟战争和西班牙继承战争。还有两个较小的冲突：权力下放战争和统一战争。战争决定了路易十四的外交政策，他的个性塑造了他的外交方针。在"商业、复仇和愤怒的混合体"的驱使下，路易意识到战争是提升他的荣耀的理想途径。在和平时期，他集中精力准备下一场战争。他教导他的外交官，他们的工作是为法国军队创造战术和战略优势。

2. Napoleon Bonaparte/拿破仑·波拿巴

Napoleon Bonaparte（August 15，1769—May 5，1821）was a French statesman and military leader who rose to prominence during the French Revolution and led several successful campaigns during the French Revolutionary Wars. He was Emperor of the French as Napoleon I from 1804 until 1814 and again briefly in 1815 during the Hundred Days. Napoleon dominated European and global affairs for more than a decade while leading France against a series of alliances in the Napoleonic Wars. He won most of these wars and the vast majority of his battles, building a large empire that ruled over much of continental Europe before its final collapse in 1815. He is considered one of the greatest commanders in history, and his wars and campaigns are studied at military schools worldwide. Napoleon's political and cultural legacy has endured as one of the most celebrated and controversial leaders in human history.

拿破仑·波拿巴（1769年8月15日—1821年5月5日）是法国政治家和军事领袖，在法国大革命期间崭露头角，并在法国革命战争期间领导了几次成功的战役。从1804年到1814年，他一直是法国的皇帝拿破仑一世；在1815年的百日王朝期间，他又是一个短暂的皇帝。拿破仑统治欧洲和全球事务超过10年，同时领导法国对抗拿破仑战争中的一系列联盟。他赢得了大部分的战争和绝大多数的战役，建立了一个在1815年欧洲大陆最终崩溃之前统治欧洲大陆大部分地区的大帝国。他被认为是历史上最伟大的指挥官之一，他的战争和战役在世界各地的军事学校都有研究。作为人类历史上最著名和最具争议性的领导人之一，拿破仑的政治和文化遗产经久不衰。

Unit 3　Culture and Education/文化和教育

I　Culture/文化

1. Art/艺术

The origins of French art were very much influenced by Flemish art and by Italian art at the time of the Renaissance. French artists developed the rococo style in the 18th century, as a more intimate imitation of old baroque style. The French Revolution brought great changes, as Napoleon favored artists of neoclassic style. At this time France had become a center of artistic creation. In the second part of the 19th century, France's influence over painting became even more important, with the development of new styles of painting such as Impressionism and Symbolism. The most famous impressionist painters of the period were Camille Pissarro, Édouard Manet, Edgar Degas, Claude Monet and Auguste Renoir. The second generation of impressionist-style painters, Paul Cézanne, Paul Gauguin, Toulouse-Lautrec and Georges Seurat, were also at the avant-garde of artistic evolutions. Beside paintings, famous sculpture work also includes the *Thinker* by Auguste Rodin.

法国艺术的根源受文艺复兴时期的弗兰芒艺术和意大利艺术影响较深。18世纪洛可可风格起源于法国,是一种具有旧巴洛克风格特点的新艺术。法国大革命给法国的艺术带来了巨大的变化,因为拿破仑偏爱新古典主义风格的艺术家,此时的法国已成为艺术创作的中心。19世纪下半叶,法国绘画的影响力进一步扩大,出现了印象派与象征主义风格。该时期著名的印象派大师有卡米耶·毕沙罗、爱德华·马奈、埃德加·德加、克洛德·莫奈和奥古斯特·雷诺阿。一些第二代印象派画家,如保罗·塞尚、保罗·高更、亨利·德图卢兹-洛特雷克和乔治·修拉也处于艺术进化的前沿。除了绘画,著名的雕塑作品还包括奥古斯特·罗丹的《思想者》。

2. Cuisine/美食

French cuisine is renowned for being one of the finest in the world. According to the regions, traditional recipes are different, the North of the country prefers to use butter as the preferred fat for cooking, whereas olive oil is more commonly used in the South. France's most renowned products are wines as well as a large variety of different cheeses. A meal often consists of three courses, entrée, main course, cheese and/or dessert, sometimes with a salad offered before the cheese or dessert. French cuisine is also regarded as a key element of the quality of life and the attractiveness of France. A French publication, the Michelin guide, awards Michelin stars for excellence to a select few establishments. The acquisition or loss of a star can have dramatic effects on the success of a restaurant.

法国菜是世界上最受欢迎的菜系之一。法国菜的一些基本配方因地区而异,例如北方偏好黄油作为烹饪的首选用油,而南方偏好橄榄油。法国最著名的产品是葡萄酒以及各种不同的奶酪。法国人就餐讲究礼仪,一般包括三道菜,第一道菜是开胃浓汤或者冷盘,接着才是主菜,最后是奶酪或者甜点,有时也在奶酪或甜点之前提供沙拉。法国菜被认为是生活品质和法国吸引力的关键因素。法国的一份出版物《米其林指南》将杰出的米其林之星奖授予少数几家机构,星级的上调和下调可以显著地影响餐厅的商业前途。

3. Fashion/时尚

Fashion has been an important industry and cultural export of France since the 17th century, and modern "haute couture" originated in Paris in the 1860s. Today, Paris, along with London, Milan, and New York City, is considered one of the world's fashion capitals, and the city is home or headquarters to many of the premier fashion brands. The association of France with fashion and style dates largely to the reign of Louis ⅩⅣ when the luxury goods industries in France came increasingly under royal control and the French royal court became, arguably, the arbiter of taste and style in Europe. But France renewed its dominance of the high fashion industry in the years 1860—1960 through the establishing of the great fashion houses such as Chanel, Dior, and Givenchy. The French perfume industry is world leader in its sector and is centered on the town of Grasse.

自17世纪起,时尚设计及时尚用品(如奢侈品和化妆品)制造一直是法国的重要行业,其中"高级服装定制"起源于19世纪60年代。如今,巴黎与伦敦、米兰和纽约一起被认为是世界时尚之都。巴黎是许多顶级时尚品牌的总部所在地。法国与时尚的联系源于路易十四统治时期,当时法国的奢侈品行业在王室控制下蒸蒸日上,法国宫廷也便自然站在欧洲时尚的最前沿,成为欧洲时尚潮流的主宰。1860—1960年的100年间,法国出现众多奢侈品及时装品牌,包括香奈儿、迪奥和纪梵希,得以巩固其在时尚款式方面的主导地位。法国的香水产业世界领先,众多香水制造商汇聚于小镇格拉斯。

Ⅱ Education/教育

The schooling system in France is centralized, and is composed of three stages, primary education, secondary education, and higher education. Primary and secondary education are predominantly public, run by the Ministry of National Education. In France, education is compulsory from six to sixteen years old, and the public school is secular and free. While training and remuneration of teachers and the curriculum are the responsibility of the state centrally, the management of primary and secondary schools is overseen by local authorities. Primary education comprises two phases, nursery school and elementary school. Nursery school aims to stimulate the minds of very young children and promote their socialization and development of a basic grasp of language and number. Around the age of six, children transfer to elementary school, whose primary objectives are learning about writing, arithmetic and citizenship. Secondary education also consists of two phases. The first is delivered through colleges (middle schools) and leads to the national certificate. The second is offered in high schools and finishes in national exams leading to a baccalaureate or certificate of professional competence.

Higher education is divided between public universities and the prestigious and selective Grandes écoles, such as the Paris Institute of Political Studies, HEC Paris for Economics, Polytechnique and the Paris School of Mines that produce high-profile engineers, or the National School of Administration for careers in the civil service of the state.

法国教育制度是高度中央集权的、组织化的,可以分为3个阶段:初等教育、中等教育和高等教育。中小学教育主要是公立的,由国家教育部管理。在法国,6至16岁的义务教育是公立的,公立学校是免费的。虽然教师的培训、薪水和课程由国家统一负责,但中小学的管理由地方当局监督。小学教育包括两个阶段:幼儿园和小学。幼儿园旨在激发幼儿的思维,促进他们的社会化和发展,基本掌握语言和数字。6岁左右,儿童升入小学,其主要目标是学习写作、算术和公民意识。中等教育也包括两种:第一种是通过社区学院(中学)提供并获得国家证书;第二种是在高中提供,并完成国家高中毕业会考,从而获得中学毕业证书或专业能力证书。

高等教育分为公立大学和有声望的私立大学,如巴黎政治学院、HEC巴黎经济学院、综合理工学院和造就高知名度工程师的巴黎矿业学院,以及培养国家行政人员的国家行政学院。

Unit 4　Major Attractions/主要景点

I　Eiffel Tower/埃菲尔铁塔

The Eiffel Tower is an iron tower located in the Champ de Mars in Paris. Its name comes from the engineer's, Gustave Eiffel. Built in 1889 for the International Exhibition, it has become a cultural icon of France and one of the most recognizable structures in the world. With more than 7 million visitors every year, it is the most visited paid monument in the world. The Eiffel tower is listed as a historical monument since June 24th, 1964.

With a height of 312 meters at the beginning, the Eiffel Tower remained for 41 years the highest monument in the world. It has 4 floors. Over the years, the height was increased several times with the setup of antennas for radio and television programs. It now measures 324 meters high.

The Eiffel Tower was designed by engineers Maurice Koechlin and Emile Nouguier. Gustave Eiffel then redeemed the rights. This project was intended to be the "highlight of the 1889 exhibition taking place in Paris", which also celebrated the centenary of the French Revolution. Built by 250 workers in two years, two months and five days, the Eiffel Tower is finally inaugurated on 31 March 1889. But the expected attendance happens only from the 1960s, with the rise of international tourism.

The Eiffel Tower is often illuminated for events: fireworks for July 14th (Bastille day), night illuminations and colorful dressing for various events.

埃菲尔铁塔坐落于巴黎的战神广场,因建造埃菲尔铁塔的工程师古斯塔夫·埃菲尔而命名。1889年巴黎世界博览会的入口就被设在了埃菲尔铁塔下,埃菲尔铁塔也因此被全世界所知,并成为巴黎乃至法国的标志。每年,埃菲尔铁塔接待超过700万的世界各地的游客,并且成为全世界付费建筑群中接待游客数最多的建筑。自1964年6月24日起,巴黎埃菲尔铁塔被认定为法国的历史建筑。

埃菲尔铁塔高312米,曾经保持近41年的世界最高建筑物的美名。埃菲尔铁塔由4层楼组成。随着岁月的累积,埃菲尔铁塔的高度也在不断"增加",许多电视和电台的天线被安装在了铁塔之上,让今天的埃菲尔铁塔的高度达到了324米。

埃菲尔铁塔的构图理念来自于建筑师莫里斯·克什兰和埃米尔·努圭尔。之后,居斯塔夫·埃菲尔将其购买并建造而成。埃菲尔铁塔是为了1889年的巴黎世界博览会和纪念法国大革命胜利100周年而建。为了完成这座世界瞩目的埃菲尔铁塔,建筑师居斯塔夫·埃菲尔自费做了近百次实验,由250位工人经两年零两月又五天的时间,并最终于1889年3月31日建造完成。但是,埃菲尔铁塔真正成为世界的旅游景点则是从1960年才开始。

埃菲尔铁塔经常为各种活动点亮,如7月14日的烟火表演(巴士底狱日),每天晚上整点举行亮灯仪式,并且在其他特殊节日时,埃菲尔铁塔也都会"穿上"特殊的应景服装。

Ⅱ Louvre Museum/罗浮宫博物馆

Louvre Museum is one of the largest museums in the world, located in the center of Paris, in the 1st district. Nearly 35,000 objects from prehistory to the 21st century are exhibited over an area of 60,600 m². With more than 8 million visitors each year, it is the most visited museum in the world.

The museum is located in the Louvre Palace, once a fortress built in the late 12th century under Philip Ⅱ. Remains of the fortress are visible in the basement of the museum. The building was extended many times to form the present Louvre Palace. In 1682, Louis ⅩⅣ chose the Palace of Versailles as his house, leaving the Louvre as a place to display the royal collection. In 1692, the building was occupied by the Académie des Inscriptions et Belles-Lettres and the Académie Royale de Peinture et de Sculpture. The Académie remained at the Louvre for 100 years. During the French Revolution, the National Assembly decreed that the Louvre should be used as a museum, to display the masterpieces of the nation. The museum opened 10 August 1793 with an exhibition of 537 paintings. Due to structural problems of the building, the museum was closed in 1796 until 1801. The museum collection increased under Napoleon, it was renamed the Napoleon museum. After the defeat of Napoleon at Waterloo, many works seized by his armies were returned to their original owners. The collection was further increased during the reigns of Louis ⅩⅧ and Charles Ⅹ. During the Second French Empire the museum gained 20,000 pieces.

巴黎罗浮宫博物馆是世界最大的博物馆之一,位于巴黎市中心的第一区。收藏着近35,000件从史前至21世纪的收藏品,展出面积6万多平方米。罗浮宫博物馆每年接待超过800万的世界各地的游客,并因此成为世界接受游览人数最多的博物馆。

罗浮宫,曾是12世纪末腓力二世统治下建造的一座堡垒,在博物馆的地下室可以看到堡垒的遗迹。这座建筑经过多次扩建,形成了现在的罗浮宫。1682年,法国国王路易十六选择凡尔赛宫作为寝宫,将罗浮宫作为了展示皇家展览品的主要场所。1692年起,罗浮宫作为皇家雕塑与绘画学院的所在地,直至100年后被迁出。在法国大革命期间,法国国民议会正式将罗浮宫认定为博物馆,并向公众展示法国国家的各项杰出作品。博物馆在1793年8月10日正式向公众开放,以其537幅油画和皇室收藏品让全世界的游客慕名而来参观欣赏。博物馆曾因建筑结构的问题在1796年至1801年暂停对公众开放。在拿破仑的领导下,罗浮宫的藏品数也迅速增加,并且罗浮宫也被改名为拿破仑博物馆。但在滑铁卢后,很多在战争中被搜缴的藏品也物归原主。罗浮宫的藏品也在路易十八和查理十世的统治下,进一步增加,直至法兰西第二帝国时期,罗浮宫的藏品已将近20,000件。

Ⅲ　Palace of Versailles/凡尔赛宫

The Palace of Versailles, or simply Versailles, is a royal castle about 18 kilometers southwest of the French capital. In 1682, the court of Versailles was the center of political power in France and the king lived there permanently. Versailles is famous not only for its magnificent castle, but also to be the symbol of the system of absolute monarchy of the Ancien Régime.

The castle covers 110,000 square metres divided into 2,300 rooms, including 1,000 open at the museum. The park of Versailles covers 1,110,000 square metres with 1,000,000 square metres of gardens, and includes the Petit and Grand Trianon, the Queen's Hamlet, the Grand and Petit Canal, a menagerie, an orangery and the water part of the Swiss.

凡尔赛宫,简称凡尔赛,是法国首都巴黎西南约18千米的一座皇家城堡。1682年,凡尔赛宫是法国的政治权利中心,法国国王在那里永久居住。凡尔赛宫不仅因其宏伟的城堡而闻名,而且是古代君主专制制度的象征。

凡尔赛宫占地11万平方米,共有2,300间大小不同的房间,其中有1,000间对公众开放。凡尔赛宫全园占地面积达111万平方米,其中园林100万平方米,包括小特里亚农宫和大特里亚农宫、皇后农庄、大运河和小运河、动物园、橘园和瑞士水域。

Part Two
Outbound Tour Guide Operation/出境领队实务

Unit 1   Situational Dialogues/情景对话

Ⅰ Dialogue 1   Luggage Claiming

(*A*: *airport staff   B*: *tour leader*)

B: Excuse me, Sir, where is the luggage claim area[①]?

A: Go downstairs and the luggage claim is at your left.

B: How can we find our luggage?

A: You can check the flight information and you will find your flight number above each carousel and the carousel for your luggage is also shown there.

B: Do we have to show our boarding passes to claim our luggage?

A: No, but you need to double-check and make sure you get the right ones.

B: OK. By the way, where can we find luggage carts?

A: They are over there.

B: But it seems they are all locked together.

A: You need to put coins into the coin slot to unlock. For each cart, you need to pay one dollar.

B: I see. Thank you very much.

A: You are welcome.

(*after claiming luggage*)

B: Excuse me. Can you help me?

A: Yes. What's the problem?

B: One of my group members' suitcase is broken. A wheel is lost. Who should be responsible for this? Where can I go to report it?

A: I'm sorry to hear that. You can go to the luggage inquiry[②] for help.

B: Can they repair it right away?

A：Yes，if it is not a big problem. But if the suitcase is irreparable，we'll either buy him a new one or pay him cash with 10% annual depreciation.

B：Thank you. Can you suggest some places to buy a watch，some jewelries，and fashionable clothing? I want to go and look around in Paris.

C：I highly recommend Galeries Lafayette Haussmann which is one of the best shopping malls in France，Mont Blanc③ on Avenue des Champs Elysees④ where the world's top designer can customize a unique watch and jewelry for you，and you can go to Yves Saint Lauren⑤ store to try the most fashionable clothes.

B：Thank you for your detailed information.

A：My pleasure.

Notes：

①luggage claim area：行李领取处。

②luggage inquiry：行李问讯处。

③Mont Blanc：万宝龙国际是位于德国的一家精品钢笔、手表与配件的制造商，以"白色六角星"商标作为识别。

④Avenue des Champs Elysees：香榭丽舍大道，它是巴黎时尚社会的尊贵代名词，永远引领着全球最前沿的时尚。

⑤Yves Saint Lauren：圣罗兰，法国著名奢侈品牌。

Ⅱ Dialogue 2 Moulin Rouge

(*A：tourist B：local guide*)

A：Mr. Guide，do we have any night program arranged for today?

B：There isn't any planned program for tonight. But as you are in Paris，you have plenty of choices.

A: Good. Can you suggest and introduce some special programs to us?

B: Visitors to Paris generally go to one of the two famous cabaret halls. One is the Lido on the Champs-Elysees in the centre of the city, and the other is the Moulin Rouge near the White Square at the foot of Montmartre in the north.

A: How different are they from each other?

B: If Lido is in the style of American Broadway, the Moulin Rouge, with its long, red glinting impeller on the roof, is more in authentic French style.

A: Naturally, we prefer the one in authentic French style. So, can we have more information about it?

B: Of course. Impressionist Auguste Renoir's Moulin Rouge put the theatre on the world stage. There are also three films themed on Moulin Rouge. One is *French Cancan* directed by Jean Renoir, and the other two films share one name Moulin Rouge, but they are made in different periods of time.

A: What is Cancan?

B: In the second half of the 19th century, street artists from around the world came to Montmartre to display their works and performances. The area became a very special place full of artistic atmosphere. As a result, many small cafes and bars came along to locate themselves on the meandering pebble road and enjoying prosperous businesses. Some special lady dancers came to these small cafes and bars. They wore long dresses with intricate laces and danced with music of crazy rhythm, wiggling their hips, lifting their legs high enough to reach the ceiling. The British at the time called the dance Cancan, which was considered debauched and obscene, and banned it in England.

A: But they were not opposed in Paris, I guess.

B: You are right. Cancan was very popular in Montmartre. The annual carnival dancers took to the streets and danced as crazy. People in the city came from all directions to watch it.

A: Why the French at that time were so different from the English?

B: The later sociologists analyzed the reasons and pointed out that after the failure in the Franco-Prussian War in 1871, the French were dispirited. In addition, the reality was full of scandals and conflicts, the whole nation felt extremely despaired. Melancholy, however, was not a characteristic of the Gaul, who soon learned to replace it with cynicism, and this contributed to an atmosphere of indulgence in Paris.

A: That was not the Moulin Rouge cabaret yet, was it? How did it become such a wonderful performance later?

B: On October 6, 1889, Moulin Rouge Theatre was formally established in the Cancan music. But it was not wonderful at that time. Painter Toulouse-Lautrec depicted the greedy audience in his watercolor painting, and he himself also indulged in Moulin Rouge with the dancers day and night, which destroyed his life. The only thing the dancers desired is to meet a man who can treat them well.

A: I'm sure the situation is totally different now.

B: Yes. Now Moulin Rouge is a large dancing hall and a tourist attraction in Paris. The audiences are different now. They come to discover and understand Paris. The dancers, though they keep some characteristics of the former dancers, for instance, almost topless and dressed in gorgeous feather clothing, they dance as professionals with great dedication, not just to please some particular men.

A: Great. I have to see the performance today. Do you know the schedule?

B: Yes. I happen to have one right here with me. Here you are.

A: Oh, it's almost the time. Thank you so much. I have to hire a taxi and get going now. Otherwise, I'll miss it. Good-bye.

B: Good-bye and enjoy yourself.

Ⅲ Dialogue 3 A Glimpse of the Champs-Elysees

(*A: tourist   B: tour Guide*)

A: Hello, Mr. Tour Guide. Can you do us a favor?

B: Yes, of course. But what is it?

A: As you know, we are free tomorrow. So we want to have a walk on our own in the downtown of Paris. What is your suggestion?

B: The Champs-Elysees, of course.

A: What are we supposed to see there?

B: This is a big question. Let me give you a brief introduction to it.

A: Perfect. It's so kind of you.

B: Thank you. For glory and grandeur, the Champs-Elysees is the most famous avenue in the world. If the monuments and symmetrical landscaping don't convince you, remember that Champs-Elysées means "elysian fields① " which indicates that someone thought this street was heaven on earth. The monuments and history connected to this avenue are worth more than the reality of the place today.

A: "Heaven on earth!" That's what we use to refer to Hangzhou and Suzhou in China.

B: Yes. Though the stylish cafés on the avenue have now given way to a generally commercial atmosphere with enormous hub-stores such as Sephora, and even McDonalds, they were once the famed meeting points for politicians and intellectuals. It is worth strolling along the massive sidewalks with their elegant facades and leafy plane trees.

A: It must be a very nostalgic strolling.

B: For those who know some of its history, yes. The older avenue was once protected by severe building codes, limiting construction to the highest aesthetic standards and creating an avenue which was frequented almost exclusively by high-end Parisian society. In recent years, however, with metro access and a more flexible zoning law, the Champs-Elysées has drifted toward mass tourism and consumerism.

A: Well, sometimes you just can't help it.

B: Anyway, the Champs-Elysées is one of the iconic Paris boulevards. It draws a perfectly straight line from the Louvre, through the Tuilerie Gardens and the Place Concord, bisects the Arche de Triomphe where it becomes the avenue de la Grande Armée, and culminates at the base of the modern Arche de la Défence.

A: It seems to be quite long. So where should we start our walking and is there any place to recover ourselves on the way. We are not young any more.

B: A stroll through the Tuilerie Gardens is highly recommended. You can exit the Louvre and retire to the park to recover. Within the park you will discover that there are cafés and benches to use to take a break as well as the popular central fountain where you can try to snag the metal chairs people use to sunbathe on. On the north and south end of the park are two very interesting museums—The Jeu de Paume which is used exclusively for photography, and the Orangerie which houses a splendid impressionist collection. The Orangerie was originally built as a nursery for orange trees, but was later selected by Monet as the resting place for his famous painting, *The Water Lilies*, which was the museum's centerpiece.

A: Wow. I must see it.

B: The Place de la Concord provides the quintessential "Parisian view". From here you can see the Arch in the distance, the massive avenue, the National Assembly, the Madeleine church, the famous Hotel de Crillon, the Grand Palais, the Obelisk of Luxor, and the Eiffel Tower rising behind it. While the scene is breathtaking, it helps to remember that thousands of people were executed in the center of the square during the revolution, including Louis ⅩⅥ and Marie-Antoinette.

A: To better understand this avenue, I have to read more about French history.

B: Now it's a straight shot to the Arch visible at the end of the avenue. It's worth taking this walk in the evening when the lights are lit, or even better yet, at Christmas, when thousands of light bulbs hang in the giant trees.

A: I can even imagine the beauty of the scene now.

B: On your left you will eventually see two imposing buildings—one with a distinctive glass roof. They are the Grand Palais and its little sibling the Petit Palais. They were built for the World Fair in 1900 and continue to be used for major exhibitions.

A: I feel I have visited the avenue already by just listening to you. It is such a great help for our trip there tomorrow. Thank you so much.

B: You are very welcome.

Notes:
① elysian fields:极乐世界。

Unit 2　Case Study/案例分析

Ⅰ　案例一:擅自增加购物点、取消行程的投诉处理

杭州旅游者朱女士、王女士偕4岁幼女参加杭州某旅行社组织的法瑞意11日游。旅行结束后朱女士向杭州市旅游质监所投诉:领队在行程中擅自增加购物点,擅自取消行程约定的新天鹅堡景点,并要求退还全部团费。

1. 调查事实和处理结果

该团为三家旅行社共同组团,全团45+1人,由旅行社委派领队兼导游带团。与旅行社签订旅游合同的共23人(含投诉人2大1小),其中20人联名出具书面证明。确认真实情况是:

(1)领队根据行程单在巴黎奥斯曼大街、卢塞恩卡佩尔塔周边等处安排自由活动,由旅游者自行逛街购物,并不存在擅自增加购物场所的行为。

(2)未能进入新天鹅堡内游览是因同团旅游者手机遗忘在冰淇淋店内,赶回去取耽搁了出发时间,导致超过关堡时间15分钟才到达,从而无法入内。领队与全团旅游者(包括投诉人)签有书面协议,旅游者同意放弃入堡游览项目,接受旅行社退还门票及补偿每人20欧元,并在此后的7个正餐均提高用餐标准(从原定的五菜一汤变为六菜一汤)的补偿方案。

旅行社将20名旅游者联名出具的证明和全团旅游者签名书面确认放弃入堡项目、接受补偿的协议作为附件,向杭州市旅游质监所书面陈述其调查得出的真实情况。杭州市旅游质监所先查阅双方签订的旅游合同及行程单,再经过取证调查,认定旅行社方无责。而对方索赔金额要求过高,双方无法达成一致意见,市旅游质监所终止了调解工作。

投诉人对此结果十分不满,继而到12345市长热线投诉市旅游质监所不作为,又请某媒体帮助维权,终因旅行社方在各环节的操作中不存在明显瑕疵,最终只能偃旗息鼓。

2. 经验和教训

旅游者过度维权的现象时有发生,此案最终能切实维护了旅行社自身的正当利益,主要是做到了以下几点。

(1)与旅游者签订的旅游合同及附件行程单等比较正确规范,按市旅游质监所的说法是"行政上没有问题"。

(2)安排商业街自由活动让旅游者自行购物可以进入行程单,行程单上有旅游者签字确认。如果进入指定的购物场所,必须要签有补充协议;如果安排另付费旅游项目,必须要签有补充协议。

(3)无论何种原因需调整变更行程单已约定的旅游项目,必须有经旅游者签字确认的行程变更协议书。

同时也应指出,该领队与旅游者签订的取消入堡协议中,讲清了未能入堡的原因以及旅游者同意放弃此项目的意愿,但对退款补偿的具体金额以及旅游者收到退款的凭据方面还存在瑕疵。建议领队们在处理当场退款变更行程的类似情况时,以"收条"形式请旅游者签字比较妥当,一则让旅游者收款后签署收条,比较容易接受,二则也是旅游者已收到钱款的凭据。此类收条应注意包括几个要点:变更行程的原因、变更行程方案、旅游者同意此变更方案并已收到补偿款的具体金额、全体旅游者签名并签署日期等。

Ⅱ 案例二：游客境外意外受伤的处理

杭州旅游者王先生参加了某旅行社2018年10月7日—10月19日法瑞意德奥13日游。2019年11月20日，王先生向杭州市市长公开电话投诉，转至杭州市旅游质监所受理。

1. 投诉的事由及诉求

王先生在2019年10月15日游览奥地利维也纳美泉宫时，不慎摔倒钩破了裤子，希望通过已购买的境外旅游意外险理赔。王先生投诉旅行社故意拖延逃避，不给其办理申请理赔的相关事宜。要求有关部门协调解决。

2. 调查事实和处理结果

（1）王先生在游览维也纳美泉宫时，被花草遮掩的金属栏杆勾住裤子而摔倒，裤子被钩破，当时导游询问其伤情是否需要去医院诊治，王先生认为仅是皮外伤并无大碍，不用去医院治疗。

（2）王先生来旅行社要求通过保险途径理赔钩破的裤子，公司请他提供购裤凭证作为理赔依据时，他无法提供购裤凭据，导致理赔工作无法进行，责任并不在旅行社。

经杭州市旅游质监所协调，旅行社补偿王先生人民币500元，王先生撤诉。

3. 经验或教训

直接导致旅行社做出让步的原因是，在杭州市旅游质监所调解现场，王先生开始指责旅行社侵害其知情权，在合同中没有清楚告知受委托社信息。合同虽然明确约定了"同意拼团"，但在受委托社名称栏中填写了"联合发团"，下面又填了受委托社的上海地址和业务经营许可证号码。这涉嫌违反了《旅游法》第九条第二款的规定"旅游者有权知悉其购买的旅游产品和服务的真实情况"，以及《旅行社条例》第五十五条第三款规定"未取得旅游者同意，将旅游业务委托给其他旅行社"，可"处2万元以上10万元以下的罚款，情节严重的，责令停业整顿1个月至3个月"的行政处罚。

因此，无论业务部门基于何种考虑，试图隐瞒受委托社信息的做法是不可取的。应在旅游合同中载明，或在旅游合同的附件"旅游行程单"（出团通知书）栏目中载明受委托社的信息，包括受委托社名称、地址、旅行社经营许可证号码三项内容。旅游目的地地接社信息也应在旅游合同或其附件中明示地接社名称、地址、联系人、联系电话四项内容，否则或将受到"处2万元以上10万元以下罚款，情节严重的，责令停业整顿1个月至3个月"的行政处罚。

Chapter 7　Spain/西班牙

Part One
Briefing on Spain/西班牙概况

Unit 1　Overviews/总览

I　Basic Information/基本信息

西班牙

National Flag/国旗	National Emblem/国徽

The flag of Spain, as it is defined in the Spanish Constitution of 1978, consists of three horizontal stripes: red, yellow, and red, the yellow stripe being twice the size of each red stripe. Traditionally, the middle stripe was defined by the more archaic term of gualda, and hence the popular name rojigualda. The origin of the current flag of Spain is the naval flag of 1785. It was chosen by Charles Ⅲ himself among 12 different flags designed by Antonio Valdés y Bazán. The flag remained marine-focused for much of the next 50 years. It was not until 1843 that Queen Isabella Ⅱ of Spain made the flag official.	The national emblem of Spain represents Spain and the Spanish nation. It appears on the flag of Spain and is used by the Government of Spain, the Cortes Generales, the Constitutional Court, the Supreme Court, and other state institutions. Represented in its design are the medieval kingdoms that would unite to form Spain, the Royal Crown, national sovereignty, the constitutional monarchy, the Spanish national motto: Further Beyond, and the Pillars of Hercules. The Monarch, the heir to the throne and some institutions like the Senate, the Council of State or the General Council of the Judiciary are also embodied in the emblem.

National Flag/国旗	National Emblem/国徽
根据1978年《西班牙宪法》,西班牙国旗由三个水平条纹组成:两条红色和一条黄色,黄色条纹的大小是每个红色条纹的两倍。国旗称为rojigualda,意为血与金。 西班牙目前的国旗起源于1785年的海军旗。它是由查尔斯三世亲自从安东尼奥·瓦尔德斯·巴赞设计的12种不同的旗帜中选出的。在接下来的50年中,该旗始终作为海军用旗,直到1843年,西班牙女王伊莎贝拉二世才正式宣布将其用作国旗。	西班牙的国徽纹章代表西班牙国家与民族。它同样呈现在西班牙的国旗上,并被西班牙政府、科尔特斯州立法院、宪法法院、最高法院和其他国家机构广泛使用。其设计中体现了早期联合建立西班牙的中世纪王国、皇家王室、国家主权、君主立宪制、西班牙民族座右铭——"通向更远方",以及海格力斯之柱。君主、王位继承人以及参议院、州议会或司法总理事会等机构在国徽纹章上也有体现。

Other Basics/其他基本信息	
Full Name/国家全称	The Kingdom of Spain/西班牙王国
Total Area/国土面积	506,000 km²/506,000平方千米
Population/人口	47,350,000(2021年7月)
Nationality/民族	89.67% Spaniards,10.33% others/89.67%西班牙裔,10.33%其他族裔
Capital/首都	Madrid/马德里
National Anthem/国歌	"Marcha Real"/《皇家进行曲》
National Flower/国花	Carnation/康乃馨
National Bird/国鸟	Imperial Eagle/西班牙帝雕
Divisions/行政区划	50 provinces in total under 17 autonomous communities and 2 autonomous cities /17个自治区及2个自治市,下设50个省
Language/语言	Spanish/西班牙语
Major Political Parties/主要政党	Podemos, PSOE, Ciudadanos, Partido Popular and Vox/"我们能"党、工人社会党、公民党、人民党、声音党
Government Type/政府类型	Unitary Parliamentary Constitutional Monarchy/单一议会君主立宪制
Religious Belief/主要宗教信仰	96.0% Catholicism/96.0%天主教
Currency/货币	Euro/欧元
Time Difference with Beijing/与北京时差	−7(Summer Time −6)/比北京晚7小时(夏时制晚6小时)

II　Physical Geography/自然和地理

Spain is the fifty-second largest country in the world and the fourth largest country in Europe. Mainland Spain is a mountainous country, dominated by high plateaus and mountain chains. Mount Teide is the highest mountain peak in Spain and is the third largest volcano in the world from its base. Spain is a transcontinental country, having territory in both Europe and Africa.

On the west, Spain borders on Portugal. On the south, it is bordered by Gibraltar (a British overseas territory) and Morocco. On the northeast, along the Pyrenees mountain range, it borders France and the Principality of Andorra.

Spain also includes the Balearic Islands in the Mediterranean Sea, the Canary Islands in the Atlantic Ocean and a number of uninhabited islands on the Mediterranean side of the Strait of Gibraltar, known as places of sovereignty.

西班牙的地域面积居世界第52位、欧洲第4位。西班牙是一个多山的国家,以高原和山脉为主。西班牙的最高峰是泰德峰,也是世界第三大火山。西班牙是一个横贯大陆的国家,在欧洲和非洲都有领土。

西班牙西邻葡萄牙,南边隔着直布罗陀海峡与非洲的摩洛哥相望,东北隔比利牛斯山脉与法国和安道尔相连。

西班牙领土还包括地中海的巴利阿里群岛、大西洋的加那利群岛以及直布罗陀海峡地中海一侧许多无人居住的岛屿,这些岛屿被称为西属主权地。

III　Government and Administration/西班牙政府机构

Spain is a country of constitutional monarchy, with a hereditary monarch, a bicameral parliament and the General Courts. The executive branch consists of a Council of Ministers of Spain presided over by the Prime Minister, nominated and appointed by the monarch and confirmed by the Congress of Deputies following legislative elections.

The legislative branch is made up of the Congress of Deputies with 350 members, elected by popular votes based on proportional representation to serve four-year terms, and a Senate with 265 seats which are directly elected by popular votes, and serve four-year terms.

Spain is organizationally structured as a so-called "State of Autonomies." It is one of the most decentralized countries in Europe, along with Switzerland, Germany and Belgium. For example, all autonomous communities have their own elected parliaments, governments, public administrations, budgets, and resources.

西班牙是君主立宪制国家,有世袭君主、两院制议会和一般法院。首相领导的政府行使行政权。首相由国王提名,由国王任命,并在依法选定后由国会代表大会确认。

立法权由两院制的议会施行,议会由参众两院组成:众议院有350名议员,各地按人口比例民选产生,任期4年;参议院为地区代表院,有265名参议员,由普选产生,任期4年。

西班牙的组织结构为"自治状态"。它与瑞士、德国和比利时一样,是欧洲管理体制高度分散的国家之一。例如,所有自治区都有自己的议会、政府、公共管理机构、预算和资源。

Unit 2   History and People/历史和人民

Ⅰ History/历史

1. Muslim Era and Reconquista/穆斯林统治时期与收复失地运动

In the 8th century, nearly all of the Iberian Peninsula was conquered by Moorish Muslim armies from North Africa. Only a small area in the mountainous north-west of the peninsula managed to resist the initial invasion.

Under Islamic law, Christians and Jews were given the subordinate status. This status required Christians and Jews to pay a special tax but have legal and social rights inferior to those of Muslims.

Between 718 and 1492, Christian countries in the northern Iberian Peninsula of Western Europe gradually defeated the Moorish Muslim regime in the south, which is called Reconquista. The Reconquista began with the conquest of the Visigoth Kingdom by Umayyad Arabia in 718 and the founding of the Kingdom of Asturias, and ended with the capture of Granada by Spain in 1492.

公元8世纪,北非的摩尔穆斯林军队几乎征服了整个伊比利亚半岛。半岛西北山区只有一小部分地区抵抗住了最初的入侵。

根据伊斯兰教法,基督教和犹太教的民众仅具有从属地位。这种身份规定基督教和犹太教的民众需要缴纳特别税,同时其法律和社会权利低于穆斯林。

718至1492年间,位于西欧伊比利亚半岛北部的基督教各国,逐渐战胜了南部摩尔穆斯林政权,这被称为收复失地运动。收复失地运动以718年倭马亚阿拉伯征服西哥特王国及阿斯图里亚斯王国建国为开端,以1492年西班牙攻陷格拉纳达为终。

2. Spanish Empire/西班牙王国

In 1469, the crowns of the Christian kingdoms of Castile and Aragon were united by the marriage of Isabella Ⅰ of Castile and Ferdinand Ⅱ of Aragon. 1478 commenced the completion of the conquest of the Canary Islands and in 1492, the combined forces of Castile and Aragon captured the Emirate of Granada from its last ruler Muhammad Ⅻ, wiping out the last remnant of the 781-year presence of Islamic rule in Iberia. After the completion of the Reconquista, the Crown of Castile began to explore across the Atlantic Ocean in 1492, expanding to the New World and marking the beginning of the Golden Age of the Spanish Empire. The kingdoms of Spain were united under Habsburg reign in 1516, which unified the Crown of Castile, the Crown of Aragon and other smaller kingdoms. Up to the 1650s, Habsburg Spain was among the most powerful states in the world.

During this period, Spain was involved in all major European wars, including the Italian Wars, the Eighty Years' War, the Thirty Years' War, and the Franco-Spanish War. In the later 17th century, however, Spanish power began to decline, and after the death of the last Habsburg ruler, the War of the Spanish Succession ended with the relegation of Spain. Spain was then under the rule of Bourbon. The Bourbon Reforms attempted the renewal of state institutions, with some success, but as the century ended, instability set in with the French Revolution, the Peninsular War and the War of Spanish Independence.

1469年,卡斯蒂利亚公主伊莎贝拉一世与阿拉贡王子费迪南德二世联姻,标志了卡斯蒂利亚和阿拉贡的联合,从而使西班牙全境政治达成统一。他们1478年征服了加纳利群岛,1492年见证了收复失地运动的最后一个阶段——从统治者穆罕默德十二世手中夺回格拉纳达,消灭了伊比利亚伊斯兰统治781年的最后残余。之后,他们从1492年开始在大西洋上探索,扩展到新大陆,标志着西班牙王国黄金时代的开始。1516年,在哈布斯堡王朝统治下,西班牙王国进一步统一了卡斯蒂利亚王权、阿拉贡王权和其他较小王权。直到17世纪50年代,西班牙哈布斯堡王朝都是世界上最强大的国家之一。

在此期间,西班牙也参与了欧洲所有主要的战争,包括意大利战争、八十年战争、三十年战争和法西战争。然而,在17世纪后期,西班牙的国家权力开始衰落,在最后一位哈布斯堡王朝统治者去世后,西班牙王位继承战争的结束也标志了西班牙王国的衰落。处于波旁王朝统治之下的西班牙,尝试了一些国家机构的改革,取得了一定成功,但是随着世纪末法国大革命和半岛战争,以及西班牙独立战争的打响,国内政局日益动荡。

3. Spanish Civil War and Francoist Spain/西班牙内战与佛朗哥时期

The Spanish Civil War broke out in 1936. For three years the Nationalist forces led by General Francisco Franco and supported by Nazi Germany and Fascist Italy fought the

Republican side, which was supported by the Soviet Union, Mexico and International Brigades but not by the Western powers due to the British-led policy of non-intervention. The war was viciously fought and violent deeds were committed by all sides. In 1939, General Franco won the victory and began his dictatorship. During Franco's rule, Spain was officially neutral in World War II and remained largely economically and culturally isolated from the outside world. With Franco's death in November 1975, Juan Carlos succeeded to the position of King of Spain and head of state. With the approval of the new Spanish Constitution in 1978 and the restoration of democracy, the State devolved much authority to the regions and created an internal organization based on autonomous communities.

西班牙内战于1936年爆发。历时3年,由西班牙共和军和人民阵线对抗以弗朗西斯科·佛朗哥为核心的西班牙国民军和西班牙长枪党等右翼团体;人民阵线得到苏联、墨西哥和国际纵队(由于英国主导不干涉政策,西方列强未支持)的援助,而佛朗哥的国民军则有纳粹德国和法西斯意大利的支持。内战带来了大量的伤亡和暴行。1939年,佛朗哥取得了胜利,开始了独裁统治。佛朗哥执政期间,西班牙在第二次世界大战中保持中立,同时在经济和文化上基本与外部世界隔绝。佛朗哥于1975年11月去世,胡安·卡洛斯继任西班牙国王和国家元首。随着1978年新《西班牙宪法》的批准和民主的恢复,国家将许多权力下放给地区,并建立了一个以自治区为基础的政治结构。

II People and Figures/人民及名人

Spain's population density is lower than that of most Western European countries and its distribution across the country is very unbalanced. With the exception of the region surrounding the capital, Madrid, the most populated areas lie along the coast. Spain has a number of descendants of populations from former colonies, especially Latin America and North Africa. Smaller numbers of immigrants from several Sub-Saharan countries have recently been settling in Spain.

西班牙的人口密度低于大多数西欧国家,人口在整个西班牙地区的分布不均。除了首都马德里以外,人口大都聚集在沿海地区。西班牙有许多后殖民人口的后裔,尤其是来自拉丁美洲和北非的移民后裔。也有一些来自撒哈拉国家的移民最近开始在西班牙定居。

1. Isabella I of Castile/伊莎贝拉一世

Isabella I (April 22, 1451—November 26, 1504) reigned as Queen of Castile from 1474 until her death. Her marriage to Ferdinand II of Aragon in 1469 became the basis for the unification of Spain. After a struggle to claim her right to the throne, she reorganized the governmental system, and unburdened the kingdom of the enormous debt her brother had left behind. The reforms she and her husband made had an influence that extended well beyond the borders of their united kingdoms. Isabella and Ferdinand are known for completing the Reconquista, and for supporting and financing Christopher Columbus's 1492 voyage that led to the discovery of the New World and the establishment of Spain as the first global power which dominated Europe and much of the world for more than a century.

伊莎贝拉一世(1451年4月22日—1504年11月26日)从1474年起担任卡斯蒂利亚女王,直到去世。她于1469年与阿拉贡的费迪南德二世结婚,奠定了西班牙统一的基础。在争取自己的王位权利后,她重组了政府体系,并为王国解除了她哥哥留下的巨额债务。她与丈夫进行的改革所产生的影响力远远超出了其联合王国的范围。伊莎贝拉和丈夫费迪南德完成了收复失地运动,为克里斯托弗·哥伦布1492年的航行提供支持和资金。这一航行导致了新大陆的发现,并确立了西班牙在接下来一个世纪中作为主宰欧洲乃至世界大部分地区的全球大国的地位。

2. Francisco Franco/弗朗西斯科·佛朗哥

The general and dictator Francisco Franco (December 4, 1892—November 20, 1975) ruled over Spain from 1939 until his death. He rose to power during the Spanish Civil War when, with the help of Nazi Germany and Fascist Italy, his Nationalist forces overthrew the democratically elected Second Republic. Adopting the title of "El Caudillo" (The Leader), Franco persecuted political opponents, repressed the culture and language of Spain's Basque and Catalan regions, and exerted absolute control over the country. His reign was marked by both brutal repressions with thousands killed, and economic prosperity, which greatly improved the quality of life in Spain. Some of the political restrictions gradually eased as Franco got older, and upon his death the country transitioned to democracy.

弗朗西斯科·佛朗哥(1892年12月4日—1975年11月20日)是西班牙历史上重要的将军和独裁者,从1939年统治西班牙直至其去世。他在西班牙内战期间上台执政,在纳粹德国和法西斯意大利的帮助下,他的民族主义力量推翻了民主选举产生的第二共和国。佛朗哥以"领袖考迪罗"的头衔,迫害政治反对派,压制西班牙巴斯克和加泰罗尼亚地区的文化和语言,推行绝对控制权力。佛朗哥的统治既有残酷的镇压,数千人被杀,又有经济繁荣,极大地提高了西班牙的生活质量。佛朗哥执政后期,一些限制逐渐放宽,他去世后,西班牙过渡成为民主国家。

Unit 3 Culture and Education/文化和教育

I Culture/文化

1. Flamenco/弗拉明戈

Flamenco, in its strictest sense, is a professionalized art-form based on the various folkloric music traditions of southern Spain in the autonomous community of Andalusia. In a wider sense, the term refers to a variety of Spanish musical styles developed as early as in the 19th century. The oldest record of flamenco dates to 1774 in the book *Las Cartas Marruecas* by José Cadalso. Flamenco has been influenced by and associated with the Romani people in Spain. However, its origin and style are uniquely Andalusian.

On November 16, 2010, UNESCO declared flamenco one of the Masterpieces of the Oral and Intangible Heritage of Humanity.

从狭义上讲,弗拉明戈是一种专业化的艺术形式,其基础是西班牙南部安达卢西亚自治区的各种民间音乐传统。从广义上讲,弗拉明戈指的是从19世纪开始发展起来的各种西班牙音乐风格。弗拉明戈最古老的记录可追溯到约瑟·卡德索尔所著的《拉斯卡塔斯·马鲁卡斯》。弗拉明戈受西班牙吉普赛人的影响深远。但是,它却依然带着起源地安达卢西亚的独特风格。

2010年11月16日,联合国教科文组织将弗拉明戈列为人类口头和非物质遗产。

2. Bullfighting/斗牛

The best-known form of bullfighting is Spanish-style bullfighting. It is an iconic tradition in which three bullfighters have to fight two bulls each and, ultimately, kill them. A bullfight is always held in a round-shape arena or venue called plaza de toros. While some forms are sometimes considered to be a bloody sport, in Spain, it is defined as an art form, a traditional spectacle and a cultural event. In Spain, bullfighters are almost as popular as football stars, often supported by sponsors and appearing in press. A particular breed of cattle, the Spanish Fighting Bull, is used for this type of bullfighting. These bulls must be bred in large ranches, and in conditions as similar as possible to the way they would live in the wild.

西班牙斗牛是最著名的斗牛形式。这是西班牙非常具有代表性的传统运动,3名斗牛士必须分别与2头公牛作战,最终杀死它们。斗牛通常在一个圆形的竞技场举行,也叫作斗牛场。尽管斗牛有时被认为非常血腥暴力,但在西班牙,它也被认为一种艺术形式,一种传统的表演和一种文化活动。在西班牙,斗牛士几乎和足球明星一样受欢迎,通常能得到赞助商的支持并出现在媒体上。斗牛用的牛也是一种特殊的牛,这些公牛必须在大牧场中饲养,并且生活条件应与野外环境保持尽可能一致。

3. Pablo Picasso and His Artworks/毕加索的艺术

Pablo Ruiz Picasso (October 25, 1881—April 8, 1973) was a Spanish painter, sculptor, printmaker, ceramicist, stage designer, poet and playwright. Regarded as one of the most influential artists of the 20th century, he is known for co-founding the Cubist movement, the invention of constructed sculpture, the co-invention of collage, and for the wide variety of styles that he helped develop and explore. Among his most famous works are the proto-cubist *Les Demoiselles d'Avignon* (1907), and *Guernica* (1937), a dramatic portrayal of the bombing of Guernica by the German and Italian air forces during the Spanish Civil War.

巴勃罗·鲁伊斯·毕加索(1881年10月25日—1973年4月8日)是西班牙著名画家、雕塑家、版画家、陶艺家、舞台设计师、诗人和剧作家。他是20世纪最有影响力的艺术家之一,以共同创立立体主义运动、创作雕塑作品、共同发明拼贴画以及协助发展和探索多种风格而闻名。他最著名的作品包括原始立体主义的《亚维农的少女》(1907年)和《格尔尼卡》(1937年),这是对西班牙内战期间德国和意大利空军轰炸格尔尼卡的生动展现。

Ⅱ Education/教育

The Spanish education is compulsory and free for all children aged between 6 and 16 years old and is supported by the national government together with the governments of each of the country's 17 autonomous communities.

Elementary school and middle school are considered basic (obligatory) education. These are Primaria (6—12 years old), which is the Spanish equivalent of elementary / primary school. It consists of six years, structured as three cycles, from first grade through to sixth grade. Secundaria (12—16 years old) consists of four years, structured as two cycles, from seventh to tenth grade.

Bachillerato or Bachiller consists of two optional additional final years in high school (mandatory education is until students are 16 years old), which is required if the student wants to attend University. Once students have finished Bachillerato, they can take their University Entrance Exam.

Spain is also working towards reforming vocational education and modernizing education to halt and reverse the rising unemployment rates.

Spanish school terms are generally similar to the English three-term system, but with slightly shorter holidays at Christmas (December 22—January 7) and Easter (one week—40 days after Ash Wednesday), and longer in the summer (normally from 23 June to 15 September). Schools practice the trimester system (September to December, January to March/April, March/April to June).

西班牙的教育系统对所有6至16岁的儿童都是义务免费的,并得到国家政府以及17个自治区的支持。

小学和初中(6—12岁)是基础义务教育,从一年级到六年级,共分6年,3个周期。中等教育(12—16岁)分为4年,结构为两个周期,从七年级到十年级。

高中在西班牙并非为义务教育,义务教育到16岁为止。高中教育一般包括初中后的两年,如果学生想上大学,则需要完成高中教育。学生完成高中教育后,即可参加大学入学考试。

西班牙同时在努力改革职业教育并使教育现代化,从而缓解失业率上升的趋势。

西班牙学校的学期与英语国家三学期的制度大致相似,但是圣诞节(12月22日—1月7日)和复活节的假期稍短,暑假则稍长(通常为6月23日—9月15日)。学校使用的三学期制大致分为9月至12月,1月至3月/4月,3月/4月至6月。

Unit 4 Major Attractions/主要景点

Ⅰ Sagrada Família/圣家堂

Sagrada Família is a large unfinished Roman Catholic minor basilica in Barcelona, Catalonia designed by Catalan architect Antoni Gaudí (1852—1926). Its towering and unique architectural design make the church the most well-known tourist attraction in Barcelona. The building is part of a UNESCO World Heritage Site.

On March 19, 1882, the construction of the Sagrada Família began under the direction of architect Francisco de Paula del Villar. In 1883, when Villar resigned, Gaudí took over as the chief architect, transforming the project with his architectural and engineering style, combining Gothic and curvilinear Art Nouveau forms. Gaudí devoted the remainder of his life to the project, and he is buried in the crypt. At the time of his death in 1926, only less than a quarter of the project was completed. Relying solely on private donations, the Sagrada Família's construction progressed slowly and was interrupted by the Spanish Civil War. In July 1936, revolutionaries set fire to the crypt and broke their way into the workshop, partially destroying Gaudí's original plans, drawings and plaster models, which led to 16 years' work to piece together the fragments of the master model. On November 7, 2010, Pope Benedict XVI consecrated the church and proclaimed it a minor basilica.

圣家堂是位于西班牙加泰罗尼亚首府巴塞罗那的一座未完工的天主教教堂,由安东尼·高迪(1852—1926)设计。其高耸与独特的建筑设计,使得该教堂成为巴塞罗那最为人所知的观光景点。这座建筑是联合国教科文组织的世界遗产的一部分。

圣家堂从1882年3月19日在建筑师弗朗西斯科·德·保拉·德尔·维拉尔的指挥下开始修建。1883年,维拉尔辞职,高迪接任首席建筑师。高迪用他的建筑和工程风格改造项目,结合了哥特式和曲线艺术新形势。高迪把他余生都献给了这个项目,他被埋葬在地下室里。在他1926年去世时,这项工程只完成了不到1/4。因为资金的来源主要靠个人捐款,工程进度缓慢,也因为西班牙内战,建筑工程不得不中断。1936年7月,革命者纵火焚烧了地下室,并闯入了车间,摧毁了高迪的部分原始计划、图纸和石膏模型,这导致了后来长达16年的修复主模型碎片的工作。虽然该教堂并非主教座堂,但教皇本笃十六世于2010年11月7日造访此教堂时将其册封为宗座圣殿。

II Puerta del Sol (Spanish for "Gate of the Sun")/太阳门广场

The Puerta del Sol (Spanish for "Gate of the Sun") is a public square in Madrid, one of the best known and busiest places in the city. This is the center of the radial network of Spanish roads. The square also contains the famous clock whose bells mark the traditional eating of the Twelve Grapes and the beginning of a new year. The New Year's celebration has been broadcast live on national television since December 31, 1962.

太阳门是马德里市的一个公共广场,也是马德里最著名、最繁忙的地方之一。它是西班牙公路网的中心点。广场上还有著名的钟,西班牙传统上,伴随十二响钟声吃下十二颗葡萄的跨年传统就是起源于此。自1962年12月31日起,西班牙国家电视台开始现场转播此处的新年庆祝活动。

III The Alhambra/阿尔罕布拉宫

The Alhambra is a palace and fortress complex located in Granada, Andalusia, Spain. The Alhambra was so called because of its reddish walls (in Arabic, also as Red Castle). It is located on top of the hill al-Sabika, on the left bank of River Darro, to the west of the city of Granada and in front of the neighborhoods of the Albaicin and the Alcazaba.

The Alhambra is a UNESCO World Heritage Site and the inspiration for many songs and stories. It is now one of Spain's major tourist attractions, exhibiting the country's most significant and well-known Islamic architecture, together with 16th-century and later Christian building and garden interventions.

阿罕布拉宫位于西班牙安达卢西亚的格拉纳达,是一座宫殿和要塞建筑群。阿罕布拉之所以这样叫是因为它的墙是红色的(在阿拉伯语里也叫红色城堡)。它位于阿尔萨比卡山顶,达罗河左岸,格拉纳达市以西,阿尔巴金和阿尔卡扎巴社区前面。

阿罕布拉是联合国教科文组织的世界遗产,也是许多歌曲和故事的灵感来源。它现在是西班牙的主要旅游景点之一,展示了西班牙最重要和最著名的伊斯兰建筑,以及16世纪和后来的基督教建筑和花园。

Part Two
Outbound Tour Guide Operation/出境领队实务

Unit 1　Situational Dialogues/情景对话

Ⅰ Dialogue 1　Customs Clearance

(*A*：*tour leader*　*B*：*inspector*)

B：Good morning, welcome to Spain. Your passport, please.

A：Good morning, Sir. Here you are.

B：Do you have anything to declare?

A：No, I don't think so.

B：Well, would you mind opening this bag?

A：Of course not, although I might not be able to close it again.

B：What's this?　Cigarettes?

A：Yes, they are for my own use.

B：One, two, three... There are ten packs, just a carton of cigarettes.

A：That's under the limit.

B：Yes, but what is this?

A：Oh, it's coffee, for my friend.

B：The 2 boxes of coffee weigh 1,000 grams together. According to Spanish law, only 500 grams of coffee per person is allowed to enter the country. On the excess, we will impose tariffs. I'm afraid you will have to choose.

A：Ok. I'll pay the tariffs.

B：What are they?

A：Medicines.

B：Let me see. These are western medicines for high blood pressure and heart disease. But what are these?

A：These are Chinese medicines for cough and cold.

B: I'm sorry I have to confiscate them because I have no idea about them. How about these? They look like herbs.

A: These are Chinese tea, jasmine tea.

B: Tea is OK. You have brought with you some pork, haven't you?

A: Yes. These are dried meat in vacuum packages. They are sealed.

B: According to Spanish policy, you have to declare the kinds of meat you bring in otherwise you'll be fined.

A: But this is the first time I've come to Spain and I don't know about this. Can you just take them away with no fines?

B: No. You have to pay the fines and I'll confiscate the meat.

A: OK.

B: Do you have any other luggage?

A: No.

B: OK, you may go through now.

A: Thank you.

B: Have a nice stay in Spain.

A: Thanks.

Ⅱ Dialogue 2 Bullfighting in Spain

(*A: Chinese tourist   B: local guide*)

A: Good morning, Sir. When I was planning my trip to Spain by searching on the Internet, the first thing showing up was Bullfighting in Spain. What kind of event is it? Why is it so popular?

B: Bullfighting in Spain is probably one of the best-known popular customs around the world. Bullfights are considered one of the symbols of the Hispanic culture. They are not only held in Spain but also in Portugal, France, and part of Latin America, where some customs may vary. However, Spain has the longest season and is the country in which most of the bullfights take place.

A: What is the origin of bullfighting? When did Spanish begin to have the custom?

B: Bullfighting has existed for thousands

of years and it has been popular in Spain for nearly a millennium, though some say it has existed in Spain since the time of Emperor Claudius two thousand years ago. Bulls started to play an important role in religious ceremonies Iberian tribes organized in prehistoric times. Then, fights against bulls were introduced as a spectacle. In the Middle Age, aristocrats fought them on horseback. Later on, in the 18th century, humble people started to practice it on foot.

A: So long a history of it! But I guess the present bullfighting is very different from that in the 18th century.

B: In fact, modern bullfighting has evolved very little, adopting its current rules from 250-year-old customs. Actually, bullfighting is a universe of its own. Made of hundreds of rules, thousands of traditions and a little bit of superstition, bullfighting evokes one of the most passionate and controversial discussions in and out of Spain.

A: What are the major rules then, if I may ask?

B: It is a Three-Act Spectacle. Every bullfight follows the same pattern and is organized identically. The event starts with a parade of all the participants. It is basically a presentation of the matadors and the rest of their team. Once the parade is over, the matadors are ready to start their fights—one at a time and following a certain order. The senior matador goes first.

A: Are the bulls finally killed?

B: Yes, of course. That is the controversy. With the rise of the animal rights movement, an ever increasing number of people have been critical of bullfighting, both within Spain and in the rest of the world. The number of websites in opposition to the activity far exceeds the number in favor.

A: Have things got changed? What is the state of bullfighting in Spain now?

B: In 2010, the government in Barcelona banned bullfighting in Catalonia, but Madrid and Andalusia continue to host bullfighting events throughout the summer. The stadiums are usually full, both with curious tourists and die-hard fans.

A: Well, I can't say anything against it. But I myself would rather not go to see it. Many thanks for your detailed information. I have learned a lot from it.

B: You are welcome.

Ⅲ Dialogue 3 Spanish Literature and Don Quixote de la Mancha

(*A*: *Chinese tourist B* : *local guide*)

A: Hello, Mr. Guide. From your introduction yesterday, I can tell that you have read a lot of books, especially those of Spanish literature.

B: Thank you. I do love reading and I'm quite interested in Spanish literature.

A: Talking about Spanish literature reminds me of one of our middle school texts about how Don Quixote fought against the windmill. Is it the most famous work of the Spanish literature?

B: Yes. Spanish literature has a huge array of must-read books, but *Don Quixote* written by Miguel de Cervantes is the most important book of all the Spanish literature, although there are some other iconic works such as *El Cantar del Mio Cid*, which tells the story of the legendary hero Rodrigo Díaz de Vivar, *Lazarillo de Tormes*, the novel which launched the genre of the picaresque novel and *Romancero Gitano*, the most famous Spanish book of poems, dedicated to the gypsy world.

A: What is *Don Quixote* really about?

B: Alonso Quixano is an Hidalgo, a low-ranking Spanish person of nobility. He is about 50 years old and lives in a settlement near the La Mancha region in Spain towards the beginning of the 17th century. He loves reading literature about knights and fantastic stories about chivalry, princesses, magicians, and enchanted castles. In fact, he is so involved with these fantasies that he slowly starts to lose touch with reality and begins to believe that he is one of these fictional heroes. He then bestows himself the name Don Quixote because it rhymes with the name of the famous knight Lanzarote, and sets off on an adventure with a ridiculous new costume and the hope of committing heroic deeds.

A: Miguel de Cervantes, the author of this novel must be a person of great imagination. It is in a way like Wu Cheng'en, the author of *Journey to the West*, one of the greatest Chinese classics.

B: Good comparison. I love *Journey to the West*. It is a fascinating novel with gripping stories. But Cervantes' imagination may have something to do with his life experience.

A: What strange things happened to him in his life?

B: We don't know much about his childhood education, but one thing is sure that by

1570 he had enlisted as a soldier in a Spanish infantry regiment stationed in Naples. In 1575, he set sail for Spain in September for promotion to the rank of captain. On this voyage his ship was attacked and he was captured by pirates. Three years later, he was bailed out from captivity. Not surprisingly, this, the most adventurous period of his life supplied subject matter for his literary works.

A: As the saying goes, "Adversity and loss make a man wise." No wonder he could write such a great novel. Thank you indeed for your telling me so much about Spanish literature.

B: It's my pleasure.

Unit 2　Case Study/案例分析

I 案例一：擅自离团受伤的处理

1. 案例简介

王先生参加某国际旅行社组织的西班牙 8 日游,在报名时王先生向旅行社咨询中途是否可以离团 1 天,因为想去巴塞罗那参加一个商业活动。旅行社告诉他不可以离团,如果参加商业活动就应当办理商务签证,而不是参加旅游团。王先生承诺随团旅游。到了巴塞罗那后,王先生仍然按照原计划参加了当地的商业活动,但事先没有和领队商量,领队和他通话后才得知事件经过,只能要求他尽快回到旅游团。当天下午王先生电话告诉领队,他在商业活动中不慎扭伤了脚踝,已经在朋友的帮助下住进了医院。领队得知情况后,要求地接旅行社派人前往医院探望,了解王先生的伤情,并提供了适当的帮助。王先生回国后,要求旅行社承担相关医疗费用,旅行社以非旅行社责任事故为由,拒绝承担赔偿责任。

2. 案例分析

请问:

(1)在出境旅游中是否允许旅游者脱团?

(2)王先生脱团期间的伤害事故应当由谁承担责任?

专家意见:

(1)按照我国法律规定,出境旅游中旅游者不得擅自脱团。我国《旅游法》规定,出境旅游者不得在境外非法滞留,随团出境的旅游者不得擅自分团、脱团。显然,王先生的行为违反了法律规定。

（2）王先生脱团期间的伤害后果应当由王先生自己承担。我国《旅游法》规定，由于旅游者自身原因导致包价旅游合同不能履行或者不能按照约定履行，或者造成旅游者人身损害、财产损失的，旅行社不承担责任。

Ⅱ 案例二：旅行社遗漏客人护照的处理

1. 案例简介

陈先生夫妇参加了某国际旅行社组织的西班牙、葡萄牙10日旅游团。领队在上海机场分发护照时发现，陈先生的护照未在团队护照中，领队和旅行社联系后，得知护照遗漏在旅行社。旅行社马上派人把护照送到候机室，飞机已经飞走。由于陈先生无法出境，他的夫人也要求留下，旅行社希望他夫人继续行程，并承诺陈先生可以在第二天赶上团队，遭到拒绝，陈先生夫妇同时滞留在机场。旅行社一方面妥善安排陈先生夫妇的住宿和餐饮（费用由陈先生先行支付），同时积极和有关部门协调，第二天飞往西班牙和团队会合。由于团队已经游览了一天，地接社愿意单独用小车送陈先生夫妇补上漏游的景点。陈先生明确表示，由于身体的原因，只愿意随团旅游，不需要再补景点。游程结束后，陈先生夫妇要求该国际旅行社全额返还在机场的食宿费用，赔偿西班牙景点的损失、缩短一天行程的损失和由于旅行社违约造成的精神损失。

2. 案例分析

请问：

（1）旅行社是否必须全额承担陈先生夫妇在机场的食宿费用？为什么？

（2）对于陈先生夫妇提出的其他赔偿请求，旅行社应当如何处理？

专家意见：

（1）旅行社应当承担陈先生在机场的食宿费用，而不应当承担陈夫人的食宿费用。根据我国《合同法》的规定，当事人一方违约后，对方应当采取适当措施防止损失的扩大。没有采取适当措施致使损失扩大的，不得就扩大的损失要求赔偿。也就是说，旅行社的确未能为陈先生提供合同约定的服务，导致陈先生行程被延误，但陈夫人可以继续行程却没有继续，人为地扩大了损失，旅行社可以拒绝赔偿，其损失由陈夫人自己承担。

（2）由于陈先生夫妇拒绝了当地旅行社提出的游览方案，放弃了第一天行程中游览的景点，旅行社可以拒绝陈先生夫妇的赔偿请求。陈先生行程缩短一天，的确给他造成了一定的损失，由于缺乏法律的明确规定，旅行社应当给予适当补偿。至于精神损失，在我国的民事立法中，只认可侵权行为引起的精神损害，对于合同违约尚未确立精神损害赔偿原则，陈先生夫妇要求精神损害的请求难以实现。

Chapter 8

Russia/俄罗斯

Part One
Briefing on Russia/俄罗斯概况

Unit 1　Overviews/总览

I　Basic Information/基本信息

National Flag/国旗	National Emblem/国徽
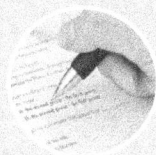	
The flag of Russia（Russian Federation）is a tricolour flag consisting of three equal horizontal fields: white on the top, blue in the middle, and red on the bottom. The flag was first used as an ensign for Russian merchant ships and became official as the flag of the Tsardom of Russia in 1696. There are varying interpretations as of to what the colors on the Russian flag mean. The most popular is as follows: The white color symbolizes nobility and frankness, the blue for faithfulness, honesty, impeccability, and chastity, and red for courage, generosity, and love.	The national emblem（coat of arms）of the Russian Federation derives from the earlier coat of arms of the Russian Empire which was abolished with the Russian Revolution in 1917. Though modified more than once since the reign of Ivan Ⅲ（1462–1505）, the current coat of arms is directly derived from its mediaeval original, with the double-headed eagle having Byzantine and earlier antecedents from long before the emergence of any Russian state. The general tincture corresponds to the early fifteenth-century standard. The shape of the eagle can be traced back to the reign of Peter the Great（1682–1725）, although the eagle charge on the present coat of arms is golden rather than the traditional, imperial black.
俄罗斯（俄罗斯联邦）的国旗是三色旗，由3个相等的水平区域组成:顶部为白色,中间为蓝色,底部为红色。国旗最初被用作俄罗斯商船的旗号,于1696年正式成为沙皇俄国的国旗。俄罗斯国旗的颜色有多种象征意义,普遍解读如下:白色象征着高贵和坦率;蓝色象征着忠诚、诚实、完美和贞洁;红色象征着勇气、慷慨和爱。	俄罗斯联邦国徽来自于1917年俄国革命时废除的早期俄罗斯帝国的国徽,虽然自伊凡三世(1462—1505)统治开始经过了多次修订,但当前的国徽是直接修订于中世纪的版本,绘有一只拜占庭和在俄罗斯人的政权产生之前很长时间里的先驱所使用的双头鹰。其色彩布局取自15世纪早期的标准。鹰的造型可追溯到彼得大帝(1682—1725)统治时期,尽管盾徽上鹰的颜色是金色而不是传统的黑色。

Other Basics/其他基本信息	
Full Name/国家全称	Russian Federation/俄罗斯联邦
Other Names/其他称呼	Russia/俄罗斯、俄国
Total Area/国土面积	17,098,246 km²/17,098,246平方千米
Population/人口	146,000,000（2020年10月）
Nationality/民族	77.0% Russian, 3.7% Tatar, 1.4% Ukrainian, 1.2% Armenian, 1.1% Bashkir, 1.0% Chuvash/俄罗斯族（77.0%）、鞑靼族（3.7%）、乌克兰族（1.4%）、亚美尼亚族（1.2%）、巴什基尔族（1.1%）、楚瓦什族（1.0%）
Capital/首都	Moscow/莫斯科
National Anthem/国歌	"State Anthem of the Russian Federation"/《俄罗斯联邦国歌》
National Flower/国花	Chamomile/洋甘菊
National Bird/国鸟	Eagle/鹰
Divisions/行政区划	85 federal subjects including 22 republics, 9 krais, 46 oblasts, 3 federal cities, 1 autonomous oblast, and 4 autonomous okrugs/85个联邦主体（22个自治共和国、9个边疆区、46个州、3个联邦直辖市、1个自治州、4个民族自治区）
Language/语言	Russian/俄语
Major Political Parties/主要政党	United Russia, the Communist Party, the Liberal Democratic Party, and A Just Russia/统一俄罗斯、俄罗斯联邦共产党、俄罗斯自由民主党、公正俄罗斯
Government Type/政府类型	Federal Dominant-party Semi-presidential Constitutional Republic under an Authoritarian System/联邦半总统制立宪共和国
Religious Belief/主要宗教信仰	Russian Orthodox/俄罗斯东正教
Currency/货币	Russian Ruble/俄罗斯卢布
Time Difference with Beijing/与北京时差	−5 hours/比北京晚5个小时

II Physical Geography/自然和地理

Russia is a country extending over much of northern Eurasia. Comprising much of eastern Europe and northern Asia, it is the world's largest country in total area. Due to its size, Russia displays both monotony and diversity. As with its topography, its climates, vegetation, and soils span vast distances. From north to south the East European Plain is clad sequentially in tundra, coniferous forest (taiga), mixed and broadleaf forests, grassland (steppe), and semi-desert (fringing the Caspian Sea) as the changes in vegetation reflect the changes in climate. The country contains forty UNESCO biosphere reserves.

Located in the north of the Northern Hemisphere, most of Russia is much closer to the North Pole than to the equator. The country includes one-eighth of the Earth's inhabited land area. Its European portion, which occupies a substantial part of continental Europe, is home to most of Russia's industrial activity and is where, roughly between the Dnieper River and the Ural Mountains, the Russian Empire took shape. Russia includes the entire northern portion of Asia.

Extending for 57,792 kilometers, the Russian border is the world's longest. Along the 20,139-kilometer land frontier, Russia has boundaries with 14 countries: Norway, Finland, Estonia, Latvia, Lithuania, Poland (via the Kaliningrad Oblast), Belarus, Ukraine, Georgia, Azerbaijan, Kazakhstan, Mongolia, the People's Republic of China and Democratic People's Republic of Korea.

Approximately two-thirds of the frontier is bounded by seawater. Virtually all of the lengthy northern coast is well above the Arctic Circle; except for the port of Murmansk—which receives currents that are somewhat warmer than would be expected at that latitude, due to the effects of the Gulf Stream—that coast is locked in ice much of the year. Thirteen seas and parts of two oceans—the Arctic and Pacific—wash Russian shores.

俄罗斯是一个横跨欧亚大陆北部大部分地区的国家。它包括东欧和北亚的大部分地区,是世界上总面积最大的国家。由于幅员辽阔,俄罗斯地貌呈现出既统一又多样的特点。和它的地形一样,它的气候、植被和土壤跨度很广。由于植被的变化反映了气候的变化,从北到南,东欧平原依次为苔原、针叶林、混交林和阔叶林、草原(草原)和半沙漠(里海边缘)。俄罗斯有40个联合国教科文组织生物圈保护区。

俄罗斯大部分地区位于北半球的北部,离北极比赤道近得多。这个国家包含了全球人居土地面积的1/8。它的欧洲部分占据了欧洲大陆的很大一部分,是俄罗斯大部分工业活动的所在地,大约在第聂伯河和乌拉尔山脉之间,这块区域也是俄罗斯帝国形成的地方。俄罗斯包括了整个亚洲北部地区。

俄罗斯边境全长57,792千米,是世界上边境最长的国家。沿着20,139千米的陆地边界,俄罗斯与14个国家接壤:挪威、芬兰、爱沙尼亚、拉脱维亚、立陶宛、波兰(途经加里宁格勒州)、白俄罗斯、乌克兰、格鲁吉亚、阿塞拜疆、哈萨克斯坦、蒙古、中华人民共和国和朝鲜。

俄罗斯大约2/3的边境被海水包围。几乎所有漫长的北海岸都远远高于北极圈;除了摩尔曼斯克港——由于墨西哥湾流的影响,该港接收的洋流比该纬度的预期温度要高一些——海岸一年中大部分时间都被冰封。13个陆缘海和两大洋的一部分——北冰洋和太平洋——都冲刷着俄罗斯海岸。

Ⅲ Government and Administration/俄罗斯政府机构

According to the Constitution of Russia, the country is an asymmetric federation and semi-presidential republic, wherein the President is the head of state and the Prime Minister is the head of government. The president is elected by popular vote for a six-year term (eligible for a second term, but not for a third consecutive term). Ministries of the government are composed of the Premier and his deputies, ministers, and selected other individuals; all are appointed by the President on the recommendation of the Prime Minister (whereas the appointment of the latter requires the consent of the State Duma).

The Russian Federation is fundamentally structured as a multi-party representative democracy, with the federal government composed of three branches:

Legislative: The bicameral Federal Assembly of Russia, made up of the 450-member State Duma and the 170-member Federation Council, adopts federal law, declares war, approves treaties, has the power of the purse and the power of impeachment of the President.

Executive: The President is the Commander-in-Chief of the Armed Forces, can veto legislative bills before they become law, and appoints the Government of Russia (Cabinet) and other officers, who administer and enforce federal laws and policies.

Judiciary: The Constitutional Court, Supreme Court and lower federal courts, whose judges are appointed by the Federation Council on the recommendation of the President, interpret laws and can overturn laws they deem unconstitutional.

根据《俄罗斯宪法》,俄罗斯是一个联邦制及半总统制共和国,总统为国家元首,总理为政府首脑。总统由民众投票选出,任期6年(可连任第二届,但不能连任第三届)。政府各部由总理及其副手、部长和选定的其他个人组成;所有人都是由总统根据总理的建议任命的(而总理的任命需要得到国家杜马的同意)。

俄罗斯联邦的基本结构是多党代议民主制,联邦政府由3个部分组成:

立法:由450人的国家杜马和170人的联邦委员会组成的俄罗斯两院制联邦议会,通过联邦法律,宣战,批准条约,拥有财权和弹劾总统的权力。

行政:总统是武装部队的总司令,可以在立法法案成为法律之前否决这些法案,并任命俄罗斯政府(内阁)和其他官员,负责管理和执行联邦法律和政策。

司法:包括宪法法院、最高法院和下级联邦法院,法官由联邦委员会根据总统的推荐任命,负责解释法律并可以推翻他们认为违宪的法律。

Unit 2　History and People/历史和人民

I　History/历史

1. Tsardom of Russia/沙皇俄国

The Tsardom of Russia was the centralized Russian state from the assumption of the title of Tsar by Ivan Ⅳ in 1547 until the founding of the Russian Empire by Peter the Great in 1721.

From 1551 to 1700, Russia grew by 35,000 km^2 per year. The period includes the upheavals of the transition from the Rurik to the Romanov dynasties, many wars with the Polish-Lithuanian Commonwealth, Sweden and the Ottoman Empire as well as the Russian conquest of Siberia, leading up to the ground-changing reign of Peter the Great, who took power in 1689 and transformed the Tsardom into a major European power. During the Great Northern War, he implemented substantial reforms and proclaimed the founding of Russian Empire after the victory over Sweden in 1721.

从1547年伊万四世获得沙皇头衔到1721年彼得大帝建立俄罗斯帝国,沙皇俄国一直是中央集权的国家。

从1551年到1700年,俄罗斯每年增长35,000平方千米。这一时期包括从鲁里克王朝向罗曼诺夫王朝过渡的剧变,与波兰-立陶宛联邦、瑞典和奥斯曼帝国的多次战争以及俄罗斯征服西伯利亚,最终,彼得大帝于1689年上台,将沙皇俄国变成了欧洲的主要大国。在北方大战期间,他进行了重大改革,并在1721年战胜瑞典后宣布建立俄罗斯帝国。

2. October Revolution/十月革命

The October Revolution, officially known in Soviet historiography as the Great October Socialist Revolution and commonly referred to as the October Uprising, the October Coup, the Bolshevik Revolution, the Bolshevik Coup or the Red October, was a revolution in Russia led by the Bolshevik Party of Lenin who was instrumental in the larger Russian Revolution of 1917—1923.

The revolution was led by the Bolsheviks, who used their influence in the Petrograd Soviet to organize the armed forces. Bolshevik Red Guards forces under the Military Revolutionary Committee began the occupation of government buildings on 7 November

1917. The following day, the Winter Palace (the seat of the Provisional government located in Petrograd, then capital of Russia) was captured.

The slogan of the October Revolution was All Power to the Soviets, meaning all power to grassroots democratically elected councils.

十月革命在苏联历史学上被正式称为十月社会主义革命,通常也被称为十月起义、十月政变、布尔什维克革命、布尔什维克政变或红色十月,是由布尔什维克党领导的俄罗斯革命。列宁在1917—1923年的俄国大革命中发挥了重要作用。

这场革命是由布尔什维克领导的,他们利用自己在彼得格勒苏维埃中的影响力组建武装力量。军事革命委员会下属的布尔什维克红卫兵部队于1917年11月7日开始占领政府大楼。翌日攻克冬宫(当时俄国首都彼得格勒的临时政府所在地)。

十月革命的口号是"一切权力归苏维埃",意思是一切权力归于基层民选委员会。

3. Soviet Union/苏联时期

In 1922, after a civil war ending in the Bolsheviks' victory, the USSR was formed by a treaty which united the Russian, Transcaucasian, Ukrainian and Byelorussian republics.

On 23 August 1939, after unsuccessful efforts to form an anti-fascist alliance with Western powers, the Soviets signed the non-aggression agreement with Nazi Germany. After the start of World War II, the formally neutral USSR invaded and annexed territories of several Eastern European states, including Poland and the Baltic states. In June 1941, Germany invaded the Soviet Union, opening the most extensive and bloodiest theater of war in history. Soviet casualties accounted for the highest proportion of the war in the effort of acquiring the upper hand over the Axis forces at intense battles such as Stalingrad and Kursk. In most of the territories occupied by the Red Army after its westward advance, local communists assumed power and formed governments allied with the USSR. The post-war division of Europe into capitalist and communist halves led to increased tensions with the United States-led Western Bloc, known as the Cold War. In 1985, the last Soviet premier, Mikhail Gorbachev, sought to reform and liberalize the economy through his policies of glasnost (openness) and perestroika (restructuring). These policies caused political instability arising from nationalist and separatist movements.

As part of an attempt to prevent the country's collapse, a referendum was held on March 1991, which was boycotted by three republics and resulted in a majority favoring the preservation of the union as a renewed federation. Gorbachev's power was greatly diminished after Russian President Boris Yeltsin's high-profile role in facing down a coup d'état by party hardliners. In late 1991, Gorbachev resigned, and the Supreme Soviet of the Soviet

Union convened and formally dissolved the union.

1922年,在以布尔什维克的胜利为结束的内战之后,俄罗斯、白俄罗斯、乌克兰和外高加索等共和国合并,成立首个社会主义国家——苏联。

在与西方列强结成反法西斯联盟的努力失败后,1939年8月23日,苏联与纳粹德国签署了《苏德互不侵犯条约》。第二次世界战开始后,正式中立的苏联入侵并吞并了几个东欧国家的领土,包括波兰和波罗的海国家,这招致德国纳粹不满,两国关系破裂。1941年6月,德国入侵苏联,开启了历史上最广泛、最血腥的战区。在斯大林格勒和库尔斯克等激烈的战争中,苏联为争取轴心国军队占据优势,伤亡人数最多。在红军西进后占领的大部分领土上,由地方共产党人掌权,组成了与苏联结盟的政府。战后欧洲分裂为资本主义和共产主义两部分,这导致苏联与美国领导的西方集团的紧张关系加剧,即冷战。1985年,时任苏联总理的米哈伊尔•戈尔巴乔夫试图通过他的开放政策和改革政策来改革和开放经济。这些政策造成了由民族主义和分裂主义运动引起的政治不稳定。

作为防止国家崩溃的努力的一部分,1991年3月苏联举行了一次全民公决,遭到3个共和国的抵制,结果大多数人赞成保留联邦作为一个新的联邦。在俄罗斯总统叶利钦高调出面镇压党内强硬派的政变后,戈尔巴乔夫的权力大打折扣。1991年底,戈尔巴乔夫辞职,苏联最高苏维埃召开会议,正式解散苏联。

Ⅱ People and Figures/人民及名人

Russia's population density is about 8.4 people per square kilometer, making it one of the most sparsely populated countries in the world. The population is most dense in the European part of the country thanks to the milder climate, centering on Moscow and Saint Petersburg. 74% of Russian population is urban, making Russia a highly urbanized country.

Russia is a multinational state with 194 ethnic groups. The populations of these groups vary enormously, from millions (e.g., Russians, Tatars) to under 10,000 (e.g., Samis, Kets).

俄罗斯人口密度约为每平方千米8.4人,是世界上人口最稀疏的国家之一。俄罗斯欧洲部分人口最密集,气候温和,以莫斯科和圣彼得堡为中心。俄罗斯74%的人口位于城市,这使俄罗斯成为高度城市化的国家。

俄罗斯是一个多民族国家,在其疆域领土内居住着194个民族的人民。民族与民族之间,人口差异显著,从几百万(如俄罗斯人、鞑靼人)到万人以下(如萨米人、凯茨人)不等。

1. Peter the Great/彼得大帝

Peter the Great (June 9, 1672—February 8, 1725) ruled the Tsardom of Russia and later the Russian Empire from 7 May 1682 until his death in 1725, jointly with his elder half-brother, Ivan Ⅴ before 1696. Through a number of successful wars, he expanded the Tsardom into a much larger empire that became a major European power and also laid the groundwork for the Russian navy after capturing ports at Azov and the Baltic Sea. He led a cultural revolution that replaced some of the traditionalist and medieval social and political systems with ones that were modern, scientific, Westernized and based on the Enlightenment. Peter's reforms made a lasting impact on Russia, and many institutions of the Russian government trace their origins to his reign. He is also known for founding and developing the city of Saint Petersburg, which remained the capital of Russia until 1917.

彼得大帝(1672年6月9日—1725年2月8日)于1696年之前与他的同父异母兄弟伊凡五世共同统治沙皇俄国,后来从1682年5月7日直到1725年去世,作为唯一的沙皇统治了俄罗斯帝国。通过战争,他将沙皇俄国变成欧洲大国,并在占领了亚速和波罗的海的港口后为俄罗斯海军奠定了基础。他领导了一场文化革命,用现代的、科学的、西方化的和启蒙运动为基础的社会制度和政治制度取代了一些传统主义和中世纪的社会和政治体系。彼得的改革对俄罗斯产生了深远影响,俄罗斯政府的许多机构都将其起源追溯到他的统治时期。他还以建立和发展圣彼得堡市而闻名,圣彼得堡市一直到1917年都是俄罗斯的首都。

2. Vladimir Lenin/列宁

Vladimir Ilyich Ulyanov (April 22, 1870—January 21, 1924), better known by his alias Lenin, was a Russian revolutionary, politician, and political theorist. He served as head of government of Soviet Russia from 1917 to 1924 and of the Soviet Union from 1922 to 1924. Under his administration, Russia and then the wider Soviet Union became a one-party communist state governed by the Russian Communist Party. Ideologically a communist, he developed a variant of Marxism known as Leninism; his ideas were posthumously codified as Marxism–Leninism.

弗拉基米尔·伊里奇·乌里扬诺夫(1870年4月22日—1924年1月21日),又称列宁,是俄罗斯共产主义革命家、政治家和政治哲学理论家,1917年至1924年任苏俄政府首脑,1922年至1924年任苏联政府首脑。在他治理下,俄罗斯及之后的苏联成为接受布尔什维克(后来的苏联共产党)统治的一党制社会主义国家。列宁思想体系的根基是马克思主义,而其发展的政治理论则称为列宁主义。

3. Joseph Stalin/斯大林

Joseph Vissarionovich Stalin (December 8, 1878—March 5, 1953) was a Georgian revolutionary and Soviet politician who led the Soviet Union from the mid-1920s until 1953 as General Secretary of the Communist Party of the Soviet Union (1922—1952) and Premier (1941 – 1953). Despite initially governing the Soviet Union as part of a collective leadership, he eventually consolidated power to become the country's de facto dictator by the 1930s. A communist ideologically committed to the Leninist interpretation of Marxism, Stalin formalized these ideas as Marxism-Leninism, while his own policies are known as Stalinism.

约瑟夫·维萨里奥诺维奇·斯大林(1878年12月18日—1953年3月5日)是格鲁吉亚革命者和苏联政治家,从20世纪20年代中期至1953年领导苏联,担任苏联共产党总书记(1922—1952)和总理(1941—1953)。尽管最初是作为苏联领导集体的一员,但他最终巩固了权力,在20世纪30年代成为该国的事实上的唯一领导者。斯大林是一位致力于列宁主义对马克思主义解释的共产主义者,他将这些思想形式化为马克思列宁主义,而他自己的政策被称为斯大林主义。

Unit 3　Culture and Education/文化和教育

I　Culture/文化

1. Lev Nikolayevich Tolstoy/列夫·尼古拉耶维奇·托尔斯泰

Lev Nikolayevich Tolstoy (September 9, 1828—November 20, 1910), usually referred to in English also as Leo Tolstoy, was a Russian writer who is regarded as one of the greatest authors of all time. He is best known for the novels *War and Peace* (1869), *Anna Karenina* (1877), and *Resurrection* (1899). He also wrote plays and numerous philosophical essays. He received multiple nominations for Nobel Prize in Literature every year from 1902 to 1906, and nominations for Nobel Peace Prize in 1901, 1902 and 1910, and his miss of the prize is a major Nobel Prize controversy.

列夫·尼古拉耶维奇·托尔斯泰(1828年9月9日—1910年11月20日)是俄罗斯作家,被认为是有史以来最伟大的作家之一。他以小说《战争与和平》(1869)、《安娜·卡列尼娜》(1877)和《复活》(1899)而闻名。他还写有剧本和许多哲学论文。从1902年到1906年,他每年都获得多项诺贝尔文学奖提名,1901年、1902年和1910年也获得过诺贝尔和平奖提名。他从未获得诺贝尔文学奖是诺贝尔文学奖的一大争议。

2. Matryoshka Doll/俄罗斯套娃

Matryoshka dolls, also known as Babushka dolls, Russian Tea dolls, stacking dolls, or Russian dolls, are a set of wooden dolls of decreasing size placed one inside another. The name "matryoshka", literally "little matron", is a diminutive form of Russian female first name "Matryona" (Матрёна) or "Matryosha".

A set of matryoshkas consists of a wooden figure, which separates at the middle, top from bottom, to reveal a smaller figure of the same sort inside, which has, in turn, another figure inside of it, and so on.

The first Russian nested doll set was made in 1890 by wood turning craftsman and wood carver Vasily Zvyozdochkin from a design by Sergey Malyutin, who was a folk crafts painter at Abramtsevo. Traditionally the outer layer is a woman, dressed in a sarafan, a long and shapeless traditional Russian peasant jumper dress. The figures inside may be of either gender; the smallest, innermost doll is typically a baby turned from a single piece of wood. Much of the artistry is in the painting of each doll, which can be very elaborate. The dolls often follow a theme; the themes may vary, from fairy tale characters to Soviet leaders. In the west, Matryoshka dolls are often referred to as "babushka dolls", babushka meaning "grandmother" or "old woman".

俄罗斯套娃,也被称为头巾玩偶、俄罗斯茶玩偶、堆叠玩偶,或俄罗斯玩偶,是一套木制玩偶,一般由多个一样图案的空心木娃娃一个套一个组成。"Matryoshka"这个名字,字面意思是"小主妇",是俄罗斯女性名字"Matryona"(Матрёна)或"Matryosha"的缩略形式 。

一套俄罗斯套娃由一组木娃娃组成,大的木娃娃从中间、顶部和底部分开,露出一个同样类型的较小的木娃娃在里面,而里面又有另一个木娃娃,以此类推。

1890年,第一套俄罗斯嵌套玩偶由木材加工工匠和木雕师瓦西里·兹维约兹多奇金根据阿布拉姆塞沃民间工艺画家谢尔盖·马尔尤丁的设计制作而成。传统上,外层是一个女人,穿着萨拉凡,一个长而不成形的传统俄罗斯农民套头衫礼服。里面的娃娃可以是任何一种性别;最小的、最里面的娃娃通常是一个木制的小婴儿。每一个娃娃身上的绘画图案都有很强的艺术性,可以非常精细。娃娃通常遵循一个主题;主题可能各不相同,从童话人物到苏联领导人。在西方,俄罗斯套娃通常被称为"babushka娃娃",babushka的意思是"祖母"或"老妇人"。

3. Russian Ballet/俄罗斯芭蕾舞

Ballet is the national honor of Russian and the "visiting card" of the Russian culture. Originated in Italy and France, here it found its "second home country". It is in Russia that classical ballet traditions have been kept and developed to present them to the whole world again afterwards.

The first ballet school was opened in St. Petersburg in 1738. After a few decades, another school was opened in Moscow. Thus started the rivalry of the two ballet traditions—

of St. Petersburg and Moscow, and the two theatres – the Mariinsky and the Bolshoy–that has continued ever after. You can find the confirmation of that rivalry by just studying the playbills in both cities.

In the 19th century, many classical ballet masterpieces were born, such as *The Sleeping Beauty*, *The Nutcracker*, *The Swan Lake*, *Raymonda*, *La Bayadère*, and *Don Quixote*. The music to the former three was written by P.I. Tchaikovsky, which also was a breakthrough, as nowhere in the world the "great" composers had worked for ballet before. Due to their wonderful music and filigree choreography, these performances are still winning great successes on the Russian and the world stages.

芭蕾舞是俄罗斯的民族骄傲,俄罗斯文化的"名片"。芭蕾舞虽然诞生于法国和意大利,但却在这里找到了"第二故乡"。恰恰是在俄罗斯,古典芭蕾舞得以保留并发展,并在其后重新向全世界展示。

1738年在彼得堡创办了俄罗斯第一所芭蕾舞学校。几十年后,在莫斯科也创办了另一所芭蕾舞学校。由此开始了彼得堡和莫斯科这两种芭蕾舞传统以及两家剧院(马林斯基剧院和大剧院)的角逐,并一直持续到今天。只要研究一下两个城市的海报就可以确认这一点了。

在19世纪,俄罗斯创作了许多古典芭蕾舞杰作:《睡美人》《胡桃夹子》《天鹅湖》《莱蒙达》《舞姬》《堂吉诃德》。前三个芭蕾舞作品的音乐都由柴可夫斯基创作而成,这也是一个突破:在这之前,世界上任何地方都没有大作曲家为芭蕾舞创作音乐。由于出色的音乐和精细的舞蹈,所有这些芭蕾舞剧直到今天在俄罗斯和世界的舞台上都大获成功。

Ⅱ Education/教育

Education in Russia is compulsory for children between the ages of 6 and 15. It consists of primary school education for ages 6 to 10, followed by senior school for ages 10 to 15. If a pupil of secondary school wishes to go on in higher education, he or she must remain to complete secondary school for 2 more years, from ages 15 to17.

Primary and secondary school includes 11 years of study. Every school has a core curriculum of academic subjects. After completing this stage, pupils are awarded the Attestat o Srednem (Polnom) Obshchem Obrazovanii (Certificate of Secondary Complete General Education).

At 15 years old, children may choose to enter a vocational school or non-university institute. They typically offer programs of academic subjects and a program of training in a technical field until students reach 17 or 18. Such institutions used to be called technikum, but now most of them are known as colleges.

The Russian school year is comprised of 4 terms with vacations in between: 1 week in November, 2 weeks in January, 1 week in March and nearly 3 months in summer. School is held from September 1 until the final week of May, with exams in June.

俄罗斯规定6至15岁的儿童必须接受义务教育。其中包括6—10岁的小学教育,其次是10—15岁的高中教育。如果中学的学生希望继续接受高等教育,则他或她必须从15—17岁继续完成两年中学的学习。

中小学包括11年的学习时间。每所学校都有核心的学术课程。完成此阶段后,学生将被授予中学教育证书。

15岁时,学生可以选择进入职业学校或非综合性大学进行学习。这些机构通常提供学术课程和技术领域的培训课程,直到学生达到17或18岁。这类机构曾经被称为职业学校,但现在大多数都被称为学院。

俄罗斯一学年有4个学期,假期包括11月1周,1月2周,3月1周,暑假近3个月。学校9月1日开学,5月的最后一周结束,6月举行考试。

Unit 4　Major Attractions/主要景点

I　Lake Baikal/贝加尔湖

Lake Baikal is a unique natural sight protected by UNESCO. And it's fair: this huge lake in the shape of a crescent, stretching from southwest to northeast for 620 kilometers, is considered "the most" in many ways.

First of all, it's the deepest lake in the world. Its maximum depth is 1,642 meters, while the average is about 742 meters. The lake is so deep because it is located right in a tectonic fault. Secondly, it accommodates about 20% of the world's fresh water and is considered to be the largest freshwater lake by volume on our planet. Still the water in Lake Baikal is one of the cleanest, clearest and oxygen-richest in the world. The visibility in the water can reach up to 40 meters in fine weather. Third, the flora and fauna of Lake Baikal are unique: more than 1,000 local species of plants and animals are that can't be found anywhere else. For example, a charming freshwater seal—the Baikal seal.

Baikal is annually visited by more than 2 million tourists from all over the world.

Nevertheless, there are many places on the lake that look completely virginal (sometimes charming but dangerous) as in ancient times. Given an opportunity to spend time on the lake and in the surrounding area long enough, everyone can find something to their liking.

It can be swimming in or ship cruising on the lake, fishing or looking at the Circum-Baikal Railway—an engineering masterpiece, acquainting with the local traditions or hiking on ecological trails, scuba diving, windsurfing, enjoying thermal water treatment and even skiing in winter.

贝加尔湖是受联合国教科文组织保护的独一无二的自然胜地。这一巨大的湖泊呈月牙状,自西南向东北延伸620千米,拥有很多方面的"之最"。

首先,这是世界上最深的湖泊。最大深度可达1,642米,平均深度约742米。湖泊深度如此之大,是由于贝加尔湖处于构造断层上。其次,贝加尔湖储存了世界上20%的淡水,因此成为地球上淡水储水量最大的水域。与此同时,贝加尔湖湖水是世界上最清澈澄冽,且富含氧气最多的。天气晴朗时,可看到湖底40米深处。再次,贝加尔湖的植物和动物独一无二:此处有1,000多种动植物是贝加尔湖特有的,例如,一种迷人的淡水海豹——贝加尔湖海豹。

每年有超过200万来自世界各地的游客来到贝加尔湖。尽管如此,湖面上仍有许多地方像远古时期一样,看起来完好无损(有时美丽与危险并存)。如果有机会长期待在湖泊及周边地区,每个人都能找到自己喜欢的东西。

人们可以在湖中游泳或乘船游弋,钓鱼或观看工程杰作——环贝加尔湖铁路,熟悉当地传统,在生态小路上徒步,潜水,冲浪,在温泉水中疗养,冬天还能进行山地滑雪。

II The Moscow Kremlin/莫斯科克里姆林宫

This is the place where Moscow was founded in almost 9 centuries ago. In the Middle Age, the fortress served as the residence of the Russian sovereigns. The tradition is kept. At present, it is the residence of the President of Russia.

Among the rampant walls and towers made of red bricks hide authentic cathedrals of the 15th to 17th centuries (architectural complex of the Cathedral Square) as well as interesting museums. Most of them are armories, a unique treasury where imperial regalia, jewelry, weapons, and masterpieces of ornamental arts of the 14th to 19th centuries are kept.

Places worth visiting include the Assumption Cathedral (where the Russian Tsars were crowned), the Archangel's Cathedral (the burial place of Russian Tsars), the Annunciation Cathedral (the Royal home church), and ancient premises of the Patriarch's Palace. If you climb up the Ivan Great Bell-Tower from where an impressive view opens, don't miss the

Tsar Bell and the Tsar-Cannon whose size is amazing.

大约9个世纪前,正是在这个地方诞生了莫斯科。中世纪时期,这座城堡是俄罗斯统治者的官邸。这种传统被保留了下来——这里如今是俄罗斯总统府。

威严的红砖宫墙和塔楼后隐藏着真正的15—17世纪大教堂(大教堂广场建筑群)以及有趣的博物馆。其中主要的是军械库,这可是罕见的宝库,这里陈列着14—19世纪的皇室勋章、珠宝、兵器及装饰艺术杰作。

圣母升天大教堂(俄罗斯沙皇加冕的地方)、天使长大教堂(俄罗斯沙皇的陵寝)、天使长报喜大教堂(沙皇家庭教堂)、宗主教宫殿的古老厅堂都值得一看。如果登上伊凡大帝钟楼,可以欣赏壮丽的景色。一定不要错过以身形庞大著称的"钟王"和"炮王"。

Ⅲ St. Petersburg/圣彼得堡

St. Petersburg is one of those Russian cities whose historical center was completely preserved. That is why you can walk along its streets without any plan—sooner or later you will come across an interesting attraction anyway. However, there are a number of locations where you can feel the spirit of the city only by seeing them with your own eyes.

Nevsky Prospect, 4.5 km long and crossing the city center from the west to the east, is the main grand street of the city. It accommodates the majority of luxury palaces as well as cafés and shops with various levels. From here you can practically get to any attraction on foot.

One of the must-see sights is the Hermitage with one of the world's best collections of works of art (especially by Italian and Dutch painters). The great museum is located in the former imperial palace where the luxury of the rooms is on a par with the beauty of the exhibits. The large Palace Square (Dvortsovaya Ploshchad) in front of it with the Bronze Horseman monument is also very beautiful. The largest collection of Russian art is presented in the Russian Museum. Both museums are huge and deserve a full-day visit.

You can also visit the Peter and Paul Fortress that first used to serve as a defense bastion, then a prison where many famous people were kept, and now the State Museum of the History of St. Petersburg. The Peter and Paul Cathedral with its beautiful golden decorations also deserves attention. The Kunstkamera, or "the cabinet of curiosities", founded by the great Russian Emperor Peter Ⅰ is also a popular attraction. It is famous first of all for its collection of various exhibits of abnormalities preserved in alcohol, whose appearance even makes some people faint. There is also a good ethnographic collection. Among the newer museums, the Grand Maket Russia Interactive Museum, a miniature model of Russia, is quite popular.

　　圣彼得堡是俄罗斯城市中少有的完整保存历史中心的城市之一。所以,可以随性在这座城市街头散步,因为不管到哪都能看到有趣的名胜。当然,如果错过了某些地方,那就不一定能完全感受到这座城市的精髓。

　　涅瓦大街——城市的主街道,全长4.5千米,东西向横穿市中心。大部分的豪华宫殿矗立在街道两边,这里同时也汇聚了各价位的咖啡馆及商店。由此出发可到达城市的任意名胜。

　　埃尔米塔日博物馆是必去之地,它是世界上最优秀艺术品(特别是意大利、荷兰大师们的作品)收藏博物馆之一。庞大的博物馆就位于昔日的皇宫内,豪华的展厅相较展品毫不逊色。博物馆前是美丽、壮阔的宫廷广场,其上屹立着"青铜骑士"雕像。俄罗斯风格艺术藏品最多的是俄罗斯博物馆。这两座博物馆都规模庞大,都值得花上一整天的时间去参观。

　　你也可以去彼得保罗要塞参观,这里曾经是防御用的碉堡,之后作为监狱,关押过很多著名的犯人,现如今,这里是彼得堡历史博物馆。彼得保罗大教堂同样值得关注,这里有精美的黄金装饰。宫斯特卡米拉博物馆同样著名,又称"珍品陈列馆",是由伟大的俄罗斯大帝彼得一世建立的。这里出名主要是因为那些酒精浸泡的畸形物,有些人看到这些甚至会晕过去。当然,这里也有不错的民族学藏品。较现代的博物馆中著名的当数俄罗斯微缩博物馆,这座博物馆是俄罗斯微缩典范。

Part Two
Outbound Tour Guide Operation/出境领队实务

Unit 1　Situational Dialogues/情景对话

Ⅰ　Dialogue 1　Duty Free Shop

（*A：shop assistant　B：customer*）

A：Good afternoon, Madam. May I help you?

B：Yes, please. I'm looking for a lipstick. Do you sell it here?

A：Yes. What brand do you want?　We have a variety of different brands.

B：Great. You must have Armani then. May I have a look at them?

A：Here you are, Madam. It is lip maestro.

B：Which color is the best seller?

A：The best seller is the intense velvet color of No. 405, which is nicknamed rotten tomato.

B：And how much is it?

A：It is 2,416 Russian Ruble or 35 Euros. Would you like it?

B：Yes. I'll take it. By the way, do you also sell loose powder?

A：Yes. Any particular brand?

B：Givenchy if you have.

A：Yes. The four-color set is very popular, which sells only 47 Euros.

B：One, please. By the way, where can I buy cigarettes and liquor?

A：Over their, at the cigarettes and liquor counter.

B：I'd like to have some cigarettes and liquor. I'm going to China. Do you know the duty free limit?

A：You can bring into China two cartons of cigarettes and three bottles of liquor.

B：Thank you. Could you please give me two cartons of Winston[①] and one bottle of Vodka?

A：OK. Here are your cigarettes and liquor. Anything else?

B：I'm looking for some souvenirs. Do you have anything commemorative for us to bring back to China?

A：We have many things for you to choose from. How about amber? The amber[2] from The Baltic is the best in the world.

B：That's a good idea. Can I see some?

A：Of course. Here are many amber bracelets, necklaces, and pendants of different size. The price is determined by size and condition.

B：What are the yellow things? They looks more beautiful.

A：They are ceromel[3], just a kind of amber, but more expensive than amber.

B：I want both.

A：Sure. Take your time and choose those you like most.

B：They are lovely. What is the minimum purchase for having tax refund, by the way?

A：70 Euros. If your purchase is over 70 Euros, you get 13 percent tax refund.

B：Thank you.

Notes：

①Winston：（俄罗斯）云斯顿香烟。

②amber：琥珀。

③ceromel：蜜蜡。

Ⅱ Dialogue 2　Ballet in Russia

（A：*tourist*　B：*guide*）

A：Good morning, Mr. Guide. Before I came to Russia, I was told I must go to see the ballet in Russia. I guess Moscow must be the best city to do it. Or do you have any other suggestions?

B：That's absolutely true. I would say, a tour to Russia without seeing ballet is not a complete one. In Russia, two best places to see ballet are Moscow and St. Petersburg. But personally, I like the latter better.

A：Why? Moscow is the capital city!

B：Yes. Moscow does have the famous Bolshoi Theatre[1]. But there is a huge debate

over which ballet theatre in Russia is the best—Bolshoi in Moscow or Mariinsky in St. Petersburg. They both are great. But tickets for Bolshoi are sometimes very hard to get, due to a large number of resellers, who buy them out and try to sell them for the price 4–5 times higher than the original. However, tickets for Mariinsky are somewhat easier to get. You know what, we wanted to see the Nutcracker in Bolshoi just after the New Year, but the tickets were sold for almost $400—over 20,000 rubles and they would never cost so much in the normal ticket office, so we decided to watch it in St. Petersburg for 6,000 rubles instead.

A: I see. Is Mariinsky the only theater in St. Petersburg where people can go to see ballet?

B: No. As far as I know, there are three good theaters in St. Petersburg where you can see ballet.

A: What are they?

B: The first one is Mariinsky Theater of course. It is a world-famous theater located in the city center of St. Petersburg. It has three stages. But the main stage and the new stage are the good ones. Avoid the Concert Hall, as they usually don't show the best performances there.

A: What is the second one?

B: The second famous theater in St. Petersburg is Mikhailovsky Theatre. Located in the heart of St. Petersburg on the Square of Arts, this theatre is my favorite. I also think it's one of the most beautiful theaters in Russia—its combination of gold and red makes it look lavish. Also, it's more spacious than the main stage of Mariinsky and the chairs, in my opinion, are more comfortable.

A: What about the third one?

B: The third one is Hermitage Theatre. If both of the theaters above are not showing performances or everything is sold out, try the lovely Hermitage Theatre, which shows the *Swan Lake* and the *Nutcracker* all year long and its audience are 100% tourists (95% of them are from China). The quality of the ballet is still good. The theatre is very small but beautiful. There are more places to see St. Petersburg ballet, but I really don't recommend them, because the ones I listed above are the only three impressive theaters.

A: What are the best ballets to see in Russia?

B: If you're wondering which ballet to see in Russia, I'd recommend the following ones: *Swan Lake*, *Giselle*, *Nutcracker*, *La Fille mal gardée*, *La Sylphide*, and *Romeo and*

*Juliet*②.

A：Good. Last question. As you said that tickets for the ballet in Bolshoi Theater in Moscow is hard to get. What is the best way to buy tickets for a ballet?

B：People often buy tickets for ballet in Bolshoi theatre from resellers for obscene prices. If you don't want to be scammed or overpay, buy the tickets on the official website of Bolshoi theatre. You can buy an e-ticket there and then print it and show it at the entrance. In order to buy the ticket, you need to register. I agree that the website interface is not the prettiest, but it's functional and it's in English as well, so don't worry about that either.

A：Thank you so much for telling me such great information of the ballet in Russia. I'll seize every opportunity to enjoy it sometime.

Notes：

①Bolshoi Theatre：莫斯科大剧院，又叫波修瓦剧院。下文中的 Mariinsky Theater，Mikhailovsky Theatre，和 Hermitage Theatre 分别是马林斯基歌剧院，米哈伊洛夫斯基剧院和赫米蒂奇剧院。

②*Swan Lake*，*Giselle*，*Nutcracker*，*La Fille mal gardée*，*La Sylphide*，and *Romeo and Juliet*：《天鹅湖》《吉赛尔》《胡桃夹子》《关不住的女儿》《仙女》《罗密欧与朱丽叶》。

Ⅲ　Dialogue 3　Russian Architecture

（*A*：guide　*B*：tourist）

B：Good morning, Sir. What have you planned for us this morning?

A：Good morning. We will go to visit the famous St. Basil's Cathedral① today.

B：Great. I heard that it is a great work of architecture. So, before we see the cathedral, would you please tell us something about Russian architecture in general?

A：My pleasure. For most of its history, Russian architecture has been predominantly religious. Churches were for centuries the only buildings to be constructed of stone, and today they are almost the only buildings that remain from its ancient past.

B：What are the major features of Russian architecture?

A：The basic elements of Russian church design emerged fairly early, around the 11th century. The plan is generally that of a Greek cross with all four arms equal. And the walls are

high and relatively free of openings. The structure is usually covered with sharply-sloped roofs and a multitude of domes. The characteristic onion dome first appeared in the 11th century. On the interior, the primary feature is the iconostasis, an altar screen on which the church's icons are mounted in a hierarchical fashion.

B: On our way to the hotel, we saw many buildings with very interesting tops. What are they?

A: They are the stunning churches and graceful cathedrals that are dotted among modern skyscrapers and apartment blocks in the city's iconic skyline. The sublime architecture of these religious buildings exhibits a variety of styles: from traditional Russian to lavish Italian Renaissance to Moscow's own take on Baroque. They are the best of Moscow's beauty.

B: You said we will see. St Basil's Cathedral today. I guess it is one of them. Why is it so famous?

A: Firstly, it has a long history. It was built under the reign of Ivan IV in the mid-sixteenth century. Secondly, it is a beauty in its own right.

B: Come on. We are all ears. Let's hear more.

A: Lying at the very centre of the city, St. Basil's and Red Square act as Moscow's beating heart, from which it expands and grows. This UNESCO world heritage site was designed to resemble a bonfire, with its eclectic domes acting as flickering flames. These kaleidoscopic domes are legendary.

B: What do you mean by legendary?

A: Legend has it that, Tsar Ivan the Terrible, upon seeing St. Basil's for the first time, demanded that the architect's eyes be cut out so he could never create anything so beautiful again.

B: How cruel! Are we going to see the inside of it?

A: Yes. Inside, St. Basil's offers visitors a wonderfully peaceful atmosphere and a stunning panorama of the Moskva River[2] from its balcony—making St. Basil's a heavenly escape in the city's bustling center. I'm sure you will enjoy the visit this morning.

B: Thank you so much. Now let's go and see it. I can't wait any longer.

Notes:
①St. Basil's Cathedral:圣巴西尔大教堂,位于莫斯科红场。
②Moskva River:莫斯科河,英文为 Moscow River.

Unit 2　Case Study/案例分析

I 案例一：飞机无法按计划起飞导致游客解除旅游合同的处理

1. 案例简介

洪先生等30名旅游者和某旅行社签订了俄罗斯7日游的旅游合同。当旅游团上午8时按时到达机场时，由于突遇暴风雪，机场被迫关闭，飞机无法按计划起飞。大部分旅游者愿意等候。洪先生等5名旅游者愿意解除旅游合同，但要求旅行社赔偿全部团费的50%，理由是旅行社违约；旅行社愿意退还全额团费，但拒绝赔偿，洪先生向旅游管理部门投诉。其他旅游者在机场等候了5个小时后前往俄罗斯。这些旅游者返程后也向旅游管理部门投诉提出每人赔偿500元的要求，理由是在旅游行程比原计划匆忙了许多，缩短了在景点逗留的时间，无形中损害了旅游者权益，旅行社仍然存在违约的事实。

2. 案例分析

请问：

(1)旅行社是否应当承担50%的违约金？为什么？

(2)其他参加旅游团的旅游者提出的赔偿要求是否合理？为什么？

专家意见：

(1)旅行社不应当承担50%的违约金。导致洪先生取消行程的原因是不可抗力。我国《合同法》的规定，因不可抗力不能履行合同的，根据不可抗力的影响，部分或者全部免除违约方的违约责任。按照《旅游法》的规定，不可抗力发生后，旅游者和旅行社都可以解除合同。当洪先生提出解除旅游合同时，旅行社只需全额退还旅游费用，不需要承担赔偿责任。

(2)其他参加旅游团的旅游者提出的赔偿要求不合理。对旅游合同而言，不可抗力发生后，旅游者的旅游时间往往会被缩短，这是每一个具备完全民事行为能力的旅游者应当预料得到的后果。既然旅游者没有解除旅游合同，并自愿继续旅游行程，就应当接受行程缩短的事实，但不能就此要求旅行社给予赔偿。因为产生这样的后果仍然是不可抗力作用的结果，不可抗力是法定的免责条件。

Ⅱ 案例二:导游擅自更改行程的处理

1.案例简介

某旅行社组织了20人去境外旅游。按照行程计划,到达境外的第二天游览某景点,但地陪未与旅游者协商,擅自将行程延后一天。就在第二天晚上,一场突如其来的大雪使旅游车无法抵达该景点,游览行程被迫取消。旅游者返回后,要求旅行社按照规定双倍赔偿该景点门票,并给予补偿。旅行社总经理只愿意原价退还门票,但拒绝赔偿。理由是景点游览取消是不可抗力造成的,旅行社没有过错,旅行社不承担赔偿责任。旅游者认为,造成景点不能游览的原因是地陪擅自改变行程造成的,旅行社应当承担赔偿责任。

2.案例分析

请问:

(1)游览景点计划取消的原因究竟是不可抗力,还是旅行社违约? 为什么?

(2)旅行社应当如何向旅游者做出赔偿?

专家意见:

(1)导致景点游览取消的原因是旅行社违约,而不是不可抗力。下大雪固然是不可抗力的,但只要导游按照原计划履行合同,不擅自改变行程,该团队本来完全可以在大雪到来前完成该景点的计划,也可以避免纠纷的发生。我国《合同法》规定,当事人迟延履行后发生不可抗力的,不能免除责任。所以,旅行社应当承担违约责任。

(2)如果旅游合同对违约责任有约定,就按照约定向旅游者做出赔偿。如果没有约定,旅行社应当退还景点门票、导游服务费并赔偿等额违约金。

Chapter 9

Australia/澳大利亚

Part One
Briefing on Australia/澳大利亚概况

Unit 1   Overviews/总览

澳大利亚

I   Basic Information/基本信息

National Flag/国旗	National Emblem/国徽

The national flag of Australia has a blue field with a Union Jack in the upper hoist corner. Australia used to be one of the 6 British dependencies before the founding of the Commonwealth of Australia in 1901. It is also a symbol of the historical relations between Australia and the United Kingdom.	The national emblem of Australia is a coat of arms. A shield lies in the middle of the emblem, surrounded by a big seven-pointed star, the golden wattle, a kangaroo and an emu.
The large white seven-pointed star in the lower hoist corner represents the six federal states and two territories (Northern Territory and Capital Territory). And the Southern Cross, formed by the five stars on the right, is the dominant feature of the night sky in southern hemisphere.	The shield has badges of Australian states of New South Wales, Victoria, Queensland, South Australia, Western Australia and Tasmania. The large white seven-pointed star represents six states and two territories. Both the kangaroo and the emu hardly move backwards, representing Australia's advancement.
澳大利亚国旗以蓝色为背景，它的左上角是英国国旗，代表着在1901年澳大利亚大陆统一之前，澳大利亚曾经是6个英国的附属国之一，同时也标志着澳大利亚和英国历史上的传统关系。	澳大利亚国徽是一个盾徽，包括一个七角星、金合欢花、一只袋鼠和一只鸸鹋。
左下角是一个稍大的七角星，也被叫作联邦之星，代表六个州和两个领地（北领地和首都领地）；而由右侧五颗星组成的南十字星座是南半球夜空的主要特征。	盾牌中包含了澳大利亚的6个州，它们分别是新南威尔士州、维多利亚州、昆士兰州、南澳大利亚州、西澳大利亚州和塔斯马尼亚州。上方七角星状的联邦之星代表着6个州和2个领地。袋鼠和鸸鹋这两种动物都代表着整个国家在一直不断前进。

Other Basics/其他基本信息	
Full Name/国家全称	The Commonwealth of Australia/澳大利亚联邦
Other Names/其他称呼	Australia, the Great Southern Land/澳大利亚、伟大的南方大陆
Total Area/国土面积	7,692,000 km²/7,692,000平方千米
Population/人口	25,690,000（2020年9月）
Nationality/民族	British Australian, Asian Australian, Maoris/英裔澳大利亚人、亚裔澳大利亚人、土著毛利人
Capital/首都	Canberra/堪培拉
National Anthem/国歌	"Advance Australia Fair"/《前进,澳大利亚》
National Flower/国花	Golden Wattle/金合欢
National Bird/国鸟	Emu/鸸鹋
Divisions/行政区划	6 states and 2 mainland territories/6个州和2个特区
Language/语言	English/英语
Major Political Parties/主要政党	Liberal Party, National Party, Australian Labor Party/自由党、国家党、澳大利亚工党
Government Type/政府类型	Federal Parliamentary Constitutional Monarchy/联邦议会君主立宪制
Religious Belief/主要宗教信仰	Protestant Christian, Catholic/基督新教、天主教
Currency/货币	Australian Dollar/澳大利亚元
Time Difference with Beijing/与北京时差	+2（Summer Time +3）/比北京早2小时（夏时制早3小时）

Ⅱ Physical Geography/自然与地理

Surrounded by the Indian and Pacific oceans, Australia is separated from Asia by the Arafura and Timor seas, with the Coral Sea lying off the Queensland coast, and the Tasman Sea lying between Australia and New Zealand. The world's smallest continent and sixth largest country by total area, Australia—owing to its size and isolation—is often dubbed the "island continent", and is sometimes considered the world's largest island. Australia has 36,735 kilometres of coastline.

The Great Barrier Reef, the world's largest coral reef, lies a short distance off the north-east coast and extends for over 2,000 kilometres. Mount Kosciuszko is the highest mountain on the Australian mainland.

Australia's size gives it a wide variety of landscapes, with tropical rainforest in the north-east, mountain ranges in the south-east, south-west and east, and desert in the centre. Australia is the driest inhabited continent; its annual rainfall averaged over continental area is less than 500 mm. The population density, 2.8 inhabitants per square kilometre, is among the lowest in the world, although a large proportion of the population lives along the temperate south-eastern coastline.

澳大利亚位于印度洋和太平洋之间,四面环海,阿拉弗拉海和帝汶海将其与亚洲隔开,珊瑚海位于昆士兰海岸,塔斯曼海则位于澳大利亚和新西兰之间。澳大利亚是世界上最小的大陆,按总面积计算则是世界第六大国家。由于其幅员辽阔和与世隔绝,常常被称为"岛屿大陆",即世界上最大的岛屿。澳大利亚拥有36,735千米的海岸线。

世界上最大的珊瑚礁大堡礁位于澳大利亚东北海岸不远处,绵延2,000多千米。科修斯科山是澳大利亚本土最高的山脉。

澳大利亚地广人稀,拥有各式地貌,东北部为热带雨林,东南、西南和东部常见山脉,中部则主要被沙漠覆盖。澳大利亚是世界上最干旱的人类栖息地,其大陆地区的年平均降雨量少于500毫米。人口密度为每平方千米2.8人,大部分人口生活在温带东南海岸线上,是世界上人口密度最低的国家之一。

Ⅲ Government and Administration/政府机构

Australia is a federal parliamentary constitutional monarchy. Elizabeth Ⅱ reigns as Queen of Australia. Since she resides in the United Kingdom, she is represented in Australia by the governor-general at the federal level and by the governors at the state level.

澳大利亚是联邦议会君主立宪制国家。现任国家元首(君主)为伊丽莎白二世。由于她居住在英国,澳大利亚联邦一级总督和州一级的总督是她的代表,代替其行使职权。

1. Parliament/议会

The Commonwealth of Australia is a federal state. Parliament consists of the governor-general which represents the monarch, the Senate and the House of Representatives.

The main functions of Parliament are to pass laws, to provide, by voting for taxation, the means of carrying on the work of government, to examine government policy and administrations, including proposal for expenditure, and to debate the major issues of the day.

In the Senate (the upper house), there are 76 senators: twelve each from the states and two each from the mainland territories (the Australian Capital Territory and the Northern Territory).

The House of Representatives (the lower house) is elected by single-member electoral division and consists of 151 members of Parliament. It is in the House of Representatives that the ultimate authority for law-making resides. The chairman who conducts debates in the House of Representatives is officially called Speaker.

澳大利亚联邦是一个联邦国家。联邦议会由女王(澳总督为其代表)、参议院和众议院组成。

议会的主要职能是:颁布法律、以投票表决的方式实施政府工作、审核政府政策及包括经费支出等的行政管理方针,以及讨论当前重要议题。

参议院(上议院)有76名议员,6个州每州12名,2个大陆地区(澳大利亚首都领地、北领地)各2名。

众议院有151名议员,由单一成员选举小组选出。众议院享有立法的最高权威。众议院辩论的主席被称为议长。

2. Party/政党

There are two major political groups that usually form government, federally and in the states: the Australian Labor Party and the Coalition which is a formal grouping of the Liberal Party and its minor partner, the National Party. Within Australian political culture, the Coalition is considered centre-right and the Labor Party is considered centre-left. Independent members and several minor parties have achieved representation in Australian parliaments, mostly in upper houses.

澳大利亚通常有两个主要的政治团体组成政府,包括联邦政府和州政府。它们是澳大利亚工党和自由党—国家党联盟。自由党—国家党联盟在澳大利亚的政治文化中,被视为中右政党,而工党则被视为中左政党。独立议员和其他党派在澳大利亚议会中也有代表权,主要是在上议院。

Unit 2　History and People/历史和人民

Ⅰ History/历史

Aboriginal Australians inhabited the continent for about 65,000 years prior to European discovery with the arrival of Dutch explorers in the early 17th century, who named it New Holland. In 1770, Australia's eastern half was claimed by Great Britain and initially settled through penal transportation to the colony of New South Wales from 26 January 1788, a date which became Australia's national day. The population grew steadily in subsequent decades.

In the1850s, gold deposits were discovered in New South Wales and Victoria. A large number of gold diggers from Europe, America and China swarmed in. Australia's population began to surge and Australia got rich and developed rapidly.

On 1 January 1901, the six colonies federated, forming the Commonwealth of Australia. Australia has since maintained a stable liberal democratic political system that functions as a federal parliamentary constitutional monarchy.

在欧洲人到达之前,澳大利亚土著人已经在这片大陆居住了约65,000年。17世纪初荷兰探险家来到这里,将其命名为"新荷兰"。1770年,澳大利亚的东半部被英国占领;并从1788年1月26日开始通过刑事运输到新南威尔士殖民地定居,这一天成为澳大利亚的国庆节。在随后的几十年里,人口稳步增长。19世纪50年代,在新南威尔士和维多利亚两州发现金矿。大批来自欧洲、美洲和中国的淘金者蜂拥而至。澳大利亚人口激增,迅速致富和发展。

1901年1月1日,6个殖民地联合起来,组成了澳大利亚联邦,成为英国的自治领地。自那以后,澳大利亚一直保持着稳定的联邦议会君主立宪制的自由民主政治制度。

Ⅱ　People and Figures/人民及名人

1. Howard Walter Florey/霍华德·沃尔特·弗洛雷

Howard Walter Florey is a pathologist born in the Adelaide, who won the Nobel Prize in Physiology or Medicine in the 1945 for his contribution of successfully isolating and purifying the Penicillin. His research promotes the application of sterilization by Penicillin in clinic. Numerous lives could be saved depended on his achievement. In 1965, Howard Walter Florey was knighted by Queen Elizabeth and served as Honorary President of the Australian National University.

霍华德·沃尔特·弗洛雷是出生于阿德莱德的病理学家,他因成功分离和纯化青霉素于1945年获得诺贝尔生理学/医学奖。他的研究推进了青霉素灭菌在临床中的应用,以此挽救了许多生命。1965年,霍华德·沃尔特·弗洛雷被伊丽莎白女王授予爵士,并担任澳大利亚国立大学名誉校长。

2. Rupert Murdoch/鲁珀特·默多克

Rupert Murdoch is a world newspaper tycoon, who owns the major shares of News Corporation, including the famous newspaper *Thames* in England and the great film company in America, 20th Century Fox Film Corporation. Additionally, Rupert Murdoch used to be a skeptic of global warming. However, he now turned to be an environmental advocator. His company follows the carbon balance rule to meet the 0 carbon emission tasks.

鲁珀特·默多克是世界报业大亨。他拥有新闻集团的主要股份,包括英国《泰晤士报》和美国20世纪福克斯电影公司。值得一提的是,鲁珀特·默多克曾对全球变暖持怀疑态度,但现在他成了环境保护倡导者。他的公司遵循碳平衡规则,以实现零碳排放任务。

3. Nicole Kidman/妮可·基德曼

Nicole Kidman is a famous Australian actress who owns good reputation in fashion, film industry all over the world. The character she acted in the films such as *the Hours*, *Moulin Rouge*, could be seen as the successful masterpieces of Nicole Kidman. As a professional actress who has a good learning capacity, with lots of fantastic work, Nicole Kidman gains the great popularity and attention in the world.

妮可·基德曼是著名的澳大利亚女演员,在世界各地的时尚、电影界享有盛誉。她在电影《时时刻刻》《红磨坊》等电影中扮演角色,是其代表作。作为一名专业演员,妮可·基德曼具有良好的学习能力,并有许多出色的作品,在世界上获得了极大的欢迎和关注。

Unit 3 Culture and Education/文化和教育

Ⅰ Culture/文化

According to the Australian history, being conquered as a colony at first by the invaders from Europe, the Australian culture was deeply influenced by the western culture—the Anglo-Celtic Western culture. At the same time, the ancestors of Australia were the aborigines, leading to the multi-culture environment and primitive color of lives. Since the mid-20th century, American popular culture has strongly influenced Australia, particularly through television and cinema.

根据历史,澳大利亚最初是被欧洲侵略者征服的殖民地,因此澳大利亚文化深受西方文化—盎格鲁-凯尔特人文化的影响。同时,澳大利亚的祖先是土著居民,这使得澳大利亚拥有多元文化环境和原始的生活色彩。 自20世纪中叶以来,美国的流行文化通过电视和电影对澳大利亚产生了深远的影响。

1. Cuisine/饮食

The first settlers introduced British food to the continent, much of which is now considered typical Australian food, such as the Sunday roast. Post-World War II European migrants, particularly from the Mediterranean, helped to build a thriving Australian coffee culture, and the influence of Asian cultures has led to Australian variants of their staple foods, such as the Chinese-inspired dim sim and Chiko Roll. Vegemite, pavlova, lamingtons and meat pies are regarded as iconic Australian foods.

第一批澳洲大陆定居者带来的英国食物中有不少现在被认为是典型的澳大利亚美食，例如星期日烤肉。第二次世界大战后，欧洲移民，尤其是来自地中海的移民，建立并发展了澳大利亚的咖啡文化；而亚洲文化的影响使得澳大利亚主食有了更多种类，例如中国风味的点心和澳式春卷。蔬菜酱、奶油蛋白甜饼、拉明顿巧克力椰丝方形蛋糕和肉馅饼都是澳大利亚的标志性美食。

2. Sports and Recreation/体育和休闲

Australia is unique in that it has professional leagues for four football codes. They are Australian rules football, rugby league, rugby union, and Soccer. The Australian national cricket team has participated in every edition of the Cricket World Cup. Australia has been very successful in the event, winning the tournament five times, the record number. Australia is a powerhouse in water-based sports, such as swimming and surfing. The surf lifesaving movement originated in Australia, and the volunteer lifesaver is one of the country's icons. Nationally, other popular sports include horse racing, basketball, and motor racing.

澳大利亚拥有四种足球(橄榄球)职业联赛，分别是澳式橄榄球、英式橄榄球联盟、英式橄榄球联合会和英式足球。澳大利亚国家板球队是板球世界杯的常客，并且在这项赛事上非常成功，共赢得五次冠军。 澳大利亚更是游泳和冲浪等水上运动强国。冲浪救生运动起源于澳大利亚，救生志愿者是澳大利亚的骄傲之一。其他在全国范围内受欢迎的体育活动包括赛马、篮球和赛车。

Ⅱ Education/教育

Australia is always be awarded as the big country of education in the world from 2 aspects: the large age range for compulsory education, the large number of public schools and the high-quality education outcomes.

As for the compulsory education, early in the 1870s, the Australian Compulsory Education Laws had been passed to facilitate the trend of the social development for better progress. Although the relevant rules vary from different continents and territories, generally, children and teenagers who is aged from 5 to 16 are compulsory for the school attendance. The teenagers aged 16–17 are required to participate in vocational training or continue to the schoolwork.

Australia has 40 public universities funded by government, 2 international universities and 1 private university. The implementation and promotion of compulsory education play an important role in the Australian culture construction. As a supplement, the TAFE (Technical And Further Education) perfects the education systems in Australia. About 58% of Australian aged from 25 to 64 have the experience of attending the vocational or tertiary qualification (Australian Bureau of Statistics, 2005), the graduation rate reaches the 49%, which is the highest among OECD countries (2016). Additionally, according to Sauter, Grossman, et al. (2012), nearly one third of Australian has obtained a higher education qualification. It makes Australia the country whose educational quality reaches the top in the world.

澳大利亚一直以来都是教育大国,其义务教育的年龄范围广,公立学校数量众多,拥有高质量的教育成果。

关于义务教育,19世纪70年代初期,《澳大利亚义务教育法》的实行促进了社会的发展与进步。虽然各地区的相关规定不同,但一般来说,年龄在5至16岁之间的儿童和青少年是要接受义务教育的。16—17岁的青少年则需要继续学习或参加职业培训。

澳大利亚有40所政府资助的公立大学、2所国际大学和1所私立大学。义务教育的实施和推广在澳大利亚文化建设中起着重要作用。作为补充,TAFE(技术和继续教育)完善了澳大利亚的教育体系。25岁至64岁的澳大利亚人中约58%具有高等职业教育经验或大专学历(数据来自澳大利亚统计局,2005年),毕业率达到49%,在经合组织(OECD)国家中最高(2016年)。此外,根据索特、格罗斯曼等人(2012)的说法,将近1/3的澳大利亚人已接受高等教育,这使得澳大利亚的教育质量达到世界一流水平。

Unit 4　Major Attractions/主要景点

I　The Great Barrier Reef/大堡礁

Located in the northeast Australia, the Great Barrier Reef is the largest and longest coral reef in the world, consisting of 2,900 little coral reef islands. From Torres Strait in the north to the Tropic of Capricorn in the south, the Great Barrier Reef has the length of 2,011 kilometers and the maximum width of this reef reaches 161 kilometers. Blue coast, golden beach, the numerous corals and the amazing biodiversity attract tourists from all over the world. However, it is not only famous for its fantastic views, but also has the danger of extinction because of the global warming.

位于澳大利亚东北部的大堡礁是世界上最大、最长的珊瑚礁,由2,900个小珊瑚礁岛组成。从北部的托雷斯海峡到南回归线,大堡礁的长度为2,011千米,最宽处达到161千米。蓝色的海岸、金色的沙滩、无数的珊瑚和惊人的生物多样性吸引了来自世界各地的游客。然而,大堡礁存在因全球变暖而消失的危险,这引起了全世界的极大关注。

II Sydney Opera House/悉尼歌剧院

Sydney Opera House is a landmark of Sydney which is impressing for its shell-type design by Danish architect Jorn Utzon. It is also unique for being built on the water. The inside decoration and architectural structure used the elements of Mayan Culture and Aztec Temple, creating the style of solemn and ancient culture. In 2007, the Sydney Opera House was named as World Cultural Heritage by United Nations Educational, Scientific and Cultural Organization. Every year, there are more than 1500 different shows on this stage, attracting millions of tourists from all over the world.

悉尼歌剧院是悉尼的地标,丹麦建筑师约恩·乌特松所打造的贝壳式设计给人留下了深刻的印象。悉尼歌剧院是在独一无二的水上建筑,内部装饰和建筑结构采用玛雅文化和阿兹特克神庙的元素,营造出庄重而古老的文化风格。2007年,悉尼歌剧院被联合国教科文组织(UNESCO)认证为世界文化遗产。每年在悉尼歌剧院的舞台上上演着1500多个不同的节目,吸引了来自世界各地数百万的游客。

III Australian National University/澳大利亚国立大学

Founded by Australia's Federal Parliament in 1946, Australian National University is a world-famous public research university located in Canberra, Australia. It is the first research university in Australia. By September 2018, it has had 7 Nobel Prize winners, 49 Rhodes Scholarships, 2 Prime Minister of Australia, 12 current federal minister and 30 current ambassadors. In 2019, Australian National University ranks No. 29 in the global universities by QS World University Rankings. It is also the university ranked first in Australia for 15 consecutive years.

澳大利亚国立大学于1946年成立,是一所世界著名的公立研究型大学,位于澳大利亚堪培拉。它是澳大利亚第一所研究型大学。截至2018年9月,从澳大利亚国立大学已经走出7位诺贝尔奖获得者、49位罗兹奖学金获得者、2位澳大利亚总理、12位现任联邦部长和30位现任大使。2019年,澳大利亚国立大学在QS世界大学排名中列第29位,连续15年在澳大利亚排名第一。

Part Two
Outbound Tour Guide Operation/出境领队实务

Unit 1 Situational Dialogues/情景对话

I Dialogue 1 Tax Refund 1

At the Chemist Warehouse

（*A*：*salesgirl*   *B*：*tourist*）

A：Welcome to Australian famous Chemist Warehouse.

B：Thank you. I want to buy some health care products for my relatives and friends. Australia specializes in this.

A：Yes. This is the right place to meet your demand. Any particular requirement?

B：Yes, something for women's health.

A：OK. I recommend Women's Ultivite Multivitamin.

B：What is the function?

A：One function is to support during stress, and the second is to assist energy levels, stamina, and vitality.

B：Does it really work?

A：Yes. It is researched and developed on the basis of scientific evidence.

B：Great! Which brand do you recommend?

A：The most famous brands are Swisse[①] and Blackmore[②]. Both are big brands in the field.

B：OK. I'll buy one bottle of Swisse.

A：I suggest you buy four bottles because one bottle contains 120 tablets, which can last 3 months with a pill one day. Four bottles for a year is a period of treatment.

B：And the price?

A：64 AUD for four bottles.

B：Can I have a tax refund form, please? I'm from China.

A：Certainly, Sir. May I have your passport, please? Let me write out a tax refund form for you.

B：Here it is.

A：Here are your tax refund form and the receipt. Keep them safe, please. When you get your tax refund, you need to show both of them.

B：By the way, where can I get tax refund?

A：At any customs in Australia. When arriving at the airport, you can go to the Customs to have your form stamped or find a pablo[3] to do it yourself. But remember you have to do it on Pablo One, the blue one and Pablo Two, the red one.

B：Is there any differences between these two machines?

A：You will register your data in Pablo One, then complete tax refund on Pablo Two.

B：It seems more convenient.

A：Yes. The 64 AUD you paid includes tax and you can draw it back at the customs with this refund form.

B：Thank you very much, Miss.

A：With pleasure.

Notes：

①Swisse：澳洲保健品牌。

②Blackmore：澳洲保健品牌。

③pablo：Programme d'Apurement des Bordereaux de détaxe par Lecture Optique（镭射阅读退税单审核程序）自助服务退税机。

Ⅱ Dialogue 2　Melbourne Cup

（A：tourist　B：Australian tour guide）

A：Good morning, Sir.

B：Good morning. Did you sleep well last night?

A：Yes. I watched a bit of TV and went to sleep quite early. There was a popular topic on TV, the Melbourne Cup. Many channels were talking about it. What is it?

B：Melbourne Cup is an annual Thoroughbred horse race held in Melbourne, Australia. The race is

a handicap for horses of three-years-old and over and it is run at a distance of 3,200 meters.

A: It must be something special here, isn't it?

B: You bet. It is considered one of the most popular sporting events in Australia with millions of people tuning in each year. Its popularity has earned the event the moniker "the race that stops a nation". The name can quite literally apply to parts of Victoria where the Melbourne Cup day was given the status of a national public holiday.

A: Is it a traditional sporting event in Melbourne?

B: I should say yes, because Melbourne Cup has a long history, with the first race held back in 1861. Ever since then, there has been a steady growth in popularity, which has spilt over the borders of the continent and now attracts audiences from all over the world.

A: In what time does it take place every year?

B: The Melbourne Cup race is a part of the Melbourne Cup day, traditionally being held every first Tuesday in November. This year, the event will be held on 5 November, and the race itself will start at 3 p.m. local time. It will be held on the Flemington Racecourse in Melbourne. The entire event starts at 11 a.m. and lasts until 5:20 p.m., with 10 races in total.

A: How long does each race last for?

B: The average race time is around 3.5 minutes over the course of 3,200 meters. The race is a true spectacle of strength and endurance.

A: What is the prize for the winner?

B: Melbourne Cup is the richest two-mile handicap in the world, with a prize pool of 7.3 million dollars.

A: I'm sure many people bet on their favorite horses.

B: Without any doubt, the event gathers a huge number of punters, many of whom choose the race to be the one event to bet on for the year.

A: What is the chance to win the bet?

B: An important fact to state is that throughout its history, the Melbourne Cup has proved notoriously difficult to predict. The main proof lies in the fact that the horses considered Melbourne Cup favorites have managed to win in only 20% of cases.

A: Alright. Now I won't think any more of betting on any of the horses. I'm just kidding. I've never thought of it.

B: It is not impossible. If you plan to take part in Melbourne Cup betting, you will be able to watch the live stream of the race through the websites of a number of betting operators, namely, BetEasy, Ladbrokes, Sportsbet, and Crownbet. However, you will most likely need a positive account balance in order to access their live streaming service.

A: Forget about that. But you mentioned that the race is to be held on the Flemington Racecourse in Melbourne. Is it far from our hotel? Is it possible for us just to take a look at the racecourse to quench our curiosity?

B: If you all want to go, there won't be any problem.

A: Thank you very much. I'm looking forward to it.

Ⅲ Dialogue 3　The Great Ocean Road

(A: tourist　B: local guide)

A: Hello, Mr. Guide. We'll have a free day tomorrow. The women are going shopping. But that's not our cup of tea. Can you suggest some places of interest for us to visit?

B: There are quite a few places around worth visiting. My first suggestion would be the Great Ocean Road.

A: The Great Ocean Road! What is it?

B: The Great Ocean Road is an Australian National Heritage listed. It is a road stretches 243 kilometers along the south-eastern coast of Australia between the Victorian cities of Torquay and Allansford.

A: What is the significance of the road?

B: Built by returned soldiers between 1919 and 1932 and dedicated to soldiers killed during World War Ⅰ, the road is the world's largest war memorial. Winding through varying terrain along the coast and providing access to several prominent landmarks, including the Twelve Apostles[①] limestone stack formations, the road is an important tourist attraction in the region. Tourists visiting there can take in the scenery, get into nature, sample the local produce, meet the wild life and experience Australia's aboriginal culture.

A: Wow. Can you give us more information?

B: Victoria's dramatic south-west coastline covers an incredible range of scenery. There you can see the world-famous waves at Bells Beach or laze on the sand at Angle Sea, visit the charming old fishing village of Port Fairy and get among the buzzing arts community in Lorne. Of course, you can't miss the Twelve Apostles[①]. These craggy limestone stacks rising majestically from the Southern Ocean are a must-see.

A: What about "get into nature"?

B: From rainforests and rivers to old volcanoes and rugged coastlines, the Great Ocean Road showcases nature at its most diverse. In Great Otway National Park you'll see thundering waterfalls and sparkling gorges and walk through the tops of ancient, mossy trees. Need to stretch your legs? See deserted sandy beaches, thick forests and some of Australia's highest sea cliffs on the 91-kilometre Great Ocean Walk.

A: Ok. Let's skip the produce and move to the wild life. What are the typical Australian wild lives can we see there?

B: The Great Ocean Road is home to an abundance of native wildlife. At Tower Hill Wildlife Reserve, near Warrnambool, you can take a 60-minute tour with an Aboriginal guide who will explain the history of this unique area as you spot emus, kangaroos, koalas, and lizards.

A: Aboriginal guide! Is that also the place to experience the aboriginal culture?

B: Aboriginal stories connect the landscapes of the Great Ocean Road from Wathaurong country in Geelong to the Gunditjmara region of the west. In Geelong, you can taste bush tucker, learn about ancient remedies and hear didgeridoo playing at the Narana Aboriginal Cultural Centre. or you can visit the Brambuk centre in Halls Gap to see fascinating displays of art and artifacts and join a tour to visit some of rock art sites dating back 22,000 years in the Grampians National Park.

A: That is awesome. We have to try to see them all. Thank you so much for telling us all the useful information.

B: It's my pleasure. Hope you will have a good time tomorrow.

A: I'm sure we will.

Notes:
①the Twelve Apostles: 耶稣的十二门徒。

Unit 2　Case Study/案例分析

Ⅰ 案例一：签证没有按时签出所造成的经济损失

杭州萧山旅游者张先生等3人于2019年7月3日委托杭州某出境旅行社为其代办2019年8月1日—10日赴澳大利亚个人旅游的签证。张先生坚称是由于旅行社催办不力，造成该签证直至8月4日才签发，致使其自行购买的机票需要改签而增加了费用，预付的酒店定金也无法退还，经济损失共达17842元，要求旅行社赔偿。

1. 调查事实及处理结果

张先生等3人于2019年7月3日下午将委托代办赴澳大利亚个人旅游签证的材料交到旅行社，并缴纳了费用1800元/人。

7月7日，旅行社签证部完成了送签材料的初审，以快递形式送旅行社签证中心上海办公室。

7月8日，签证中心上海办公室收到快递并再次审核后，将送签材料于7月9日送澳大利亚驻沪领事馆办理签证，整个过程无拖延情况。

据澳大利亚驻沪领事馆官网显示，办理个人旅游签证的受理时间为5—15个工作日，按正常时间推算，7月9日送签后的15个工作日，最迟至7月30日也应出签，可是直至8月4日才出签，历时18个工作日。

旅行社质监部给杭州市旅游质监所的回复中表示：各国的使领事馆代表各自的主权国家为申请入境该国的外国人发放入境签证，任何组织和个人都无权进行干涉或施加影响，并附上了旅行社于7月25日、7月30日以及7月31日向澳大利亚驻沪领事馆连续发送的几份催签电子邮件的证据证明旅行社并无懈怠行为。

同时，旅行社接洽张先生代办澳签的工作人员也曾再三口头提醒张先生，欧美、澳新等国家的个人旅游签证存在"拒签"等不确定因素，在未出签前切勿订机票和预付酒店费用，已尽警示义务。因此，张先生等3人由于澳大利亚驻沪领事馆延缓出签而造成的经济损失，旅行社不应承担责任。

但旅行社考虑到张先生毕竟是委托旅行社为其代办签证的客户，遭受的损失也是实际存在的，同意给张先生等3人每人1000元的经济补偿。后经杭州市旅游质监所协调，双方达成和解协议，旅行社补偿张先生等3人每人1200元。

2. 经验或教训

此案例暴露的最大问题是双方没有签订书面的委托代办合同。现再次强调,旅行社提供代订机票、代订酒店、代办签证等旅游服务并收取代办费用的,均应该与旅游者签订书面的委托代办合同。对于提供代办签证服务的,更应在合同中予以明确告知,为申请人发放入境签证是各国使领馆的权利,任何组织、个人都无权干涉或施加影响;还应提示注意申请欧美、澳新等发达国家的入境签证存在"拒签"等不确定因素,在未取得入境签证前,均勿订机票或支付预订酒店等费用;须在合同中约定,若遭"拒签",支付给使领馆的申办签证费用××元和旅行社的操作费××元,共××元由旅游者承担。

Ⅱ 案例二:对合同订立,修改与终止的投诉处理

1. 案例简介

张女士一家三口和李女士夫妻俩报名参加了某旅行社组织的澳大利亚游,签订合同的时候,旅行社在包价旅游合同中载明了详细的旅游行程安排、航班和酒店信息等各事项。2019年8月10日澳洲游出发当天,由于超强台风"利奇马"的影响,8月10日上海浦东进出港航班全部由于台风不可抗力原因取消。旅行社原定8月10号上海/墨尔本航班也被迫取消,致使旅客短暂滞留。旅行社经过多方努力改签到最早飞墨尔本的航班(8月12日出发),同时旅行社积极联系澳大利亚地接社及时调整行程,并告知游客最新的旅游行程安排,尽最大努力满足旅客的需求。期间,经过协调沟通,李女士的丈夫由于工作原因,确定无法参加修改后的澳大利亚跟团游行程,要求退团,取消跟团游。张女士一家三口和李女士一人经过协调沟通后,同意于8月12日出发前往澳大利亚游。行程中,张女士在旅游拍照时,没有谨记导游的安全提醒,前往危险的地方拍摄,因为自身原因不慎扭伤,一家人要求提前结束行程,提前回国,旅行社帮助安排了他们回国事宜并垫付了张女士一家三口提前回国的新增机票费用。李女士一人参加完了全程澳大利亚游。回国后,张女士一家三口和李女士分别找到报名旅行社,要求退还原包价合同中没有履行的旅游行程的团费,并提出额外的经济补偿。并且,张女士提出,自己境外的扭伤是旅行社安排的行程不安全导致的,且不愿意承担支付提前回国的新增机票费用。请问该如何处理?

2. 案例分析

(1)关于合同终止、单方取消的分析。

张女士一家三口和李女士夫妻俩报名参加的澳大利亚游,在出行前签订了包价旅游合同。出发当天,由于超强台风"利奇马"影响,不得不改签和调整行程,他们被告知旅游行程需推迟且调整,期间旅行社尽最大努力满足旅客的需求。经过协调沟通,李女士的丈夫因为工作原因,确定无法参加修改后的澳大利亚跟团游行程,要求退团,取消跟团游。

依据我国《旅游法》第五章旅游服务合同第六十五条:旅游行程结束前,旅游者解除合

同的,组团社应当在扣除必要的费用后,将余款退还旅游者。包价旅游合同的修改或终止后,都应该将团费中扣除必要产生的费用后的余款,退还给旅游者。其中关于必要费用的认定属于旅行社实际产生的损失,而不包含合同约定中的违约金。因为,《合同法》第一百一十四条规定:当事人可以约定一方违约时应当根据违约情况向对方支付一定数额的违约金,也可以约定因违约产生的损失赔偿额的计算方法。由此可知,违约金是承担违约责任的方式之一,是以存在违约行为为前提的。

同时,超强台风"利奇马"属于不可抗力原因。我国《旅游法》第五章旅游服务合同第六十七条:因不可抗力或者旅行社、履行辅助人已尽合理注意义务仍不能避免的事件,影响旅游行程的,按照下列情形处理:

①合同不能继续履行的,旅行社和旅游者均可以解除合同。合同不能完全履行的,旅行社经向旅游者做出说明,可以在合理范围内变更合同;旅游者不同意变更的,可以解除合同。

所以,面对李女士丈夫的取消行程和退团,旅行社应当予以同意。

②合同解除的,组团社应当在扣除已向地接社或者履行辅助人支付且不可退还的费用后,将余款退还旅游者;合同变更的,因此增加的费用由旅游者承担,减少的费用退还旅游者。

所以,李女士的丈夫需要承担期间产生的相应的境外地接损失费用,而不用承担包价合同中的违约金。且旅游者解除合同是不承担违约责任的,旅游者享有任意解除权,该必要的费用是旅行社的损失。之所以根据取消行程时间不同,规定承担必要费用的不同比例,是基于该法律规定及行业操作惯例,为减轻旅行社的举证责任所做的变通之举,是损失的一种计算方法。

(2)关于合同修改的分析。

当双方因为不可抗力导致行程变更,协调过程中,张女士一家三口和李女士也一样拥有任意解除权,一旦他们同意合同变更,则增加的费用理应由自身承担,如确有减少的费用需退还他们。他们在行程结束后,回国找到报名旅行社,要求退还原包价合同中没有履行的旅游行程的团费,并提出额外的经济补偿的做法不合理。出发前合同已经重新调整,根据我国《旅游法》《合同法》重新约定旅游事项,合同已变更,所以就不存在对原包价合同的违约。

(3)关于团队滞留的分析。

《旅游法》第五章旅游服务合同第六十七条:造成旅游者滞留的,旅行社应当采取相应的安置措施。因此增加的食宿费用,由旅游者承担;增加的返程费用,由旅行社与旅游者分担。

出发前,在上海滞留期间,旅行社不仅应当积极协调处理团队事宜,还应采取相应的客人在上海相应的安置措施,例如住宿和餐食问题,因此增加的食宿费用,由旅游者承担,如果确实因为航班无法改签,团队被迫取消,导致客人需要全部返程,则增加的返程费用,由旅行社与旅游者分担。

(4)关于意外事故的分析。

行程中,张女士在旅游拍照时,没有顾忌安全(导游已有提醒),前往危险的地方拍摄,因为自身原因不慎扭伤,一家人要求提前结束行程,提前回国,旅行社帮助安排了他们回国事宜并垫付了张女士一家三口提前回国的新增机票费用。在这过程中,首先,导游做到了安全提醒工作,发生事故后,旅行社也积极配合客人解决问题,协助客人提前回国,并且垫付了他们的回程机票。旅行社尽到了安全提示、救助义务。其次,旅游者自身原因导致包价旅游合同不能履行或者不能按照约定履行,旅行社不承担责任,因此增加的费用,旅游者应该自行承担。后续,未完成的旅游行程中,若有可取消的团款费用,应退还旅游者。

依据如下:

《旅游法》第五章旅游服务合同第六十八条:旅游行程中解除合同的,旅行社应当协助旅游者返回出发地或者旅游者指定的合理地点。由于旅行社或者履行辅助人的原因导致合同解除的,返程费用由旅行社承担。

《旅游法》第五章旅游服务合同第七十条:旅行社不履行包价旅游合同义务或者履行合同义务不符合约定的,应当依法承担继续履行、采取补救措施或者赔偿损失等违约责任;造成旅游者人身损害、财产损失的,应当依法承担赔偿责任。旅行社具备履行条件,经旅游者要求仍拒绝履行合同,造成旅游者人身损害、滞留等严重后果的,旅游者还可以要求旅行社支付旅游费用一倍以上三倍以下的赔偿金。由于旅游者自身原因导致包价旅游合同不能履行或者不能按照约定履行,或者造成旅游者人身损害、财产损失的,旅行社不承担责任。在旅游者自行安排活动期间,旅行社未尽到安全提示、救助义务的,应当对旅游者的人身损害、财产损失承担相应责任。

《旅游法》第五章旅游服务合同第七十三条:旅行社根据旅游者的具体要求安排旅游行程,与旅游者订立包价旅游合同的,旅游者请求变更旅游行程安排,因此增加的费用由旅游者承担,减少的费用退还旅游者。

Chapter 10

Egypt/埃及

Part One
Republic of Egypt/埃及概况

Unit 1 Overviews/总览

埃及

Ⅰ Basic Information/基本信息

National Flag/国旗	National Emblem/国徽
The flag of Egypt is a tricolour consisting of the three equal horizontal red, white, and black bands, dating back to the 1952 Egyptian Revolution.	The current national emblem of Egypt is a shield emblem, launched in 1984, painted with the national flag of the tricolor straight bar, placed on the chest of a saladin eagle. The eagle clutched the ribbon with the words "Arab republic of Egypt".
Red represents revolution and blood, white represents a bright future, and black represents a long history suppressed by foreign countries. The flag bears Egypt's national emblem, the Egyptian eagle of Saladin centered in the white band.	埃及国徽现行国徽是一个盾徽,1984年启用,绘有国旗的三色直条,置于一只萨拉丁之鹰胸前。鹰爪抓住书有"阿拉伯埃及共和国"的饰带。
埃及国旗为三色,由红、白、黑三种水平相等的条纹组成,其历史可追溯到1952年的埃及革命时期。	
红色象征革命与鲜血,白色象征纯洁和光明前途,黑色象征过去的黑暗岁月。国旗上有埃及的国徽——萨拉丁之鹰,雄鹰在白带中央。	

Other Basics/其他基本信息	
Full Name/国家全称	Arab Republic of Egypt/阿拉伯埃及共和国
Other Name/其他称呼	Egypt/埃及
Total Area/国土面积	1,001,449 km²/1,001,449平方千米
Population/人口	100,000,000（2021年7月）
Nationality/民族	Arab，Berber/阿拉伯人、柏柏尔人
Capital/首都	Cairo/开罗
National Anthem/国歌	"My Country，My Country，My Country"/《祖国，祖国，祖国》
National Flower/国花	Lotus/莲花
National Bird/国鸟	Eagle/雄鹰
Divisions/行政区划	The 27 provinces are composed of 10 provinces of upper Egypt，7 provinces of lower Egypt，3 provinces of central part and canal，2 provinces of Sinai Peninsula，and 4 other provinces（unofficial sub-region）/27个省分别由上埃及10省、下埃及7省、中部和运河各3省、西奈半岛2省，以及其他4省组成（非官方分区）
Language/语言	Arabic. For historical reasons，English and French are also widely used in Egypt./阿拉伯语。由于历史原因，英语、法语在埃及也被广泛使用。
Major Political Parties/主要政党	National Democratic Party（ruling party），Free Egyptians Party，Nation's Future Party，New Wafd Party/埃及民族民主党（执政党）、埃及新华夫脱党、埃及自由社会主义者工党、埃及民族未来党
Government Type/政府类型	Semi-presidential System/半总统共和制
Religious Belief/主要宗教信仰	Islam/伊斯兰教
Currency/货币	Egyptian Pound/埃及镑
Time Difference with Beijing/与北京时差	-6/比北京晚6个小时

Ⅱ Physical Geography/自然和地理

Egypt covers an area of 1,001,450 square kilometers and stretches across Asia and Africa，most of it lies in northeast Africa，with the Sinai Peninsula on east of the Suez Canal in southwest Asia. Egypt has a unique geographical location：in terms of the land，it connects Asia and Africa；in terms of sea route，the Mediterranean Sea and the Indian Ocean are also connected by the Suez Canal and the red sea. So Egypt has been a battleground since the beginning of recorded history. At present, Egypt borders Libya in the west, Sudan in the south, the Red Sea, Palestine and Israel in the east, and the Mediterranean Sea in the north.

Ninety-five percent of Egypt is desert. The highest peak, Kathryn Mountain, is 2,629 meters above sea level. The world's longest river, the Nile, flows through the whole territory from south to north, with a length of 1,350 kilometers and a narrow river valley of about 3—16 kilometers on both sides, forming a delta of 24,000 square kilometers north of the capital Cairo. The river valleys and deltas on both sides of the river account for only 4% of Egypt's total area, but are home to 99% of the country's population. The Suez Canal is a major transportation link between Asia, Africa and Europe.

Egypt is dry throughout the country with little rain. The Nile delta and the northern coastal areas belong to the Mediterranean climate, with the average temperature of 12℃ in January and 26℃ in July. The average annual precipitation is 50—200 mm. The rest of the region is mainly tropical desert climate, hot and dry, desert temperature up to 40℃, annual average precipitation less than 30 mm. The "Pentecostal wind" occurs every year between April and May. The flying sand and rocks damage the crops.

埃及面积有1,001,450平方千米,疆域横跨亚、非两洲,当中大部分位于非洲东北部,另外苏伊士运河以东的西奈半岛位于亚洲西南部。埃及有着独特的地缘位置:在陆路上,它连接亚、非两洲;在海路上,通过苏伊士运河及红海连接地中海及印度洋。所以有历史记录以来,埃及都是兵家必争之地。现时埃及的西面与利比亚为邻,南与苏丹交界,东临红海并与巴勒斯坦、以色列接壤,北临地中海。

埃及全境有95%为沙漠。最高峰凯瑟琳山海拔2,629米。世界第一长河尼罗河从南到北流贯全境,境内长1,350千米,两岸形成宽约3—16千米的狭长河谷,并在首都开罗以北形成2.4万平方千米的三角洲。两岸的河谷及三角洲地带,虽然只占埃及全国总面积的4%,却是埃及99%的人口聚居所在。苏伊士运河是连接亚、非、欧三洲的交通要道。

埃及全境干燥少雨。尼罗河三角洲和北部沿海地区属地中海型气候,1月平均气温12℃,7月26℃;年平均降水量50—200毫米。其余大部分地区属热带沙漠气候,炎热干燥,沙漠地区气温可达40℃,年平均降水量不足30毫米。每年4—5月常有"五旬风",飞沙走石,使农作物受害。

Ⅲ Government and Administration/埃及政府机构

A Semi-presidential System/半总统制共和制

A semi-presidential system or dual executive system is a system of government in which a president exists alongside a prime minister and a cabinet, with the latter being responsible to the legislature of a state. Generally speaking, the president's executive power is larger than that of the prime minister, and the cabinet led by the prime minister has a relatively stable position, but the prime minister needs to exercise executive power through the cabinet.

The President is the head of state and the supreme commander of the armed forces. He is nominated by the people's assembly and elected by referendum for a four-year term (the term of the President before 2011 was six years). He can serve a second term. He has the power to appoint vice presidents, prime ministers and cabinet ministers, as well as to dissolve the people's parliament and take urgent measures in special periods. When the People's Assembly (legislature) is not in session, it may also rule by decree. On 22 May 1980, a referendum was held to amend the constitution, stipulating that the political system should be "based on a multi-party system". "The President may be re-elected for a number of consecutive terms", and the article "establishment of a consultative conference" was added.

The Parliament of Egypt, officially the House of Representatives is the highest legislature. Members are elected by popular vote for five-year terms. The main functions of parliament are: to nominate presidential candidates; to administer the formulation and amendment of the constitution; to determine the general policy of the state; to approve plans for economic and social development and state budgets and final accounts, and to supervise the work of the government.

半总统制又称双首长制、混合制,是一种同时具有总统制和内阁制(议会制)特征的共和制政体,后者负责国家立法。半总统制的总统作为国家元首有一些特殊的行政权力,一般而言其行政权力较总理大;由总理领导的内阁有相对较稳固的地位,但总理需通过内阁行使行政权。

总统是国家元首兼武装部队最高统帅,由人民议会提名,公民投票选出,任期4年(2011年前总统任期为6年),可以连任一次,拥有任命副总统、总理及内阁部长,并在特殊时期解散人民议会和采取紧急措施的权力;在人民议会(立法机关)闭会期间,还可通过颁布法令进行统治。1980年5月22日经公民投票修改宪法,规定政治制度"建立在多党制基础上""总统可多次连选连任",并增加了"建立协商会议"的条文。

埃及议会(国会众议院)是最高立法机关。议员由普选产生,任期5年。议会的主要职能是:提名总统候选人;主持制定和修改宪法;决定国家总政策;批准经济和社会发展计划及国家预算、决算,并对政府工作进行监督。

Unit 2　History and People/历史和人民

Ⅰ History/历史

1. Overview of The History/历史综述

Egypt is one of the oldest countries in the world. Its history can be traced back to 6,000 BC— 4,000 BC. Ancient Egypt is regarded as the cradle of civilization, which witnessed the early development of writing, agriculture, urbanization, organized religion and central government. Monuments such as Giza Necropolis and sphinxes, as well as Memphis, Thebes, Karnak and the valley of kings, remain an important focus of science and the public. Egypt's long and rich cultural heritage is an integral part of its national identity, which has been influenced by various foreign countries, including Greece, Persia, Rome, Arabia, Ottoman Turkey and Nubia, and is often assimilated. Although Christianity was a minority, Egypt was an important early Christian Center. It was Islamized in the seventh century.

From the 16th to the beginning of the 20th century, Egypt was ruled by foreign imperial powers: The Ottoman Empire and the British Empire. Modern Egypt dates back to 1922, when it gained nominal independence from the British Empire as a monarchy. However, British military occupation of Egypt continued, and many Egyptians believed that the monarchy was an instrument of British colonialism. Following the 1952 revolution, Egypt expelled British soldiers and bureaucrats and ended British occupation, nationalized the British-held Suez Canal, exiled King Farouk and his family, and declared itself a republic. In 1958 it merged with Syria to form the United Arab Republic, which dissolved in 1961. Throughout the second half of the 20th century, Egypt endured social and religious strife and political instability, fighting several armed conflicts with Israel in 1948, 1956, 1967 and 1973, and occupying the Gaza Strip intermittently until 1967. In 1978, Egypt signed the Camp David Accords, officially withdrawing from the Gaza Strip and recognizing Israel. The country continues to face challenges, from political unrest, including the recent 2011 revolution and its aftermath, to terrorism and economic underdevelopment. Egypt's current government is a semi-presidential republic headed by President Abdel Fattah Al-Sisi, which has been described by a number of watchdogs as authoritarian.

埃及是世界上历史最悠久的国家之一,其历史可以追溯到公元前6000年—公元前4000年。古埃及被认为是文明的摇篮,它见证了文字、农业、城市化、宗教组织和中央政府的早期发展。吉萨墓地和狮身人面像这样的标志性遗迹,以及孟菲斯、底比斯、卡纳克和帝王谷的遗址,仍然是科学和公众的重要焦点。埃及悠久而丰富的文化遗产是其国家身份的一个组成部分,它经受了各种外国的影响,包括希腊、波斯、罗马、阿拉伯、奥斯曼土耳其和努比亚,并经常被同化。尽管基督教占少数,但埃及是早期重要的基督教中心。在公元7世纪它被伊斯兰化。

从16世纪到20世纪初,埃及一直被外来帝国统治:奥斯曼帝国和大英帝国。现代埃及可以追溯到1922年,当时以君主制从大英帝国获得了名义上的独立。然而,英国对埃及的军事占领仍在继续,许多埃及人认为君主制是英国殖民主义的工具。1952年革命后,埃及驱逐了英国士兵和官员,结束了英国的占领,将英国控制的苏伊士运河收归国有,流放了法鲁克国王和他的家人,并宣布自己为共和国。1958年,埃及与叙利亚合并,形成了阿拉伯联合共和国,并于1961年解体。整个20世纪下半叶,埃及经历了社会和宗教冲突及政治动荡。1948年、1956年、1967年和1973年与以色列发生了几次武装冲突,直到1967年才断断续续地占领加沙地带。1978年,埃及签署了戴维营协议,正式撤出加沙地带,承认以色列。这个国家继续面临挑战,从政治动荡,包括最近的2011年革命及其后果,到恐怖主义和经济落后。埃及现政府是一个由阿卜杜勒·法塔赫·塞西总统领导的半总统制共和国,许多监督机构称其为独裁政府。

2. Historical Events/历史事件

(1)Suez Crisis/第二次中东战争

Suez Crisis, or The Second Arab–Israeli War, also called the "Tripartite Aggression" in the Arab world and Sinai War in Israel, was an invasion of Egypt in late 1956 by Israel, followed by the United Kingdom and France. The aims were to regain Western control of the Suez Canal and to remove Egyptian president Gamal Abdel Nasser, who had just nationalized the canal. After the fighting had started, political pressure from the United States, the Soviet Union and the United Nations led to a withdrawal by the three invaders.

苏伊士运河危机,或第二次阿以战争,也被称为阿拉伯世界的"三方侵略"和以色列的西奈战争,指的是1956年末以色列入侵埃及,随后是英国和法国。其目的是重新获得西方对苏伊士运河的控制,并推翻刚刚将运河收归国有的埃及总统贾迈勒·阿卜杜勒·纳赛尔。战争开始后,来自美国、苏联和联合国的政治压力使三方侵略者撤退。

(2)The Third Middle East War/第三次中东战争

The third Middle East war, known as the Six Day War in Israel and the June War in

Arab countries, took place in early June 1967, which is a model of "pre-emptive" war. It happened between the state of Israel and the neighboring Arab states of Egypt, Syria and Jordan. The war began on June 5 and lasted for six days. The combined forces of Egypt, Jordan and Syria were soundly defeated by Israel, making it one of the most overwhelming wars in military history of the 20th century.

第三次中东战争,以色列方面称六日战争,阿拉伯国家方面称六月战争。战争发生在1967年6月初,是"先发制人"战争的一个典范。它发生在以色列国和毗邻的埃及、叙利亚及约旦等阿拉伯国家之间。战争从6月5日开始,共进行了6天。埃及、约旦和叙利亚联军被以色列彻底打败,这也成为20世纪军事史上最具有压倒性结局的战争之一。

（3）The Egyptian Revolution/埃及革命

The Egyptian Revolution of 2011, also known as the January 25 Revolution, started on 25 January 2011 and spread across Egypt. The date was set by various youth groups to coincide with the annual Egyptian "Police holiday" as a statement against increasing police brutality during the last few years of Mubarak's presidency. It consisted of demonstrations, marches, occupations of plazas, non-violent civil resistance, acts of civil disobedience and strikes. Millions of protesters from a range of socio-economic and religious backgrounds demanded the overthrow of Egyptian President Hosni Mubarak. Violent clashes between security forces and protesters resulted in at least 846 people killed and over 6,000 injured. Protesters retaliated by burning over 90 police stations across the country.

2011年的埃及革命,也被称为"1月25日革命",始于2011年1月25日,并蔓延到埃及各地。这一天是由各青年团体确定的,正好是埃及一年一度的"警察节",以此来反对在穆巴拉克总统任期的最后几年里不断增加的警察暴行。它包括示威、游行、占领广场、非暴力公民抵抗、公民不服从行为和罢工。来自不同社会经济和宗教背景的数百万抗议者要求推翻埃及总统穆巴拉克。安全部队和抗议者之间的暴力冲突导致至少846人死亡,6,000多人受伤。作为报复,抗议者烧毁了全国90多个警察局。

II People and Figures/人民及名人

Ethnic Egyptians are by far the largest ethnic group in the country, constituting 91% of the total population. Ethnic minorities include the Abazas, Turks, Greeks, Bedouin Arab tribes living in the eastern deserts and the Sinai Peninsula, the Berber-speaking Siwis (Amazigh) of the Siwa Oasis, and the Nubian communities clustered along the Nile. There are also tribal Beja communities concentrated in the south-eastern-most corner of the country, and a number of Dom clans mostly in the Nile Delta and Faiyum who are progressively becoming assimilated as urbanisation increases.

埃及人是埃及最大的民族,占总人口的91%。少数民族包括阿巴扎斯人、土耳其人、希腊人、生活在东部沙漠和西奈半岛的贝都因阿拉伯部落、锡瓦绿洲说柏柏尔语的西威人(阿马齐格),以及尼罗河沿岸的努比亚人。还有集中在该国最东南角落的贝雅部落,以及随着城市化程度的提高逐渐被同化的多姆部落,这些部落主要分布在尼罗河三角洲和法尤姆。

1. Cleopatra VII Philopator/埃及艳后

Cleopatra Ⅶ Philopator was the last female pharaoh of the Ptolemaic Dynasty in ancient Egypt. She let a venomous snake bite her to death to end both her life and that of Egypt (though studies have shown that she was more likely to have been murdered by Octavian). Egypt became part of the Roman Empire until the fall of the Western Roman Empire in the fifth century.

克利奥帕特拉七世,通称为埃及艳后,是古埃及的托勒密王朝最后一任女法老。她让一条毒蛇咬死自己来同时结束自己和埃及的生命(不过,研究证明她死于屋大维谋杀的可能性更大一些)。从此以后,埃及成为罗马帝国的一部分,直到5世纪西罗马帝国的灭亡。

2. Menes/美尼斯

Menes (3200 BC—3000 BC) was a pharaoh of the Early Dynastic Period of ancient Egypt credited by classical tradition with having united Upper and Lower Egypt and as the founder of the First Dynasty.

美尼斯(公元前3200—公元前3000)是古埃及王朝早期的一位法老。根据古典传记,他统一了上埃及和下埃及,并建立了第一个王朝。

3. Khufu/胡夫

Khufu, known to the Greeks as Cheops, was an ancient Egyptian monarch who was the second pharaoh of the Fourth Dynasty, in the first half of the Old Kingdom period (26th century BC). Khufu succeeded his father Sneferu as king. He is generally accepted as having commissioned the Great Pyramid of Giza, one of the Seven Wonders of the Ancient World, but many other aspects of his reign are poorly documented.

胡夫,希腊人称为基奥普斯,是古埃及的一位君主,是旧王国时期(公元前26世纪)上半叶第四王朝的第二位法老。胡夫继承了他父亲斯尼夫鲁的王位。人们普遍认为他委托建造了古代世界七大奇迹之一的吉萨大金字塔。但他统治时期的许多其他方面却鲜有记载。

4. Ramesses Ⅱ/拉美西斯二世

Ramesses Ⅱ, also known as Ramesses the Great, was the third pharaoh of the Nineteenth Dynasty of Egypt. He is often regarded as the greatest, most celebrated, and most powerful pharaoh of the New Kingdom. His successors and later Egyptians called him the "Great Ancestor".

拉美西斯二世,也被称为拉美西斯大帝,是埃及第十九王朝的第三位法老。他常被认为是新王国最伟大、最著名、最有权力的法老。他的继任者和后来的埃及人称他为"伟大的祖先"。

Unit 3　Culture and Education/文化和教育

I　Culture/文化

The ancient Egyptian civilization is one of the five cradles of human civilization. Apart from building pyramids, sphinx and mummification, the ancient Egyptians also invented many things that had a profound impact on later generations. The culture of ancient Egypt was very rich. The creation of hieroglyphs had a great influence on the later Phoenician alphabet, and the Greek alphabet was based on the Phoenician alphabet. In addition, the pyramids, the lighthouse of Alexandria, the Temple of Amun and other buildings reflect the Egyptian superb architectural skills and mathematical knowledge. They also had great achievements in geometry, calendar and other aspects.

The ancient Egyptian script, created in 3500 BC, is a kind of hieroglyphics called sacred script. This type of script is one of the oldest written scripts written by human beings. It is often engraved on tombs, monuments, temple walls or stones of the ancient Egyptians, so it is called "sacred script".

古埃及文明是人类文明的五大摇篮之一。古埃及人除了建造金字塔、狮身人面像和木乃伊外,还发明了许多对后世产生深远影响的东西。古埃及的文化非常丰富。象形文字的产生对后来的腓尼基字母有很大的影响,希腊字母是以腓尼基字母为基础的。此外,金字塔、亚历山大灯塔、阿蒙神庙等建筑体现了埃及高超的建筑技艺和数学知识。他们在几何、历法等方面也取得了很大的成就。

古埃及文字,创造于公元前3500年,是一种被称为神圣文字的象形文字。这种文字是人类最古老的文字之一。它常被刻在古埃及人的坟墓、纪念碑、寺庙墙壁或石头上,因此被称为"圣书"。

1. The Pyramid and the Great Sphinx of Giza/金字塔与狮身人面像

The pyramid is a huge triangular structure made of large stones and is the tomb of the pharaoh. Because the ancient Egyptians lived and farmed on both sides of the Nile, the pyramids were built mainly in the desert. It is estimated that the ancient Egyptians built more than 80 pyramids during the 900 years from 2700 BC to 1800 BC. The great pyramid, which was built between 2589 and 2566 BC, is the largest of all. It was built for the Pharaoh Khufu.

The ancient Egyptians built the Great Sphinx of Giza near the Great Pyramid Located in the northwest of the sacrificial temple of the Pyramid of Kafra. The Sphinx sits east to west. The ancient Greeks called it the "Sphinx". It is the largest and oldest outdoor carved giant statue in Egypt. No one knows the reason for the construction of the huge stone sculpture, which is made up of the body of a lion and the face of a man. It represents the wisdom and valor of the Pharaoh. Some people believe the Sphinx may be the patron saint of the pyramids, while others believe it is a symbol of the great civilization of ancient Egypt.

金字塔是利用大石块建成的巨大三角形建筑物,是法老的墓穴。由于古埃及人在尼罗河两岸生活及耕作,金字塔主要是在沙漠地区兴建。据估计从公元前2700年至公元前1800年这900年里,古埃及人共建造了超过80座金字塔。建于公元前2589年至公元前2566年间的"大金字塔"是最大的一座金字塔,它是为法老胡夫而兴建的。

古埃及人在大金字塔附近建造了一座狮身人面像。狮身人面像位于卡夫拉金字塔祭庙的西北方。狮身人面像坐东向西,古希腊人把它叫作"斯芬克斯"。它是埃及最大、最古老的室外雕刻巨像。至今仍然没有人知道建造这座由"狮身"与"人面"组成的巨大石雕的原因。它代表着法老的智慧与勇猛。一些人相信狮身人面像可能是金字塔的守护神,另一些则认为它是古埃及伟大文明的象征。

2. The Mummy/木乃伊

It refers to the long-preserved bodies of ancient Egyptians, which survived for thousands of years because they were specially treated. First, the ancient Egyptians removed the internal organs of the bodies. Then they soaked them with special medicine, and smeared salt and spices on the bodies to drain the water. Finally, wrap the body in a long piece of cloth so that it will not rot. Mummification was made by the priests of ancient Egypt. In addition to mummification, the priests also sacrificed to the gods and carved "sacred tablets" on the walls of tombs, monuments and temples for the Pharaohs. The ancient Egyptians liked to place mummies in human coffins, and the coffin containing the mummies had been buried in the tomb.

木乃伊是指长久保存的古埃及人尸体,这些尸体能保存数千年是因为它们经过特别的处理。首先,古埃及人清除尸体的内脏;然后用特制的药物浸制这些内脏,再把盐和香料涂在尸首上,以吸干尸体上的水分;最后用长布条把尸体包裹起来,尸体便不会腐烂。制造木乃伊的人是古埃及的祭司,祭司除了把尸体制成木乃伊外,还需祭祀神明及为法老在墓穴、纪念碑和庙宇的墙上刻上"神碑体"。古埃及人喜欢把木乃伊放入人形的棺木内,而这个藏有木乃伊的棺木曾被埋葬在墓穴中。

Ⅱ Education/教育

Egypt implements universal primary school compulsory education system. There are 42,184 schools providing basic education (including primary, secondary, high education and secondary technical education). It has 37,218 public schools and 4,966 private schools. There are 34 universities in total, including 18 public universities and 16 private universities. Famous universities are Cairo University, Alexander University, Ain Shams University, Al-Azhar University and so on. The average enrollment rate in higher education was 32 percent.

埃及实行普及小学义务教育制度。全国共有基础教育(含小学、中学、高等教育和中等技术教育)学校42,184所,其中公立学校37,218所,私立学校4,966所。共有大学34所,其中公立大学18所,私立大学16所。著名的大学有开罗大学、亚历山大大学、艾因·夏姆斯大学、爱资哈尔大学等。高等教育平均入学率达32%。

Unit 4　Major Attractions/主要景点

Ⅰ Pyramid/金字塔

Pyramids in Egypt were built 4,500 years ago as tombs for the pharaohs and queens of ancient Egypt. The mausoleum is a cone-shaped building built of huge stone blocks, which is translated as "pyramid" because it looks like the Chinese character "Jin(金)". So far, 110 pyramids have been found in Egypt, most of which were built in the ancient dynasty of Egypt. The largest and most famous pyramids found in Egypt is the three-generation pyramid on the giza plateau southwest of Cairo. They are the great pyramid (also known as khufu), the pyramid of haefra and the pyramid of menkaula.

埃及的金字塔建于4,500年前,是古埃及法老和王后的陵墓。陵墓是用巨大石块修砌成的方锥形建筑,因形似汉字"金"字,故译作"金字塔"。埃及迄今已发现大大小小的金字塔110座,大多建于埃及古王朝时期。在埃及已发现的金字塔中,最大、最有名的是位于开罗西南面的吉萨高地上的祖孙三代金字塔。它们是大金字塔(也称胡夫金字塔)、海夫拉金字塔和门卡乌拉金字塔。

Ⅱ The Museum of Egyptian Antiquities/埃及古文物博物馆

The Museum of Egyptian Antiquities, known commonly as the Egyptian Museum or Museum of Cairo, in Cairo, Egypt, is home to an extensive collection of ancient Egyptian antiquities. It has 120,000 items, with a representative amount on display, the remainder in storerooms. Built in 1901 by the Italian construction company Garozzo-Zaffarani, the edifice is one of the largest museums in the region. In March 2019, the museum is open to the public. In 2020, the museum was superseded by the new Grand Egyptian Museum at Giza.

埃及古文物博物馆,俗称埃及博物馆或开罗博物馆,位于埃及开罗,收集了大量的古埃及文物。它有12万件文物,许多代表性的文物陈列在外,其余的存放在储藏室。这座由意大利建筑公司加罗佐-扎法拉尼于1901年建造的建筑是该地区最大的博物馆之一。自2019年3月起,该博物馆向公众开放。2020年,位于吉萨的新埃及大博物馆取代了该博物馆。

Ⅲ Citadel of Qaitbay/凯特贝城堡

The castle was formerly known as the lighthouse of Alexandria, one of the seven wonders of the world. In 1480, it was used to build a castle on the site of the lighthouse named after king Qaitbay.

凯特贝城堡前身为世界七大奇迹之一的亚历山大灯塔。1480年用其石块在灯塔原址修筑城堡,以国王凯特贝的名字命名。

Part Two
Outbound Tour Guide Operation/出境领队实务

Unit 1 Situational Dialogues/情景对话

I Dialogue 1 Tax Refund 2

(*A:airport staff   B:tour leader   C:Customs officer   D:staff at the TRS counter*)

B: Excuse me, Sir. I am looking for the tax refund counter. Would you please tell me how could I get tax refund?

A: Well, first, you need to take your entire luggage with you and go to the Customs. Take the lift downstairs and you will find many people queuing there. Second, please ensure that all items are carried, including liquids, cosmetics, health supplements, etc. that need to be checked in; also include valuables that you have to bring with you on the plane. Finally, when you are in line, please prepare your passport, receipts for all tax refund items, and goods that need to be refunded. At the same time, please fill out each tax refund form.

B: I see. Thank you very much.

(*one hour later*)

C: Good afternoon, Madam. Your passports, tax refund forms, and all the receipts.

B: Here you are.

C: Please show me this LV handbag and the necklace of Tiffany.

B: OK.

C: According to Australian law, Australia's consumption tax is 10%, called GST[①]. Please confirm that you can refund the amount of the consumption tax.

B: OK.

C: Which way do you choose to refund tax? Cash or credit card?

B: Credit card, please.

(*the officer stamped the tax refund forms.*)

C: Now you can check in your luggage on the departure hall, and the valuables should be carried on the plane. Then you can go to the security check and customs, and after that you can see a TRS② counter. There, you can get a tax refund.

B: Thank you very much. You are so nice.

(*one hour later*)

D: Good afternoon, what can I do for you?

B: I would like to claim a tax refund.

D: Your passport, boarding pass, all the receipts, and tax refund forms, please.

B: Here you are.

D: Do you choose to get tax refund by credit card?

B: Yes.

D: Please show me your credit card.

B: Sure. How much can I get?

D: The total amount of your payment and the refund amount will be clearly showed in the form.

B: How long will it take me to get my tax refund?

D: It takes several days for the tax refund to arrive your credit card, 10 working days or so.

B: Thank you.

D: You're welcome. Have a good trip.

Notes:

①GST: goods and service tax, 增值税（澳洲）。

②TRS: tax refund sign, 退税标志。

Ⅱ Dialogue 2   The Suez Canal

(*A: Chinese tourist B: local guide*)

A: Good evening, Sir. Dinner today is on our own. But I'd like to invite you to go with us. Don't think that is free because you'll have to answer many questions.

B: Thank you, Sir. I will try my best to answer your questions even without dinner.

A: Terrific. Maybe I can ask my questions before we go to dinner together.

B: Certainly. Go ahead, please.

A: As you know we are from China. When we were kids, we learned from our textbooks that there are three important canals in the world, the Grand Canal in China, the Panama Canal in America, and the Suez Canal in Egypt. Since we are here in Egypt today, we'd love to know more about it.

B: The Suez Canal is a major shipping lane through Egypt, which connects the Mediterranean Sea with the Gulf of Suez, a northern branch of the Red Sea. It officially opened in November 1869.

A: That's about 150 years ago. It is a much younger canal than the Grand Canal in China, which was constructed in the early years of the 7th century in the Sui Dynasty. But I suppose it is not less important.

B: You are right. Although the Suez Canal wasn't officially completed until 1869, there is a long history of interest in connecting both the Nile River in Egypt and the Mediterranean Sea to the Red Sea. Pharaoh Senusret Ⅲ is thought to be the first to connect the Mediterranean and Red seas by digging connections through branches of the Nile River in the 19th century BC. Those eventually filled with silt. Various other pharaohs, the Romans and possibly Omar the Great built other passageways over the centuries, but those, too, yielded to disuse.

A: Wow. But it is natural that they ended in disuse since it was almost 4,000 years ago.

B: The first modern attempts to build a canal came in the late 1700s when Napoleon Bonaparte conducted an expedition to Egypt. He believed that building a French-controlled canal on the Isthmus of Suez would cause trade problems for the British as they would either have to pay dues to France or continue sending goods over land or around the southern part of Africa. Studies for Napoleon's canal plan began in 1799 but a miscalculation in measurement showed the sea levels between the Mediterranean and the Red seas as being too different, causing fear of flooding the Nile Delta.

A: So Napoleon Bonaparte actually failed to build the canal due to lack of advanced technology.

B: That's true. The next attempt occurred in the mid-1800s when a French diplomat and engineer, Ferdinand de Lesseps, convinced the Egyptian viceroy Said Pasha to support building a canal. In 1858, the Universal Suez Ship Canal Company was formed and given the right to begin construction of the canal and operate it for 99 years, when the Egyptian government would take over control. At its founding, the Universal Suez Ship Canal Company was owned by French and Egyptian interests.

A: Everything seems to be ready now.

B: Yes. Construction of the Suez Canal officially began on April 25, 1859. Low-paid forced Egyptian labors using picks and shovels did the initial digging which was extremely slow and painstaking. This was eventually abandoned for steam and coal powered machines that quickly finished the work. However, it still took them ten years. It opened 10 years later on November 17, 1869, at a cost of $100 million.

A: Better late than never. It must have brought about tremendous changes in the world trade.

B: Immediately after the construction, the Suez Canal had a significant impact on world trade. In 1875, debt forced Egypt to sell its shares in ownership of the Suez Canal to the United Kingdom. However, an international convention in 1888 made the canal available for all ships from any nation to use.

A: Good convention.

B: In addition to dramatically reducing transit time for trade worldwide, the Suez Canal is one of the world's most significant waterways as it supports 8% of the world's shipping traffic. Almost 50 ships pass through the canal daily. Because of its narrow width, the canal is also considered a significant geographic chokepoint, as it could easily be blocked and disrupt this flow of trade.

A: Who has the ownership of the canal now?

B: Through fire and water, Egypt made its final payments for the canal to its original owners (the Universal Suez Ship Canal Company) in 1962, and the nation took full control of the Suez Canal.

A: Congratulations.

B: Future plans for the Suez Canal include a project to widen and deepen the canal to accommodate the passage of larger and more ships at one time.

A: I hope the plans will have been carried out by the time when I come to Egypt again.

B: Let's hope together.

A: Thank you so much for your information. It's high time we had dinner. Let's go.

Ⅲ Dialogue 3 The Sphinx

(*A: Chinese tourist B: local guide*)

B: Good morning, ladies and gentlemen. Did you have a good rest last night?

A: Good morning. We slept like a log and are ready for the day. What are we going to start with today?

B: We are visiting the Pyramids in Giza this morning.

A: The Egyptian Pyramids! That's what I have come to Egypt for! Tell us about them, please.

B: The Egyptian pyramids are ancient pyramid-shaped masonry structures located in Egypt. Sources cite either 118 or 138 as the number of identified Egyptian pyramids. Most were built as tombs for the country's pharaohs and their consorts during the Old and Middle Kingdom periods[①]. This morning, we are going to see those in Giza, including the Sphinx.

A: The Sphinx! Isn't it something similar to a Chinese dragon?

B: Well, I'm sorry but I don't know much about Chinese dragon. Could you explain a bit to me?

A: Let me try. Chinese dragons are legendary creatures in Chinese mythology, Chinese folklore, and East Asian culture at large. Chinese dragons have many animal-like forms such as turtles and fish, but are most commonly depicted as snake-like with four legs. They traditionally symbolize potent and auspicious powers, particularly control over water, rainfall, typhoons, and floods. The dragon is also a symbol of power, strength, and good luck for people who are worthy of it in East Asian culture. During the days of Imperial China, the Emperor of China usually used the dragon as a symbol of his imperial strength and power.

B: Thank you. There are certainly similarities between Sphinx and Chinese dragon. The Sphinx is a mythical creature with the head of a human and the body of a lion. In Greek tradition, it has the head of a human, the haunches of a lion, and sometimes the wings of a bird. It is mythicised as treacherous and merciless. Those who cannot answer its riddle suffer a fate typical in such mythological stories, as they are killed and eaten by this ravenous monster.

A: How interesting. Chinese dragon is also believed to be a combination of different animals. It has the eyes of shrimp, the antlers of a deer, the mouth of an ox, the nose of a dog, the whiskers of cat fish, the bristles of a lion, the scales of fish and the claws of an eagle.

B: The Great Sphinx of Giza is a giant 4,500-year-old limestone statue situated near the Great Pyramid in Giza. Measuring 73 meters long and 20 meters high, the Great Sphinx is one of the world's largest monuments. It is also one of the most recognizable relics of the ancient Egyptians..

A: How old is the Great Sphinx?

B: The most common and widely accepted theory about the Great Sphinx suggests the statue was erected for the Pharaoh Khafre in about 2603 BC—2578 BC.

A: What is the relationship of the Great Sphinx with the Great Pyrimad?

B: Hieroglyphic texts suggest Khafre's father, Pharaoh Khufu, built the Great Pyramid, the oldest and largest of the three pyramids in Giza. When he became Pharaoh, Khafre constructed his own pyramid next to his father's. Though Khafre's pyramid is 10 feet shorter than the Great Pyramid, it is surrounded by a more elaborate complex that includes the Great Sphinx and other statues.

A: If the texts were right, the Sphinx has been there for more than 4,500 years. What is it made of and how can it survive so long?

B: Good question. The statue began to fade into the desert background at the end of the Old Kingdom, at which point it was ignored for centuries. Inscriptions on a pink granite slab between the Great Sphinx's paws tell the story of how the statue was saved from the sands of time. Prince Thutmose, son of Amenhotep Ⅱ, fell asleep near the Sphinx, and the story started. In Thutmose's dream, the statue, calling itself Harmakhet, complained about its state of disarray and made a deal with the young prince: It would help him become pharaoh if he cleared away the sand from the statue and restored it.

A: Did it happen?

B: Whether or not the dream actually occurred is unknown, but when the prince did become Pharaoh Thutmose IV, he introduced a Sphinx-worshipping cult to his people. Statues, paintings, and reliefs of the figure popped up across the country and the sphinx became a symbol of royalty and the power of the sun.

A: What time was that?

B: It was from 1401 BC—1391 BC. Later, the Great Sphinx was eventually forgotten again. Its body suffered from erosion and its face became damaged by time as well. It was actually buried in sand up to its shoulders until the early 1800s. Today, the Sphinx is continuing to deteriorate due to wind, humidity, and pollution. Restoration efforts have been ongoing since the mid-1900s, some of which failed and ultimately caused more damage to the Sphinx.

A: That's too bad. I hope things will become better.

B: That is also my hope and actually the hope of the world.

Notes：

①the Old and Middle Kingdom periods：中古时期,西方文明史上意指约从公元500年到公元1500年一千年来的欧洲历史。

Unit 2 Case Study/案例分析

Ⅰ 案例一:旅游项目活动受伤的处理

肖女士在埃及参加降落伞活动时,由于工作人员操作不当,致使其小腿部位受伤。当时立即送医院进行了一个小手术,2,000多元的医疗费用由游船公司支付。经肖女士本人及其单位负责人、领队、地陪、游船公司多方协商,达成了一次性赔偿3,000元的协议。肖女士回国后,重新向旅行社提出赔偿要求,理由是小腿部位必须"美容",费用大概在5,000元左右。她认为旅行社应当承担这笔费用。旅行社拒绝承担,理由是双方已经在境外达成了一次性赔偿协议,肖女士不能出尔反尔。

1. 纠纷防范与应对

(1)有关人身伤害赔偿的法律规定。

《中华人民共和国民法典》规定,行为人因过错侵害他人民事权益造成损害的,应当承担侵权责任。侵害他人造成人身损害的,应当赔偿医疗费、护理费、交通费、营养费、住院伙食补助费等为治疗和康复支出的合理费用,以及因误工减少的收入。

(2)造成旅游者人身伤害的原因。

①旅行社及其相关企业的过错。

②旅游者自身的过错或者疏忽。

③外来第三方对旅游者的损害。

④上诉因素的综合损害。

(3)旅行社必须履行的安全保障义务。

①旅行社必须确保旅游产品和服务安全。

②旅行社及其从业人员必须认真履行告知义务。

③旅行社及其从业人员必须采取有效的预防和处置措施。

(4)旅游者人身伤害纠纷处理的基本原则。

①对于旅行社及其相关服务供应商过错造成旅游者的人身伤害,如果旅游者以违约责任追究为由,向旅行社提出赔偿请求,旅行社应当承担全部赔偿责任。

②对于旅游者自身原因或者第三方责任造成旅游者人身伤害,其伤害应当由旅游者自己或者第三方承担,旅行社不承担赔偿责任。

③由于综合因素造成旅游者的人身伤害,由于造成旅游者伤害的原因复杂,主次责任较难划分,应当报请事发地有关部门进行责任认定,根据责任大小来确定责任分担的比例。

④不论是何种原因造成旅游者的人身伤害,旅行社都应及时向有关部门报告,确定旅游者人身伤害事故的原因和责任。

2. 领队注意事项

(1)领队在自费活动前、中都要强调注意事项及安全事项。

(2)意外发生时,及时报告公司,做好取证工作,安抚客人。

(3)回程中应写好情况说明,以备后用。

Ⅱ 案例二:航班延误的处理

嘉兴桐乡旅游者钱先生等4人参加旅行社组织的2019年11月7日—11月15日埃及开罗7晚8日游,2019年12月1日向杭州市旅游质监所投诉。

1. 投诉的事由及诉求

钱先生一行完成了在埃及的旅游行程,返程时因航班延误,在开罗机场滞留近14个小时,要求旅行社赔偿。

2. 调查事实和处理结果

该团共12+1人,从开罗返程时,原定乘坐2019年11月15日的航班当地时间10:00起飞,于北京时间16:00到达杭州萧山机场。因飞机机械故障,在开罗机场滞留约14个小时,该航空公司为乘客安排午餐、晚餐和酒店的住宿,可是我团游客拒绝接受航空公司的安排,就是要求经济赔偿。后经旅行社与航空公司协商,对未接受食宿安排的旅游者,该航空公司同意给予每人200元的经济补偿。

旅行社认为,"由于公共交通经营者原因造成旅游者人身损害、财产损失的,由公共交通经营者依法承担赔偿责任,旅行社应当协助旅游者向公共交通经营者索赔。"旅行社向杭州市旅游质监所提供了航空公司出具的因机械故障导致航班延误的航班延误证明,以及该团领队与该团操作在航班延误期间,双方频繁交换信息的微信截屏。微信截屏内容反映了在航班延误期间,旅行社多方协调处理,争取航空公司现金理赔,以及领队说服旅游者不得采用"罢机"等过激行为的全过程,并表示旅行社考虑到这批旅游者均来自杭州周边县市,愿在航空公司理赔每人200元的基础上增加每人100元的交通补偿。旅行社的处理方案得到杭州市旅游质监所的认可。

3. 经验或教训

在旅游行程中遭遇航班延误情况,是每位旅途中人都不愿碰到的烦心事,可是目前的航班能准点起飞的不多,航班延误成为"常态",这对旅行社的业务操作和领队人员都是一种考验。若遭遇航班延误情况,领队应立即向委派部门的操作人员报告,以便操作人员及时与航空公司进行沟通交涉。

首先,领队应知晓我国民航总局2014年7月出台的《国内航空公司因自身原因造成航班延误给予旅客经济补偿》中强调的是"航空公司自身原因造成",而天气原因、军事演习、机械故障等非"自身原因",不属补偿范围,同时按航班延误时段分4—8小时和8小时以上两种,补偿标准在每人100元至200元之间。其次,已在我国生效的《蒙特利尔公约》也约定了"天气原因、军事演习、机械故障等情况发生延误,航空公司已经采取措施尽量避免给游客带来损失的情况下,航空公司不承担责任。"这些规定、公约内容,领队可适时向旅游者灌输。

领队应清楚相关法律规定,如我国《旅游法》第六十七条:"因不可抗力或者旅行社、履行辅助人已尽注意义务仍不能避免的事件,影响行程造成旅游者滞留时,旅行社应当采取相应措施。因此增加的食宿费用,由旅游者承担,增加的返程费用,由旅行社与旅游者分担。"领队应适时向旅游者宣讲;应耐心安抚游客情绪,避免发生"罢机""闹机"等不文明的过激行为;应告诫游客,任何不文明过激行为不但解决不了问题,反而会让其承担严重后果。

该团领队能够在航班延误近14个小时,旅游者情绪激动的情况下,引导旅游者通过合法、合理途径维权,成功地劝阻了不文明、不理智的过激行为发生,带领全团游客安全返还,实属不易。

参考文献

陈德. 新编英语国家概况：美国加拿大篇[M]. 西安：西安交通大学出版社,2013.

杰姬·盖伊. 英语国家文化与生活：出国留学英文版（美国）[M]. 天津：天津人民出版社，2017.

凯伦·史密斯. 英语国家文化与生活：出国留学英文版（澳大利亚）[M]. 天津：天津人民出版社，2017.

托尼·伯顿. 英语国家文化与生活：出国留学英文版（加拿大）[M]. 天津：天津人民出版社，2017.

谢福之. 英语国家概况（语言文化类）[M].北京：外语教学与研究出版社,2011.

宣念念，朱建. 主要英语国家概况[M]. 广州：华南理工大学出版社,2011.

浙江省旅游局,浙江省旅游管理培训中心. 领队英语[M].北京：中国旅游出版社,2014.

中华人民共和国外交部. 澳大利亚国家概况[EB/OL]. (2020-10-08)[2020-11-28]. https://www.fmprc.gov.cn/web/gjhdq_676201/gj_676203/dyz_681240/1206_681242/1206x0_681244/.

中华人民共和国外交部. 加拿大国家概况[EB/OL]. (2020-04-01)[2021-06-30]. https://www.fmprc.gov.cn/web/gjhdq_676201/gj_676203/bmz_679954/1206_680426/1206x0_680428/.

中华人民共和国外交部. 美国国家概况 [EB/OL].(2020-09-01)[2021-08-01]. https://www.fmprc.gov.cn/web/gjhdq_676201/gj_676203/bmz_679954/1206_680528/1206x0_680530/.

中华人民共和国外交部.埃及国家概况 [EB/OL].(2021-02-01)[2021-07-30].https://www.fmprc.gov.cn/web/gjhdq_676201/gj_676203/fz_677316/1206_677342/1206x0_677.

CHRISTIAN, D. A History of Russia, Central Asia and Mongolia: Inner Eurasia from Prehistory to the Mongol Empire[M]. Hoboken: Wiley,1998.

Madrid Traveller. Bull Fighting In Spain [EB/OL]. (2010-06-19)[2020-06-28]. https://www.madrid-traveller.com/bull-fighting-in-spain/.

SMITH, R. M. Spain: A Modern History[M]. Ann Arbor: University of Michigan Press, 1965.

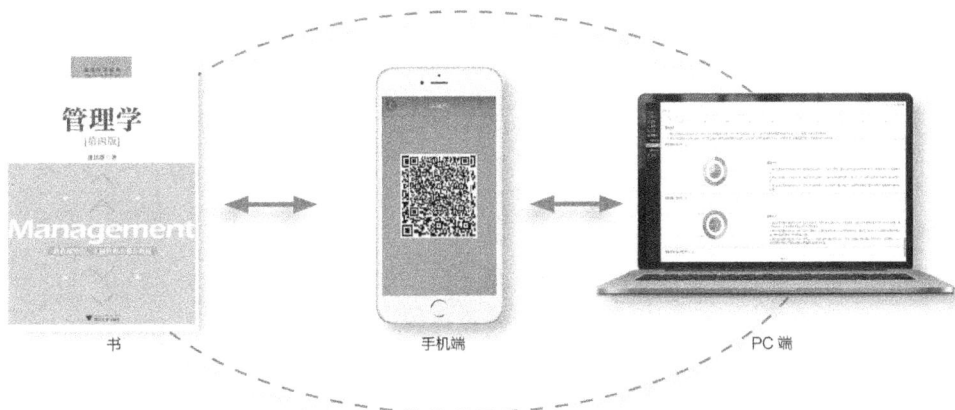
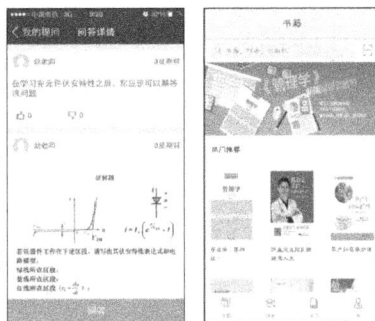

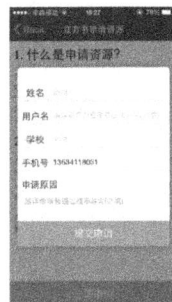